"Michael Kimmel's *Guyland* could save the humanity of many young men—and the sanity of their friends and parents—by explaining the forces behind a newly extended adolescence. With accuracy and empathy, he names the problem and offers compassionate bridges to adulthood."
—Gloria Steinem

"Kimmel is our seasoned guide into a world that, unless we are guys, we barely know exists. As he walks with us through dark territories, he points out the significant and reflects on its meaning. Just as *Reviving Ophelia* introduced readers to the culture of teenage girls, *Guyland* takes us to the land of young men."
—Mary Pipher, Ph.D., author of *Reviving Ophelia*

"An absolute bombshell of a book. A disturbing but mandatory wake-up call for all of us who are boys, love boys, or raise boys. Not only does it answer the question 'What exactly are they *doing?*' as they appear joined at the hip in sloppy, boozy apartments watching endless sporting events and video games, but it also helps us separate what is normative and what is truly worrisome. Good kids are turned around rather easily, and Kimmel helps us enter into the space these kids inhabit and show us how to help move them along the road to real adulthood."
—Madeline Levine, Ph.D., author of *The Price of Privilege: How Parental Pressure and Material Advantage Are Creating a Generation of Disconnected and Unhappy Kids*

"*Guyland* takes up where *Real Boys* left off, giving us a vivid picture of the harrowing effects that the societal 'boy code' has upon adolescents on the cusp of manhood. Kimmel interweaves cutting edge data with heart-wrenching stories of young men's struggles. This is a must-read for parents, teachers, coaches, young women who are so confused by the guys in their midst—and for guys themselves who yearn to break free of unwritten rules that leave them half a man, rather than a whole person."
—William Pollack, author of *Real Boys*

"For anyone who has ever longed to know what's really going on in a young man's life, rejoice: *Guyland* is a compassionate, unflinching dispatch from deep in the heart of young masculinity. Required reading for people who raise, teach, and love guys."
—Rachel Simmons, author of *Odd Girl Out: The Hidden Culture of Aggression in Girls*

"The hard-drinking, bullying, video-game-tuned, sometime gun-toting guys Michael Kimmel interviewed in cities across the country were not young denizens of the so-called underclass. Most were white, middle class, and college educated. But as the job market tightens around them, these young men have co-created Guyland, a

macro culture which ironically guarantees their future as its discards. In this hugely brave, compassionate, and important book, Kimmel calls on us all to see the boy in the pseudo-man, to break the silence with which we surround them, and do what it takes to help them grow into real men."
> —Arlie Hochschild, author of *The Second Shift*, *The Time Bind*, and *The Commercialization of Intimate Life*

"In this powerful book, Michael Kimmel finds that we're raising a generation of Prodigal Sons, lost on the road to manhood and wasting their substance. Afraid of competing with competent young women and confused about how to become responsible men, they retreat into self-congratulation, exploitative sex, and video games. Every parent who is about to write a check for college tuition should read this book first and discuss it with his or her son . . . and daughter."
> — Michael G. Thompson, Ph.D., co-author of *Raising Cain: Protecting the Emotional Life of Boys*

"In *Guyland* Michael Kimmel presents a searching and accurate description of the rules, expectations, and consequences of the social world inhabited by my friends and me. Rendering these pressures and their effects visible, Kimmel does all of us—both those who dwell in Guyland and those who feel those effects from the outside—a great service. I feel certain that the insights he offers, to me and guys like me, about how best to navigate this often unrecognized but powerful subculture will help us become the honest and honorable men we want to be."
> —Connor Diemand-Yauman, president of the Princeton University class of 2010

"*Guyland* paints a very vivid picture of the 'behind the scenes' of guys' lives. Whether it's girls, sports, economics, academics, or how we talk to each other, this is the first research on our generation that we can actually relate to—and not just write off as someone older than we are criticizing the decisions we make. *Guyland* is a book that all incoming freshmen should read during their first semester of college! And we will have our parents reading the book as well, because we know it will give them a better understanding of us and other guys."
> —Mike Nowak and Jim Friesema, Sigma Phi Epsilon, Eastern Illinois University, Class of 2008

GUYLAND

ALSO BY MICHAEL KIMMEL

Nonfiction

Manhood in America

The Gendered Society

Men Confront Pornography (editor)

The Gender of Desire

The History of Men

Men's Lives (co-editor)

Sociology Now (co-author)

GUYLAND

The
Perilous
World
Where Boys
Become Men

MICHAEL KIMMEL

HARPER

An Imprint of HarperCollins*Publishers*
www.harpercollins.com

HarperCollins books may be purchased for educational, business, or sales promotional use. For information, please write: Special Markets Department, HarperCollins Publishers, 10 East 53rd Street, New York, NY 10022.

"The After Hours Crowd" from *Some America* by Patrick D. Higgins, © 2008 by Patrick D. Higgins. Reprinted here with permission from the author.

FIRST EDITION

Designed by Kara Strubel

Library of Congress Cataloging-in-Publication Data is available upon request.

ISBN: 978-0-06-083134-9

08   09   10   11   12   ID/RRD   10   9   8   7   6   5   4   3   2   1

For Mitchell Tunick

———

We two boys together clinging,
One the other never leaving,
Up and down the roads going—North and South excursions making,
Power enjoying—elbows stretching—fingers clutching,
Arm'd and fearless—eating, drinking, sleeping, loving.

—WALT WHITMAN, *Leaves of Grass*

CONTENTS

The After Hours Crowd

American boys walk in packs
    playing dress up in
    small towns, boulevard
    walking along panels
    illuminated of glass.

American boys get violent
    scared straight
    sending vibes like
    small atom bombs
    fallout smells of
    musk, fear, Old Spice,
        Boy Scouts.

American boys and mall-metal podcast
    haircuts get the better
    of me, an American boy,
    hapless in fashion's prison
    culturebound to ignoramus
    brethren, fatuous
    fumbling for cigarette
    taunting nervous girl
    as she walks by alone.

American boys atomic and atomizing
    walk strong in tough
    group same shirt
    bent brim hat to
    Señor Frog shooter
    night for to make
    get drunk, get pussy,
    get real stupid drunk
    like television drunk.

We too Americans, boys
     caught somewhere
     nomadic in packs
     snapping fingers
     giggling in 7/4
     rearrangers of names
     becoming sounds blasts
     of rhythm without
     territory or time,

We too are America(n), boys,
     despite it all,
     laugh it out
     have it out
     have a drink
     have a smoke
     have a conversation
          interrupted
          by cell phone
          new conversation
          text message
             on virtual
          co-planar getting
          co-planar getting
             sick.

Let's start a fire, America.

Let's do away with
     Boys Who Will Be Boys.

Let's become something else.

—Patrick D. Higgins

PREFACE

Writing a book is never a solitary process—at least not for me. It's a conversation.

I wrote this book in part to contribute to a conversation I believe we desperately need to have in this country: a conversation about guys, and about the world in which they live. A conversation in which guys—as well as those who care about them—can participate.

This book is also based on conversations—hundreds of them—in which I was an eager participant. I talked with young men and women informally all over the country over the past several years. I learned more than I could possibly cram into this book.

Writing it required that I participate in many other conversations, with colleagues and friends, who read parts of the manuscript, facilitated research, pointed me in the right direction when I was lost. I am grateful to Danielle Currier, Mike Messner, Hank Nuwer, Rebecca Plante, and Steve Zyck. I'm grateful to Paula England for her generosity with the development of the On-Line Survey of Campus Social Life and to the other participants in the "hooking up" study.

Several of my students read and commented on various aspects of the book, either sharing their experiences or mining some vein of empirical research together. Thanks to Andrew Buskin, Ryan Hubbell, Rachel Kalish, Matt Mahler, Amy Traver.

Three of my most trusted friends—Michael Kaufman, Lillian Rubin, and Jean-Anne Sutherland—read the entire manuscript and their comments were so incisive and engaged that it took me several weeks just to absorb them all. They were provoked and frustrated by my arguments, and often by my narrative style, and they pushed back—harder than I had anticipated, but exactly as I needed. This book is so much the better for their candor and wisdom. It would have been better still had I listened to more of it.

While this book engages in a conversation, it has its origins in an argument. My agents, Gail Ross and Howard Yoon, were excited by the initial proposal for this book, and Howard suggested I think bigger, bolder, and try to understand this difficult transition from adolescence to adulthood as both a stage of life and a social world. Then Gail chimed in with stories drawn from the lives of her family and friends and I was hooked. I'm so grateful to them both. (And thanks to Rachel Simmons for being willing to share Gail!)

Just about every author says he or she wishes for a hands-on editor, one who doesn't merely publish or print the work, but who really edits it, who wrestles critically with the ideas, who enters into the conversation that any book attempts to elicit. I am enormously lucky to have found such an editor in Gail Winston, who not only engaged with both the form and content of these pages, argued passionately as an engaged reader, caring mother of two guys, as well as empathic editor. One may not enjoy "tough love" when one receives it; but one is usually eventually grateful when the end result is so much stronger and more resilient.

Ditto to Sarah Manges, who also wrestled with every idea, and every way I tried to convey them—from sociological theory to phrasing and semicolons. If I'm clear at all, I have them to thank; if I'm not, I have only myself to blame. And thanks also to Sarah Whitman-Salkin, who sweated every detail of the editing and production process, and introduced me to the work of Patrick Higgins, whose poem provides the book's epigraph. And, of course, to Patrick for allowing me to use his fine work.

For the past couple of decades, I've been part of a critical conversation about masculinity with scholars and activists around the world. There is hardly room to thank them all, but I must mention several (if I haven't already) as these conversations form the foundation for my work: Chris Beasley, Harry Brod, Marty Duberman, Carol Gilligan, Jeff Hearn, Oystein Holter, Lars Jalmert, Terry Kupers, Jorgen Lorentzen, Lisa Machoian, Bill Pollack, Don Sabo.

Several friends enriched my life, and our conversations made my work feel more urgently needed: Mary Morris and Larry O'Connor, Pam Hatchfield, Shanny Peer and Cliff Landesmann, Javier Auyero.

Nowhere has that conversation been more rewarding or enriching than the conversation I carry on with my family every single day. My parents, my sister, and my step-family, and all their partners and spouses, are always supportive; they provided—and still provide—such a firm foundation to build a life.

My son, Zachary, now nine (I'm writing this on his birthday!), is already engaged with many of the issues I describe here. He was eager to be a part of the book, and he helped me understand a lot more than the lure of video games. I hope that this book enables him to navigate Guyland better—without having to sacrifice his exuberance, his ethics, his empathy, or his laughter.

My wife, Amy, to whom all my work—indeed, my life!—should probably be dedicated, is simply what I envision when I imagine what the words "life partner" might actually mean—critic, cheerleader, collaborator, coauthor, co-parent, companion.

Nine years ago, at Zachary's naming ceremony, we each offered a wish for our newborn son. When it was my turn, I quoted the poet Adrienne Rich, who wrote "If I could have one wish for my own sons, it is that they should have the courage of women." I wished nothing more for Zachary—that he would have Amy's courage, her integrity, and her passion. I hope for that still.

For nearly half a century I've carried on a conversation about being a guy with my oldest friend, Mitchell Tunick. Since we met on that first day of sixth grade, we've navigated Guyland together—from standing in front of a mirror in my basement imitating the dance steps to "My

Girl," to the Fillmore East and Woodstock and hundreds of concerts, to now playing "Rock Band" with our sons. And every moment in between —from the darkest existential crises and losses of loved ones, to the dizziness of our team winning the Super Bowl. We've been friends, wingmen, husbands, fathers, and now godfathers to each other's sons. He's been with me every step of that journey and it's about time I thanked him for being my go-to guy.

M.S.K.
Brooklyn, NY
30 January 2008

GUYLAND

1 | WELCOME TO GUYLAND

The ignominy of boyhood; the distress
Of boyhood changing into man;
The unfinished man and his pain.

—WILLIAM BUTLER YEATS
"A Dialogue of Self and Soul" (1933)

Jeff* is 24, tall and fit, with shaggy brown hair and an easy smile. After graduating from Brown three years ago, with an honors degree in history and anthropology, he moved back home to the Boston suburbs and started looking for a job. After several months, he found one, as a sales representative for a small Internet provider. He stays in touch with friends from college by text message and email, and still heads downtown on weekends to hang out at Boston's "Brown bars." "It's kinda like I never left college," he says, with a mixture of resignation and pleasure. "Same friends, same aimlessness."

Andy is 17, a high-school senior in the San Diego area. Affable, slightly chubby, and wearing glasses, his Chargers jersey signals his interest in sports. At the moment, he's waiting to hear to which University of California campus he'll be accepted. Or if he'll be accepted. Once a

---

* Jeff is not his real name. All the names of interviewees, and some identifying details, have been changed.

reasonably good student, he says he now worries that he's spent so much time playing video games and hanging out in online communities that he hasn't studied hard enough and that his grades have suffered. "I just get kinda lost in there, your know?" he says. "My parents think I'm doing homework all the time, so I sorta keep it a secret." While he was hoping for UCLA or Santa Barbara, he is also sending in a few applications to other, less competitive state colleges, just in case. "My parents are going to freak if I don't get into UCLA," he says, wincing.

Brian is 21, a senior chemistry major at Indiana. Serious and earnest, he is putting himself through school by working two jobs off campus— waiting tables in a local restaurant on weekends and stacking books in the science library during the week when he is not in class or lab. An honors student, he wakes up at about six every morning so he can study in quiet in his dorm room.

His freshman roommate, Dave, still a friend, has approached college life somewhat differently. A business major, Dave usually wakes up around noon, hangs out at his fraternity house playing video games with his fraternity brothers until dinner, and then heads out to the local bars for the night. He estimates that he drinks five nights a week, parties all weekend, and studies only the night before finals, if then. He had been putting himself through school gambling online, but he ran into a streak of bad luck and now owes about $12,000.

We sit together in one of the many snack bars around campus. "I don't understand Dave, never did," Brian says. "But he's my friend anyway, and he invites me to the cool parties, which, I confess, I never go to."

"Listen," Dave replies, "he doesn't understand *me*? I think it's great to want to have a career and all, but Brian is, like, so tight, you know. He's such a go-getter. He doesn't get that college is about parties and fun—oh, and did I mention the drinking?" He laughs.

Jason graduated from Dartmouth almost five years ago. Now 26, he works in finance in Boston and shares a Back Bay apartment with five other guys with whom he went to school. He runs and works out, stays fit, and dates lots of different women—all in their early twenties. At night, he hangs out at the "Dartmouth bars" of Boston. "Hey, college was supposed to be the best years of your life, right?" he explains, with only a trace of defensiveness in his voice. "So where is it written that it has to end when you graduate? College is forever, man. That's what the admissions guys say—that these will be your friends forever. Well, forever is now."

These are some of the young men you will meet in this book. They're among the nearly 400 I've interviewed over the past four years—on college campuses, in neighborhood bars and coffee shops, in Internet chat rooms, and at sports events. Most of them are college educated, from good homes in reasonably affluent suburbs and urban areas. Most are white, but I talked with plenty of Latino, African-American, and Asian-American guys. Most are middle class, but I also made sure to talk with high-school grads who never went to college but instead worked in auto body shops, served in the military, and opened small businesses. Most were straight, but I spoke with quite a few gay and bisexual guys as well.

In another era, these guys would undoubtedly be poised to take their place in the adult world, taking the first steps toward becoming the nation's future professionals, entrepreneurs, and business leaders. They would be engaged to be married, thinking about settling down with a family, preparing for futures as civic leaders and Little League dads. Not today.

Today, many of these young men, poised between adolescence and adulthood, are more likely to feel anxious and uncertain. In college, they party hard but are soft on studying. They slip through the academic cracks, another face in a large lecture hall, getting by with little effort and less commitment. After graduation, they drift aimlessly from one dead-end job to another, spend more time online playing video games and gambling than they do on dates (and probably spend more money too), "hook up" occasionally with a "friend with benefits," go out with their buddies, drink too much, and save too little. After college, they perpetuate that experience and move home or live in group apartments in major cities, with several other guys from their dorm or fraternity. They watch a lot of sports. They have grandiose visions for their futures and not a clue how to get from here to there. When they do try and articulate this amorphous uncertainty, they're likely to paper over it with a simple "it's all good."

You can find them in New York's Murray Hill, or Silver Lake and Echo Park in Los Angeles, Houston's Midtown, or Atlanta's Buckhead district, sipping their mocha lattes in the local Starbucks and crowding upmarket pool halls; some are banker boys in cargo shorts, untucked striped Oxford shirts, and baseball caps; and others still sport the T-shirts or flannel shirts of their college days. They are the "friendsters" with their wi-fi computers looking for love, friendship, or hookups, or on monster.com looking for next month's job. In a scene that makes the TV show *Friends* appear more like a documentary, they double and triple up in their overpriced apartments, five or six guys in a two-bedroom pad, re-creating their collegiate lifestyle in the big city. "Murray Hill has more young people that just graduated from college than any other neighborhood in the city," gushes one very happy Manhattan realtor, who estimates that 90 percent of his rentals go to young people aged 21 to 25.

At night, they'll all troop off to bars that are branded as collegiate alumni bars, such as Beacon Hill Pub or Cleary's, Boston's "Dartmouth bars" because there are so many recent Dartmouth grads in the city who congregate there. High school may be over at eighteen, college at twenty-two, but the same social life often continues for another several years. Bars advertise "Spring Break 52 Weeks a Year!" and others promote college-party atmospheres for the post-college party set. Many post-grads move in a languorous mass, a collection of anomic nomads looking for someplace to go.

Welcome to Guyland.

Guyland is the world in which young men live. It is both a stage of life, a liminal undefined time span between adolescence and adulthood that can often stretch for a decade or more, and a place, or, rather, a bunch of places where guys gather to be guys with each other, unhassled by the demands of parents, girlfriends, jobs, kids, and the other nuisances of adult life. In this topsy-turvy, Peter-Pan mindset, young men shirk the responsibilities of adulthood and remain fixated on the trappings of boyhood, while the boys they still are struggle heroically to prove that they are real men despite all evidence to the contrary.

Males between 16 and 26 number well over 22 million—more than 15 percent of the total male population in the United States. The "guy" age bracket represents the front end of the single most desirable consumer market, according to advertisers. It's the group constantly targeted by major Hollywood studios, in part because this group sees the same shoot-em-up action film so many times on initial release. They're targeted in several of the most successful magazine launches in recent memory, magazines like *Men's Health, Maxim, FHM, Details*, and *Stuff*. Guys in this age bracket are the primary viewers of the countless sports channels on television. They consume the overwhelming majority of recorded music, video games, and computer technology, and they are the majority of first-time car buyers.

Yet aside from assiduous market research, Guyland is a *terra incognita*; it has never been adequately mapped. Many of us only know we've landed there when we feel distraught about our children, anxious that they have entered, or will be entering, a world that we barely know. We sense them moving away from us, developing allegiances and attitudes we neither understand nor support. Recently, a teacher at a middle school told me about his own 16-year-old son, Nick. "When we're together, he's excited, happy, curious, and so connected," he told me.

> "But when I drove him to school this morning, I watched an amazing transformation. In the car, Nick was speaking animatedly about something. As we arrived at his school, though, I saw him scan the playground for his friends. He got out of the car, still buoyant, with a bounce in his step. But as soon as he caught sight of his friends he instantly fell into that slouchy 'I don't give a shit' amble that teenagers get. I think I actually watched him become a 'guy'!"

Parents often feel we no longer know them—the young guys in our lives.

Just what are they doing in their rooms at all hours of the night? And what are they doing in college? And why are they so aimless and directionless when they graduate that they take dead-end jobs and move back home? When they come home for college vacations, we wonder just who is this new person who talks about ledge parties and power hours—and what happened to the motivated young man who left for college with such high hopes and a keen sense of purpose. And guys themselves often wonder where they left their dreams.

Every time we read about vicious gay-baiting and bullying in a high school, every time the nightly news depicts the grim horror of a school shooting, every time we hear about teen binge drinking, random sexual hookups, or a hazing death at a college fraternity, we feel that anxiety, that dread. And we ask ourselves, "Could that be my son?" Or, "Could that be my friend, or even my boyfriend?" Or, even "could that be *me*?"

Well, to be honest, probably not. Most guys are not predators, not criminals, and neither so consumed with adolescent rage nor so caught in the thrall of masculine entitlement that they are likely to end up with a rap sheet instead of a college transcript. But most guys know other guys who *are* chronic substance abusers, who *have* sexually assaulted their classmates. They swim in the same water, breathe the same air. Those appalling headlines are only the farthest extremes of a continuum of attitudes and behaviors that stretches back to embrace so many young men, and that so circumscribes their lives that even if they don't want to participate, they still must contend with it.

Guyland is not some esoteric planet inhabited only by alien creatures—despite how alien our teenage and 20-something sons might seem at times. It's the world of everyday "guys." Nor is it a state of arrested development, a case of prolonged adolescence among a cadre of slackers. It has become a stage of life, a "demographic," that is now pretty much the norm. Without fixed age boundaries, young men typically enter Guyland before they turn 16, and they begin to leave in their mid to late 20s. This period now has a definable shape and texture, a topography that can be mapped and explored. A kind of suspended animation between boyhood and manhood, Guyland lies between the dependency and lack of autonomy of boyhood and the sacrifice and responsibility of manhood. Wherever they are living, whatever they are doing, and whomever they are hooking up with, Guyland is a dramatically new stage of development with its own rules and limitations. It is a period of life that demands examination—and not just because of the appalling headlines that greet us on such a regular basis. As urgent as it may seem to explore and expose Guyland because of the egregious behaviors of the few, it may be more urgent to examine the ubiquity of Guyland in the lives of almost everyone else.

It's easy to observe "guys" virtually everywhere in America—in every high school and college campus in America, with their baseball caps on frontward or backward, their easy smiles or anxious darting eyes, huddled around tiny electronic gadgets or laptops, or relaxing in front of massive wide-screen hi-def TVs, in basements, dorms, and frat houses. But it would be a mistake to assume that each conforms fully to a regime of peer-influenced and enforced behaviors that I call the "Guy Code," or shares all traits and attitudes with everyone else. It's important to remember that individual guys are not the same as "Guyland."

In fact, my point is precisely the opposite. Though Guyland is pervasive—it is the air guys breathe, the water they drink—each guy cuts his own deal with it as he tries to navigate the passage from adolescence to adulthood without succumbing to the most soul-numbing, spirit-crushing elements that surround him every day.

Guys often feel they're entirely on their own as they navigate the murky shallows and the dangerous eddies that run in Guyland's swift current. They often stop talking to their parents, who "just don't get it." Other adults seem equally clueless. And they can't confide in one another lest they risk being exposed for the confused creatures they are. So they're left alone, confused, trying to come to terms with a world they themselves barely understand. They couch their insecurity in bravado and bluster, a fearless strut barely concealing a tremulous anxiety. They test themselves in fantasy worlds and in drinking contests, enduring humiliation and pain at the hands of others.

All the while, many do suspect that something's rotten in the state of Manhood. They struggle to conceal their own sense of fraudulence, and can smell it on others. But few can admit to it, lest all the emperors-to-be will be revealed as disrobed. They go along, in mime.

Just as one can support the troops but oppose the war, so too can one appreciate and support individual guys while engaging critically with the social and cultural world they inhabit. In fact, I believe that only by understanding this world can we truly be empathic to the guys in our lives. We need to enter this world, see the perilous field in which boys become men in our society because we desperately need to start a conversation about that world. We do boys a great disservice by turning away, excusing the excesses of Guyland as just "boys being boys"— because we fail to see just how powerful its influence really is. Only when we begin to engage in these conversations, with open eyes and open hearts—as parents to children, as friends, as guys themselves— can we both reduce the risks and enable guys to navigate it more successfully. This book is an attempt to map that terrain in order to enable guys—and those who know them, care about them, love them—to steer a course with greater integrity and honesty, so they can be true not to some artificial code, but to themselves.

Just Who Are These Guys?

The guys who populate Guyland are mostly white, middle-class kids; they are college-bound, in college, or have recently graduated; they're unmarried. They live communally with other guys, in dorms, apartments, or fraternities. Or they live with their parents (even after college). Their jobs, if they have them, are modest, low-paying, low-prestige ones in the service sector or entry-level corporate jobs that leave them with plenty of time to party. They're good kids, by and large. They blend into the crowd, drift with the tide, and often pass unnoticed through the lecture halls and multistory dorms of America's large college campuses.

Of course, there are many young people of this age group who are highly motivated, focused, with a clear vision and direction in their lives. Their stories of resilience and motivation will provide a telling rejoinder to many of the dominant patterns of Guyland. There are also just as many who immediately move back home after college, directionless, with a liberal arts BA that qualifies them for nothing more than a dead-end job making lattes or folding jeans. So while a few of them might jump right into a career or graduate school immediately after college, many more simply drift for a while, comforting themselves with the assurances that they have plenty of time to settle down later, after they've had their fun.

In some respects, Guyland can be defined by what guys do for fun. It's the "boyhood" side of the continuum they're so reluctant to leave. It's drinking, sex, and video games. It's watching sports, reading about sports, listening to sports on the radio. It's television—cartoons, reality shows, music videos, shoot-em-up movies, sports, and porn—pizza, and beer. It's all the behavior that makes the real grownups in their lives roll their eyes and wonder, "When will he *grow up*?!"

There are some parts of Guyland that are quite positive. The advancing age of marriage, for example, benefits both women and men, who have more time to explore career opportunities, not to mention establishing their identities, before committing to home and family. And much of what qualifies as fun in Guyland is relatively harmless. Guys grow out of a lot of the sophomoric humor—if not after their "sophomore" year, then at least by their mid–twenties.

Yet, there is a disturbing undercurrent to much of it as well. Teenage boys spend countless hours blowing up the galaxy, graphically splattering their computer screens in violent video games. College guys post pornography everywhere in their dorm rooms; indeed, pornographic pictures are among the most popular screen savers on male college students' computers. In fraternities and dorms on virtually every campus, plenty of guys are getting drunk almost every night, prowling for women with whom they can hook up, and chalking it all up to harmless fun. White suburban boys don do-rags and gangsta tattoos appropriating inner-city African-American styles to be cool. Homophobia is ubiquitous; indeed, "that's so gay" is probably the most frequently used put-down in middle schools, high schools, and college today. And sometimes gay-baiting takes an ugly turn and becomes gay-bashing.

All the while, these young people are listening to shock jocks on the radio, laughing at cable-rated T&A on the current generation's spin-offs of "The Man Show" and watching Spike TV, the "man's network," guffawing to sophomoric body-fluid humor of college circuit comedians who make Beavis and Butt-head sound quaint. They're laughing at clueless henpecked husbands on TV sitcoms; snorting derisively at guys who say the wrong thing on beer ads; snickering at duded-up metro-sexuals prancing around major metropolitan centers drinking Cosmos and imported vodka. Unapologetically "politically incorrect" magazines, radio hosts, and television shows abound, filled with macho bluster and bikini-clad women bouncing on trampolines. And the soundtrack in these new boys' clubhouses, the sonic wallpaper in every dorm room and every shared apartment, is some of the angriest music ever made. Nearly four out of every five gangsta rap CDs are bought by suburban white guys. It is not just the "boys in the hood" who are a "menace to society." It's the boys in the "burbs."

Occasionally, the news from Guyland is shocking—and sometimes even criminal. There are guys who are drinking themselves into oblivion on campus on any given night of the week, organizing parties where they spike women's drinks with Rohypnol (the date rape drug), or just try to ply them with alcohol to make them more compliant—and then video-taping their conquests. These are the guys who are devising elaborately sadomasochistic hazing rituals for high-school athletic teams, collegiate fraternities, or military squads.

It is true, of course, that white guys do not have a monopoly on appalling behavior. There are plenty of young black and Latino boys who are equally desperate to prove their manhood, to test themselves before the watchful evaluative eyes of other guys. But only among white boys do the negative dynamics of Guyland seem to play themselves out so invisibly. Often, when there's news of young black boys behaving badly, the media takes on a "what can you expect?" attitude, failing to recognize that expecting such behavior from black men is just plain racism. But every time white boys hit the headlines, regardless of how frequently, there is an element of shock, a collective, "How could this happen? He came from such a good family!" Perhaps not identifying the parallel criminal behavior among white guys adds an additional cultural element to the equation: identification. Middle-class white families see the perpetrators as "our guys." We know them, we are them, they cannot be like that.

Though Guyland is not exclusively white, neither is it an equal-opportunity venture. Guyland rests on a bed of middle-class entitlement, a privileged sense that you are special, that the world is there for you to take. Upwardly mobile minorities feel the same tugs between claiming their rightful share of good times and delaying adult responsibilities that the more privileged white guys feel. But it often works itself out differently for them. Because of the needs and expectations of their families, they tend to opt for a more traditional trajectory. Indeed, many minority youths have begun to move into those slots designated for the ambitious and motivated, just at the moment that those slots are being abandoned by white guys having fun.

Some think they're fulfilling the American Dream, yet most feel as if they're wearing another man's clothes. Take Carlos, the son of illegal immigrants, who worked in the central California fields, harvesting artichokes and Brussels sprouts. Carlos is their success story, a track star and good student, who got recruited to several colleges and landed a scholarship to USC. But now he feels torn between the pressure from his family "to be the first in everything"—the first college grad, the first doctor—and from his friends in his hometown of Gilroy to hang out with them over the summer.

Or Eric, who just graduated from Morehouse College in Atlanta. He says he's "out of step" with his other African-American friends; he is highly motivated and serious, eschews hip-hop, and always knew he wanted to get married, start a family, and get a good job. Heavily recruited out of college, he's already a regional manager for Coca-Cola in Atlanta and dating a senior at Spelman. They plan to marry next June. "Too many of my friends think gangsta is the way to go," he says, nodding at a table nearby of college guys sporting the latest do-rags and bling. "But in my family, being a man meant stepping up and being responsible. That was what being a Morehouse Man meant to me. I can live with that."

And while the American college campus is Guyland Central, guys who don't go to college have ample opportunities—in the military, in police stations and firehouses, on every construction site and in every factory, in every neighborhood bar—for the intimately crude male bonding that characterizes Guyland's standard operating procedure. Sure, some working-class guys cannot afford to prolong their adolescence;

their family needs them, and their grownup income, too badly. With no college degree to fall back on, and parents who are not financially able or willing to support a prolonged adolescence, they don't have the safety net that makes Guyland possible. But they find other ways, symbolic or real, at work or at play, to hold onto their glory days—or they become so resentful they seethe with jealous rage at the privileged few who seem able to delay responsibility indefinitely.

Greg, for example, never made it to college. He didn't regret it at the time, but now he wonders. The son and grandson of steel workers near Bethlehem, Pennsylvania, Greg knew he'd end up at Beth Steel also—except the steel plant closed and suddenly all those jobs disappeared. Even if he could go to college now, it's too expensive, and besides, he needs to save for a new car so he can move out of his parents' house. In the past two years he's worked at a gas station, Home Depot, a mini-mart convenience store, and as a groundskeeper at a local university. "I'm trying, honest, I really am," he says, with a certain resigned sadness already creeping into his 24-year-old eyes. "But there is just no way an honest white guy can make a living in this economy—not with these Bush fat cats and all the illegals."

Rather than embracing Guyland as a way of life, working-class guys instead seem to inhabit Guyland at their local sports bar, on the factory shop floor, and in the bowling league or military unit. Yet the same sense of entitlement, the same outraged response to the waning of privilege, is clear. One Brooklyn bar near my house has been home to generations of firefighters and their pals. There's an easy ambience about the place, the comfort of younger and older guys (all white) sharing a beer and shooting the breeze. Until I happen to ask one guy about female firefighters. The atmosphere turns menacing, and a defensive anger spills out of the guys near me. "Those bitches have taken over," says Patrick.

They're everywhere. You know that ad "it's everywhere you want to be." That's like women. *They're* everywhere *they* want to be! There's nowhere you can go anymore—factories, beer joints, military, even the goddamned firehouse! [Raucous agreement all around.] We working guys are just fucked.

The camaraderie of working-class guys long celebrated in American history and romanticized in Hollywood films—the playful bonding of the locker room, the sacrificial love of the foxhole, the courageous tenacity of the firehouse or police station—has a darker side. Homophobic harassment of the new guys, racial slurs, and seething sexism often lie alongside the casual banter of the band of brothers, and this is true in both the working-class bar and the university coffee house.

And although my focus is American guys, Guyland is not exclusively American terrain. Both Britain and Australia have begun to examine "Laddism"—the anomic, free-floating, unattached and often boorish behavior of young males. "Lads" are Guys with British accents—consuming the same media, engaging in the same sorts of behaviors, and lubricating their activities with the same alcohol. In Italy, they're called *bamboccioni,* or *"mammoni,"* or Mama's boys. Half of all Italian men between 25 and 34 live with their parents. In France, they're called *"Tanguys"* after the French film with that title about their lifestyle.

Guyland revolves almost exclusively around other guys. It is a social space as well as a time zone—a pure, homosocial Eden, uncorrupted by the sober responsibilities of adulthood. The motto of Guyland is simple: "Bros Before Hos." (Long "o" in both Bro and Ho.) Just about every guy knows this—knows that his "brothers" are his real soul mates, his real life-partners. To them he swears allegiance and will take their secrets to his grave. And guys do not live in Guyland all the time. They take temporary vacations—when they are alone with their girlfriends or even a female friend, or when they are with their parents, teachers, or coaches.

Girls in Guyland—Babes in Boyland

What about girls? Guys love girls—all that homosociality might become suspect if they didn't! It's *women* they can't stand. Guyland is the more grownup version of the clubhouse on *The Little Rascals*—the "He-Man Woman Haters Club." Women demand responsibility and respectability, the antitheses of Guyland. Girls are fun and sexy, even friends, as long as they respect the centrality of guys' commitment to the band of brothers. And when girls are allowed in, they have to play by guy rules—or they don't get to play at all.

Girls contend daily with Guyland—the constant stream of porno-graphic humor in college dorms or libraries, or at countless work stations in offices across the country; the constant pressure to shape their bodies into idealized hyper-Barbies. Guyland sets the terms under which girls try to claim their own agency, develop their own senses of self. Guyland sets the terms of friendship, of sexual activity, of who is "in" and who is decidedly "out." Girls can even *be* guys—if they know something about sports (but not too much), enjoy casual banter about sex (but not too actively), and dress and act in ways that are pleasantly unthreatening to boys' fragile sense of masculinity.

Some of the girls have mastered the slouching look, the indiffer-ent affect, the contemptuous attitude, the swaggering posture, the foul language, and the aggressive behaviors of guys. Since Guyland is often the only game in town, who can blame them if they indulge in a little—or a lot—of what I call "guyification?" Observe a group of college-age women. It's likely they're wearing jeans, T-shirts, oversized sweatshirts, running shoes or sandals—guywear. If not, they'll be wearing thong underwear, skimpy mini T-shirts that leave their midriffs bare, and supertight pants, leggings, or miniskirts. And for which gender are they getting all Barbied up? (Here's a quiz: Which gender invented the thong and presents it as the latest fashion accessory for women?) And listen as they call each other "guys" all the time, even when no actual guys are around. It's become the generic term for "person."

Some girls have parlayed their post-feminist assertiveness into "girl power," or *grrrl* power. A few think that they can achieve equality by imitating guys' behaviors—by running circles around them on the ath-letic field or matching them drink for drink or sexual hookup for hook-up. But it's a cruel distortion of those ideals of early feminist liberation when female assertiveness is redefined as the willingness to hike up your sweater and reveal your breasts for a roving camera in a "Girls Gone Wild" video. And sexual equality is hardly achieved when she is willing to perform oral sex on his entire group of friends.

And most girls also know the motto "Bros Before Hos." A girl senses that she is less than, not a bro, and that underneath all his syrupy flattering is the condescension and contempt one naturally has for a ho. Girls also know the joke about the difference between a bitch and a slut (their only two choices in Guyland): "A bitch will sleep with everyone but you." Girls live in Guyland, but they do not define it. They contend with it and make their peace with it, each in their own way.

Grinding to a Halt?

Guyland now even has its own literature. In both the United States and in Britain, there is a new genre, a masculine riposte to the "chick lit" fiction of Bridget Jones's diaries. In Britain, the slightly slackeresque musings of Nick Hornby lead the pack. But Hornby cleverly criticizes the very culture he is examining, and while his lads—Rob in *High Fidelity* and Will Lightman in *About a Boy*—initially drift along aimlessly, worldly wise and wise-cracking, something eventually happens to them and they grow up, settle down, and get a life.

Not so their American cousins in such recent novels as *Booty Nomad* by Scott Mebus, *Love Monkey* by Kyle Smith, and the widely praised *Indecision* by Benjamin Kunkel. These preternatural Peter Pans simply won't grow up, no matter what happens to them. Jaded and cynical well before their time, they watch, they criticize, they stand aloof and apart. They can't go back to Neanderthal masculinity; they can't move forward to embrace some sensitive new-age guydom. They're stuck where they are: in eternal boyhood. In fact, Kunkel's main character suffers from a new psychological malady, abulia, defined as the chronic inability to make a decision (hence the book's title). They cannot commit—to their girlfriends, their jobs, or even to a purposeful life. Nor do they seem especially professionally ambitious. They drift from job to job; some are fired, some quit.

No wonder literary critic Laura Miller posted the genre's obituary at the moment of its birth. In an essay in the *New York Times Book Review*, she wrote that "[i]f female readers allowed themselves to believe that most straight men spend their time holding conversations with their penises, watching the Cartoon Network, fiddling with their rotisserie baseball teams and contemplating the fine art of passing gas on subway trains, romance—and perhaps even human reproduction itself—would grind to a halt."

Why Now?

But surely, you're probably saying to yourself, this is nothing new. Guys have been acting this way since—well, since there were guys. They've always taken risks—getting drunk and driving fast, fighting, bullying smaller guys—all to prove their masculinity.

When I was a young man, there were more possibilities to swim against the current; Guyland was hardly the only arena. One could be serious, sober, stable, and responsible, as readily as wild, boisterous, and predatory. One could be independent, an individual, without being seen as a freak or a loner. There were always other cliques to join for support. Back then different schools, different neighborhoods, different workplaces, even different military units all had different local cultures. Not anymore. One of the great contradictions of our era is that there is a super-abundance of choices now, far more than ever before, and yet the range of those choices somehow feels more constricted, and more constricting, than ever. "There's 57 channels, and nothing on," Bruce Springsteen sang—and that was 250 channels ago! More choices may not mean greater freedom, just a larger number of possible alternatives that are dismissed as wannabes and also-rans.

The dramatic increase in alternatives is accompanied by an equally dramatic cultural homogenization, a flattening of regional and local differences with a single mainstream dominant culture prevailing. Accents are losing their distinct regional flair, local cuisines are losing their regional flavors (often only to re-create them for tourists), downtown villages are being replaced by strip malls on the outskirts of town featuring the same national chain stores from coast to coast. One large state university campus looks very much like any other; indeed, you'd be hard pressed, without looking at the names on the sweatshirts, to tell Ole Miss from Michigan, or Texas from Tennessee, Akron from Albany. Music, TV, and the Internet ensure that parties, and party-goers, all look the same. And the Power Hour, a drinking ritual that ushers virtually every collegiate 21-year-old into legal drinking age, features roughly the same vile alcoholic concoctions in the same ritualistic order—all experienced as spontaneous fun—no matter where you are in the country.

What this has come to mean is that while there are more possible identities for a young boy to gravitate toward—hippie, stoner, skater, nerd, prep, wigger, and a long list of others—the pressure *not* to choose one of these alternatives is also increasing. Each of these subcultures has been marginalized in high-school locker rooms and cafeterias, where Guyland in capital letters begins to hold sway over the adolescent imagination.

Nerds, geeks, wonks, and dorm rats learn to keep their heads down and avoid drawing attention to themselves if they want to be left alone and not get bullied, beat up, or worse. Other campus subcultures—Goths, punkers, anarchists, politicos—are really counter-cultures. That is, they define themselves in opposition to the dominant Guyland ethos. The former is marginalized, the second defiantly rejecting—but both define, and are defined by, Guyland. Nerds may plot their revenge together in private, but in public they usually cut a narrow swath.

What's more, the stakes are higher, the violence more extreme, the weapons more lethal. In 1967, the *New York Times* and the *Yale Daily News* reacted with mortified disdain to stories about fraternity branding; today, hundreds of pledges are ritually branded every year with nary an eyebrow raised. Emergency rooms at campus-based hospitals bulge with alcohol-related injuries and illnesses virtually every weekend, and they overflow during pledge week events. At least one pledge has died during some campus-based event every year for the past decade.

The entire landscape of Guyland is structured by the massive social and economic changes in the United States over the past several decades. As Susan Faludi documented in her book *Stiffed*, men who once found meaning and social value in their work are increasingly pushed into lower-wage service occupations; as the economy has shifted from a culture of production to a culture of consumption men experience their masculinity less as providers and protectors, and more as consumers, as "ornaments." Many men feel "downsized"—both economically and emotionally; they feel smaller, less essential, less like real men.

At the same time, women have entered every single arena once completely dominated by men. In the last three decades of the twentieth century, virtually every all-male college went coed, the military integrated, as did police stations, and firehouses, and every single profession and occupation. Where once there were so many places where men could validate their masculinity, proving it in the eyes of other men, there are today fewer and fewer places where they aren't also competing with women.

It might seem ironic that Guyland encompasses an ever-expanding age spectrum, from mid-teens through the late twenties at the same time that the social space of Guyland is shrinking enormously. But young men are seeking what used to be so easy to find by pushing the age limits of their boyhoods as far into their twenties as they possibly can. That is why they are often so defensive: they've lost the casual ease of proving themselves to other guys that they once took for granted.

Yes, young men have always wanted to prove themselves, and that is nothing new. But today that desire has a distinct tone of desperation to it. In a world where their entitlement is eroding, where the racism and sexism that supported white male privilege for decades is taking hits left and right, where women are "everywhere they want to be," and affirmative action has provided at least some opportunities to minorities, the need for a "Band of Brothers" feels stronger than ever.

Grownups in Guyland

When I talk with adults about Guyland, I'm often met with confusion. Surely, say some parents, these headline-grabbing behaviors aren't about my son. And, by and large, they're right. But they are about the world their son inhabits, what goes on around him, what he knows about and won't say. It's perhaps a world into which he retreats when he logs on, texts his friends, watches TV, or plays video games, parties, drinks, and hooks up. Many parents are eager to raise these issues with their sons and daughters. But how? What can they say?

It's ironic that American parents are often chastised as "helicopter parents"—hovering so closely and insistently in their children's lives, constraining their developing sense of autonomy—until, that is, the day they go off to college, at which point they frequently wash their hands of the whole thing and become absentee parents. Their children, straining all during their adolescence for more latitude, dutifully troop off to college with little understanding of how to manage responsibly such freedom. And freedom without responsibility is a volatile combination. All hell often breaks loose.

In an effort to prove their masculinity, with little guidance and no real understanding of what manhood is, they engage in behaviors and activities that are ill-conceived and irresponsibly carried out. These are the guys who are so desperate to be accepted by their peers that they do all sorts of things they secretly know to be not quite right. They lie about their sexual experiences to seem more manly; they drink more than they know they can handle because they don't want to seem weak or immature; they sheepishly engage in locker-room talk about young women they actually like and respect. These are the guys who want to do well in school but don't want to be seen as geeks; the guys who think they can't be cool and responsible at the same time; the pledges and pledgemasters whose hazing rituals are frequently disgusting, sometimes barbaric, and occasionally lethal. With no adults around running the show, they turn to each other for initiation into manhood.

There is, incidentally, no profound societal need served by such initiation; plenty of healthy functioning societies do without them altogether. But many of Guyland's fiercest defenders argue that initiation serves some psychological hunger that boys feel, a desperate urge to be validated as men. This only begs the question: Why do they feel such a need in the first place, and how could they possibly have their masculinity validated by their peers, when those peers are only "men" by virtue of having declared it themselves? Such rituals, absent any adult participation, are desperate frauds, and, I suspect, the participants sense this fraud, which only fuels their eagerness to participate in increasingly desperate and dangerous rites in order to prove it.

To be sure, there are plenty of arduous initiation rituals in other cultures. But, as we'll see, every other culture assigns to the grownups the task of supervising those rituals, to let the boys feel tested, but also to ensure that they all safely pass. (After all, how could a culture survive if it made its initiation rituals so rigorous that only a few boys actually succeeded?) And after their rituals, young males are validated as men and there is no going back.

American parents need to loosen up slightly when their children are younger and still living at home, and then maintain contact, and develop solid relationships with their grown children once they leave home. By the time their sons hit their teen years, many mothers have been pushed aside to facilitate their coming to manhood. A boy must, we hear constantly, let go of her apron strings and bond with his father, the epitome of masculinity. But mothers are no less necessary in the lives of their teenage boys than they were when he was in diapers. If mothers represent compassion, empathy, love, and nurturance, he will need those qualities in abundance.

And fathers are equally vital. I've heard too many stories of fathers—even those who have been involved in their sons' early lives—who begin to distance themselves once their sons navigate, seemingly successfully, through puberty and adolescence. More than one college guy has had the experience that Josh, a 21-year-old junior at a small elite New England college had. "I know it's a goddamned cliché," he told me, "but I swear to God, I called home last weekend and my dad answered, and I said 'Hey Dad, how are you?' and he said—I swear—'Hold on, I'll get your mother.' I couldn't believe it." It's not that fathers are absent in the literal sense, but many begin to detach emotionally once they've completed their "work" in raising a son who has managed to survive adolescence without becoming a drug addict, a felon, or a victim of some other felon!

Other fathers are more complacent, identifying with their sons' behaviors, perhaps recalling their own adolescent missteps. We know that we did some of the same crazy things, took some of the same insane risks, and we came through it okay. So let the boy sow his wild oats, make his own mistakes. There's no harm. Some even overidentify and become complicit.

We need to enable our sons (and daughters) to be resilient, to be able to withstand some of the temptations of Guyland, to develop and trust their own moral compass so they can navigate the more treacherous waters and emerge as healthy adult men and women. We need to support them as they find and test their own internal voices of resistance and individuality, with a sense of honor and integrity on which others can rely.

Part of it, as I said, has to come from parents. But parents cannot do it alone. Part of that help has to come from the communities in which we live. As a society, we must be active, engaged, and interventionist, helping America's guys find a path of emotional authenticity, moral integrity, and physical efficacy, and thereby ease themselves more readily into an adulthood in which they can truly stand tall. We can—and must—empower boys to be more than complicit bystanders. We can help just *guys* to become *just* guys.

Typically, we assume that this can be approached solely by psychological interventions, by counseling boys to find a moral center, encouraging their resilience, providing adequate role models and clear messages. These are all necessary, but they are not enough. They assume that by helping the boys find their way out of Guyland, the social and cultural frameworks that sustain and encourage it will simply atrophy from a lack of participants. Starved of individuals willing to play along, the game will end.

While salutary, such efforts put the cart before the horse, ignoring the social and cultural mechanisms that sustain Guyland and underlie its persistence. Confronting Guyland does not turn guys into a gaggle of wimps but a generation of men—able to do the right thing, to stand up and be counted, to fear only their own fears of not fitting in, of being bullied and cowed into submission.

Getting Inside Guyland

In this book, I draw on thirty years of experience in education, thirty years of talking with tens of thousands of college and high-school men. I've given lectures and conducted workshops at nearly 300 colleges and universities and nearly 100 high schools in the United States, and perhaps another 100 at universities abroad. I've conducted research at the nation's military academies, and I've worked with dozens of athletic teams and fraternities. I became well acquainted with Guyland at Virginia Military Institute and The Citadel, and also at the University of Colorado, when I served as an expert witness in court cases involving those schools.

As a sociologist, my field of expertise, the study of men and masculinity, is a relatively new subfield of the study of "gender." It provides a different vantage point from that usually taken by psychologists who write about men and boys. I base my work not on the experiences of the guys who come to see me as patients or clients, as a therapist might. While such stories are rich with detail, sociologists always find it less persuasive to generalize from therapy patients: what about the guys who *aren't* in therapy? We need to hear both the stories behind the statistics and the statistics themselves, the large general patterns of behavior and the individual ways that guys navigate their way through Guyland.

My research for *Guyland* has taken me to just about every state in the country, to dorm rooms and fraternity lounges, local bars and restaurants, tailgate parties, truck stops, and billiard parlors. Some guys I've interviewed online, others on the phone, and still others in chat rooms. With several colleagues, I've participated in one of the largest-ever studies of campus sexual behavior. And I've organized and run focus groups of gamers, online gamblers, porn watchers, and sports junkies to hear them talk to each other about their hobbies and obsessions.

The book brings together psychological insights into these guys' interior anguish and a sociological analysis of what larger social forces have brought them to this state. Guys tell me that they feel they are making up the rules as they go along, with neither adequate adult guidance nor appropriate road maps, and, at the same time, that they feel they are playing by rules that someone else invented and which they don't fully understand. This book explores that contradiction.

Let me make it clear: Most of the guys I meet are good guys, searching earnestly for a way to carve out a life for themselves that has meaning and integrity. But far too many are easily influenced by the bullies and the big shots, the guys who think they are making up the rules and, in any event, are the most committed to enforcing them. Many guys are simply too afraid of being taken for a wimp, and so they oblige, unwittingly perpetuating Guyland, and preventing themselves from breaking free.

Guyland sells most guys a bill of goods telling them that a constellation of behaviors are the distilled essence of manhood, which could not be farther from the truth. We need, collectively and individually, in our relationships and families, schools and churches, shopping malls and freeways, to enable young guys to see through the facade and navigate a path toward adulthood. We need to turn the world back, right side up.

They're counting on it. In order to love young men, to be compassionate about their world and their choices, we need, as a society, to look at Guyland squarely, to no longer turn a blind eye to their world and resign ourselves to boys just being boys. They are counting on us being involved in that now-expanded transition from adolescence to adulthood.

And, as the father of a 9-year-old boy, I'm counting on it too. My young son encompasses a full range of emotions—aggressive and competitive, emotionally alert and empathic, capable of flights of giddy sensitivity and gross-out fart jokes. And yet I know—and can already see—Guyland is waiting on the horizon. Guyland is looming in the occasional comments by classmates and friends about cooties and what boys and girls can and cannot do, and in the teasing and shoving that often accompanies any expression of compassion or care.

And yet my son reminds me every day of the poverty of that resigned statement that "boys will be boys." He—and all our boys—will be people. And, with our help, they will also become men—the kind of men who their families and communities can truly be proud of and admire.

2 | "WHAT'S THE RUSH?": GUYLAND AS A NEW STAGE OF DEVELOPMENT

When do you become an adult? How do you know? What are the markers of adulthood today? Is it when you can legally drink? Get married? Drive a car? Vote? Serve in the military?

Demographers typically cite five life-stage events to mark the transition to adulthood: leaving home, completing one's education, starting work, getting married, and becoming a parent. Of course, not all adults would actually check off all those markers, but they represent a pattern, a collection of indicators. In 1950, when social scientists first identified these markers of adulthood, they all clicked in at almost exactly the same time.

My parents' story is typical. They got married in 1948, after my father returned from the wartime Navy, and both he and my mother began their careers. At first, like so many of their generation, they lived in the bottom floor of my grandparents' home, saving their money to flee the city and buy a house in the New York suburbs—part of the great wave of suburban migration of the 1950s. My mother, and her five closest lifelong friends, all had their first children within two years of their weddings, and their second child three years later—all within five years of graduating from college.

Flash forward to my generation. A few years ago, I went to my twenty-fifth college reunion. Some of the women in my graduating class had college-age children; indeed, one or two already had a child at my alma mater. At the time, my wife and I were just deciding about whether or not to start a family. As I looked around, my former classmates were arranged across the spectrum—some with toddlers in strollers and others with adolescents in full pubescent rebellion. One former class-mate had just become a grandmother! In one short generation, our class had extended child-bearing from a period within a year or two of graduation to a full generation.

We also took our time completing our education, getting married, settling into our careers, and leaving home. More than half went to graduate or professional schools; many of my classmates were in their late twenties to early thirties when they completed their education (I was 30). Many had interrupted their educations (as I had) to test out a possible career path. Some waited until their late twenties or early thirties to get married; others married right after college and divorced within a few years of their weddings.

The pendulum is swinging in the same direction for the next generation. The U.S. census shows a steady and dramatic decline in the percentage of young adults, under 30, who have completed these demographic markers. In 2000, 46 percent of women and 31 percent of men had reached those markers by age 30. In 1960, just forty years earlier, 77 percent of women and 65 percent of men had reached them.

The passage between adolescence and adulthood has morphed from a transitional moment to a separate life stage. Adolescence starts earlier and earlier, and adulthood starts later and later. This stage of life—call it "the odyssey years" as does *New York Times* columnist David Brooks, or "adultolescence," or "young adulthood"—now encompasses up to two full decades, beginning at puberty and ending around one's 30th birthday. Everyone knows that 30 is the new 20. But it's equally true these days that 12 is the new 20.

A New Life Stage

We often fret how our children "grow up so fast" as we watch our precocious preteens doing things we would not even have considered until we were at least 16. On the other hand, "When will he ever grow up?" is the refrain of many older parents whose 26-year-old is also doing the same things he was doing at 16—including living at home! Both are true. Kids are growing up faster than ever, and they're staying un-grownup longer than ever, too. The "seasons of a man's life," those supposedly naturally evolving developmental stages, have undergone a dramatic climate change. In the effort to avoid an early frost, this generation is prolonging its Indian summer—sometimes for decades.

In many respects this is understandable. After all, to a guy, growing up is no bargain: It means being a sober, responsible, breadwinning husband and father. It means mortgage payments, car payments, health insurance for the kids, accountability for your actions. Just think about how manhood is portrayed on network television, where shows like *Everybody Loves Raymond* and *According to Jim* feature grown men being infantilized by their wives, unable to do the simplest things for themselves, clueless about their kids' lives, and begging for sex—or reduced to negotiating for it in exchange for housework. "Where's the fun in that?" they ask, and rightly so. Adulthood is seen as the negation of fun. It sucks. Who can blame them for not wanting to jump right in with both feet? If that's your idea of adulthood, of marriage, and of family life, it makes sense that you'd want to postpone it for as long as possible, or at least take the time to figure out a way to avoid the pitfalls so that your own life doesn't turn out that way. Here's Ted, 25, a Northwestern graduate who is working "in a soulless office" in Chicago's Loop:

> At least I got time. I mean, I'm only 25, and I'm gonna live to what, 90? So, like, why hurry on the marriage and kids thing? And besides, this gives me lots more time to meet the perfect woman, and figure out the perfect career. What's the rush?

In some ways, these young people grew up too fast. As children they were overscheduled and overobserved, every utterance and gesture parsed endlessly for clues to their developmental progress. They've coped with divorces; navigated their ways through the treacherous middle-school waters of mean girls and bullies, cliques and teams; thrown themselves into extracurricular activities and sports in order to write brilliant college application essays. They often feel that they've spent their entire childhoods being little grownups—being polite, listening attentively, and prepping for college since elementary school.

"I feel like my whole life has been one long exercise in delayed gratification," says Matt, a graduate student in psychology at the University of Wisconsin:

I mean, in high school, I had to get good grades, study hard, and do a bunch of extracurricular things so I could get into a good college. Okay, I did that. Went to Brown. Then, in college, I had to work really hard and get good grades so I could get into a good graduate school. Okay, I did that. I'm here at Wisconsin. Now, though, I have to work really hard, publish my research, so I can get a good tenure track job somewhere. And then I'll have to work really hard for six years just to get tenure. I mean, by the time I can exhale and have a little fun, I'll be in my mid–30s—and that's too old to have fun anymore!

Matt is paving the way for his career, but he can't wait to regress; adulthood is a burden.

"My grandfather died at 66," Matt says, "and he was already working and supporting a family at age 23. I expect to live to my nineties—so what's the rush? I got 30 more years than he had!"

What happened? What happened to the clearly defined path from adolescence to adulthood? What has made it expand so dramatically? The answers to these questions lead us back to some significant changes in American society—economic and demographic shifts that have had a profound impact on young people today. Before we get inside Guyland, it is important to understand the historical trajectory, set the cultural context, and map the terrain in which guys now become men. Not because these changes are either good or bad: They're neither—and both. Rather because without understanding the economic, social, and cultural context, we cannot adequately understand the pressures and the realities that face young men as they try to become adults in America today.

A Brief History of Adolescence

Once, Americans understood that a boy became a man when he completed school, got a job, and began to raise a family. In the nineteenth century, the passage from boyhood to manhood took place, for most boys, in their early teens, when they left school for the farm or factory. It wasn't that far from the truth for a Jewish boy to declare, at his bar mitzvah, that "today I am a man."

Just over a century ago, in 1904, the famous psychologist G. Stanley Hall published his massive tome, *Adolescence,* demarcating a psychological stage between childhood puerility and adult virility. Coinciding roughly with the biological changes of puberty, and coincident with its time period (roughly 12 to 15), adolescence was described as a time of transition, a time when the boy (or girl, of course, though Hall conveniently overlooked them himself) develops his adult identity, tests himself, and finds out who he really is. He enters the stage a boy, but he leaves a full-fledged man, able to negotiate his way through the thicket of adult life issues: job, family, responsibility.

Hall saw adolescence as a "storm," a perilous time of dramatic and rapid transformation. Shielded from the demands of work, boys could engage with the question of identity. But at the turn of the century, and even as late as the 1920s and 1930s, boys still entered the workplace, and adulthood, at 16. It was only when high-school graduation rates began to rise, throughout the first half of the twentieth century, that the adolescent years began to expand. By the time America entered World War II, the high-school graduation rate was at an all-time high, and a new word, "teenager," had entered the American vocabulary. Critics worried that this "sudden and dramatic prolongation of adolescence" meant that over half of those who had "passed the terminal age of adolescence" were not acting as adults—physically, socially, or economically.

And Americans have been worrying about teenagers ever since.

Some worried about teen sexuality, especially after the publication of the two volumes of the Kinsey Reports on American sexual behavior. Some worried about "juvenile delinquency," another new term from the era—lonely disaffected boys who sought approval from their peers by increasingly dangerous stunts and petty crime. "Let's Face It" read the cover of *Newsweek* in 1956, "Our Teenagers Are Out of Control." Many youths, the magazine reported, "got their fun" by "torturing helpless old men and horsewhipping girls they waylaid in public parks."

Perhaps the most influential thinker on this new stage of development was psychologist Erik Erikson. His path-breaking books, *Childhood and Society* (1950) and *Identity: Youth and Crisis* (1968), identified the seven life-stages of individual psychological development that became a mantra in developmental psychology classes for decades. By labeling adolescence as a "moratorium," a sort of prolonged time-out between childhood and adulthood, Erikson tamed and sanitized Hall's fears that adolescence was a maelstrom, a chaos of uncontrolled passions.

This moratorium was a time for regrouping, reassessing oneself before undertaking the final quest for adult identity, "a vital regenerator in the process of social evolution," as Erikson put it. Rather than rushing headlong into work and family lives, as children did in earlier societies, adolescence slows down the process to allow young people to accomplish certain identity tasks. The venerable institutions that once structured a young person's socialization—family, church, school—could no longer provide those identity needs, and thus, though plagued by doubts, adolescents were beginning to take those tentative steps toward autonomy by themselves, before facing the responsibilities of adulthood that loomed ominously ahead. In a sense, Erikson did for adolescence what Dr. Spock did for babies: reassured parents that the everyday crises their children were experiencing were simply a normal and healthy part of growing up, and that there was little they could do to screw it up.

Sociologist James Coleman had a somewhat less sanguine view. In *The Adolescent Society* (1961), he argued that the gradual recession of education, religion, and family as the primary institutions of socialization left a vacuum, and high-schoolers had largely become the agents of their own socialization. Anti-intellectualism abounded, sports reigned supreme, and everyone simply wanted to be popular! Hardly tremulous individualists, Coleman saw adolescents as frighteningly dependent on peer culture, and boys, especially, as desperate to prove their masculinity in the eyes of other boys. This certainly seems to be the case today, as guys continue to turn to one another for the validation of manhood that was once provided by the community of adults.

Biology and Science Weigh In

One reason why adolescence starts so much earlier today is that puberty, the collection of physiological markers of adolescence, now occurs four to five years earlier than it did about a century ago. Improvements in nutrition, sanitation, and healthcare have lowered the average age of puberty about one year for every twenty-five years of development. Each generation enters puberty about a year earlier than its predecessor. In the years just before the Civil War, the average age for the onset of puberty was 16 for girls, and 18 for boys; today it is about 12 for girls, and 14 for boys. Anyone who has actually spent more than five minutes in the company of contemporary 12-year-old girls and 14-year-old boys knows that these pubescent children are already well into their adolescence.

But just as adolescence reaches us earlier and earlier, what we now know about the brain suggests that it stretches longer and longer. Biologically, though puberty begins earlier, full physiological maturation still doesn't take place until well into our twenties. By 18, neuropsychological development is far from complete; the brain continues to grow and develop into the early twenties. (In a bit of a stretch, one biologist suggests that this immature brain lacks the "wiring" for placing long-term benefits over shorter-term gains, which explains how we are "hardwired" for high-risk behaviors like drug taking, smoking, and drinking when we're young.)

Markers of Adulthood: Marriage and Family

The five classic demographic markers—education, marriage, parenthood, career, and residential independence—have not simply shifted over the past generation. They've scattered across a time span that now stretches to more than a decade for a large swath of American youth. Take marriage and family. In 1950, the average age of marriage was 20.3 for women and 22.8 for men. Close to half of all women were married by age 20. By 1975, the median age had climbed about a year for both. But today it is 27.4 for men and 25.8 for women. And young people are having their first child four years later than they did in 1970.

Many of these changes have been pushed along, in part, by changes in women's lives, which have not only dramatically affected young women but young men as well. The entry of overwhelming numbers of middle-class women into the workplace is largely responsible for the postponement of marriage and child-rearing for both sexes. Today, with women appearing to be every bit as professionally competent, career-oriented, and ambitious as men, and equally capable of earning a living wage, there is no longer the same sense of urgency for men to move toward "getting a good job" to eventually provide for the material needs of a wife and children.

In much the same way, the sexual revolution of the 1960s, coupled with the invention of the birth control pill, has had a profound impact on the lives of young women, which again, in turn, has changed the lives of young men. Before the sexual revolution, young adulthood certainly didn't promise the smorgasbord of sexual experiences that it does today. Premarital sex, while certainly in existence, was nowhere near as ubiquitous. In fact, given the injunctions against it, particularly for women, it might not be too off the mark to suggest that many young people got married *in order to* have sex.

In this sense, ironically, women's newfound freedom invites men to delay adulthood even longer. With no family to support, no responsibilities to anyone other than themselves, and young women who appear to be as sexually active and playful as they could possibly ever fantasize, they're free to postpone adulthood almost indefinitely. They now assume, rightly, that since they'll live into their eighties, they have all the time in the world to commit to a career and marriage. They keep all their options open, even into their thirties (and sometimes their forties), and see their early jobs and relationships more as placeholders than as stepping-stones to adult life. There is no reason to get a real job if you don't actually need one. No reason for marriage, or even a serious relationship, if sex is really all you want. Why *should* they grow up, they wonder?

In part, this might be because parenthood and family life are no longer as appealing as they may have been in the past. Today's young people come from much less stable and settled family lives; they're far more likely to have been raised in a single-parent home and, if not, are living in a culture where divorce is the norm for half of the population. "I'm in no rush to get married, and even less in a rush to have a kid," says Jeff, a UC, San Diego, senior. "I watched my own parents get a divorce, and it became pretty clear that they got married and started having kids—namely, me—before they were ready. I'm not going to make that mistake."

Their reticence is the result of both high expectations for their own relationships and fears that their love lives will resemble their parents'. Afraid to commit, yet desperate to connect, they form close friendships with members of the opposite sex, but often make sure that sex is just about hooking up at the moment, and not about building a relationship.

"Serial Jobogamy"

They feel similarly about their careers. Middle-class kids know that their career is supposed to be more than a job; it is supposed to be financially rewarding, emotionally rich and satisfying, and offer them a sense of accomplishment and inner satisfaction. Work, for them, is an "identity quest." And while there is certainly nothing wrong with wanting a satisfying and financially rewarding professional life, many have absolutely no idea of what's available, what they want to do, or how they might begin. They have utterly unrealistic expectations about the range of jobs they might find satisfying, and no real understanding of the level of commitment and diligence involved in developing those careers. They all seem to want to write for television, become famous actors, or immediately become dot-com entrepreneurs. Whatever they do, they want to make an impact—starting on Day 1. One employment recruiter calls them "the Entitlement Generation" since they have such "shockingly high expectations for salary, job flexibility, and duties but little willingness to take on grunt work or remain loyal to a company."

While their parents fret, and wonder "when is he going to get a good job?" the truth is he'd be lucky to find a job at all. In 2000, 72.2 percent of Americans aged 20 to 24 were employed; four years later, it was 67.9 percent, barely two-thirds. The career expectations of a generation raised to feel special, their self-esteem protected at every turn, spiral upward at the same time that their economic forecast looks increasingly bleak. The secure economic foundation on which previous generations have come of age has eroded. For both the traditional blue-collar and white-collar guys, globalization has changed everything. Working-class guys face a decline in manufacturing jobs, a decline in union protection, and an increase only in the least secure dead-end service sector jobs, with neither pension nor health benefits. Middle-class guys watch their fathers get "outsourced," "downsized," "reallocated"—and they know those are just nice words for the difficult task of finding a new job at mid-life in a less certain job market than ever.

Both groups know that corporations are no longer loyal to their employees—just consider all those companies that picked up and moved out of towns they had helped to build, watching indifferently as entire communities unraveled. They've watched as corporate executives lined their pockets with the pension funds of their own employees. They've seen that despite all the promises, there's been no "trickle down" of the bloating at the top. All the tax breaks for the wealthy and wealthier have only strapped the middle class even further to their credit card debts. So why should they be loyal to the company? Or to the economy? Or to some vision of the future? They have come to believe that the only way to get rich in this culture is not by working hard, saving and sacrificing, but by winning the lottery.

Unlike virtually every single previous generation of Americans, the income trajectory for the current generation of young people is downward. Between 1949 and 1973, during that postwar economic boom, men's earnings doubled and the income gap narrowed. But since the early 1970s, annual earnings for men aged 25 to 34 with full-time jobs has steadily declined, dropping 17 percent from 1971 to 2002. Of male workers with only a high-school diploma, the average wage decline from 1975 to 2002 was 11 percent. Only half of all Americans in their mid-twenties earn enough to support a family. Two-thirds of this current generation "are not living up to their parents' standard of living," commented Andrew Sum, the Director of the Center for Labor Market Studies at Northeastern University.

The gap between college-educated and noncollege-educated has increased as well. In the late 1970s, male college graduates earned about 33 percent more than high-school graduates; by the end of the 1980s, that gap had increased to 53 percent "When I graduated from high school, my classmates who didn't want to go to college could go to the Goodyear plant and buy a house and support a wife and family," Steven Hamilton of the Cornell University Youth and Work Program told *Time* magazine. "That doesn't happen anymore."

Nor do they have much protection. Once they're 18 or 19, young people are only covered as dependents on their parents' medical and healthcare plans if they go to college. All government healthcare covers children only through their eighteenth year. (They lose healthcare under these programs on their nineteenth birthday.) And many young people work at low-wage, temporary, low- or no-benefit jobs, or remain dependent on their parents.

There is no mistaking the economic signs: This generation of young people is downwardly mobile. Gen X'ers and Gen Y'ers will earn less than their parents did at every single age. Young adults, those 18 to 26 years old are the lowest ranked in earned income of all age groups. Their household income is the second lowest (right above 65 and older). "On most socioeconomic measures, the young were the worst-off age group in 1997—and the gap has widened since," notes Tom Smith, the director of the General Social Survey, that has tracked Americans' life experiences since 1972.

The only economic sector in which jobs are being created is entry-level service and sales. In *Generation X*, author Douglas Coupland calls it "McJob"—"low-paying, low-prestige, low-dignity, no future job in the service sector." Young people, along with immigrants, minorities, and the elderly, are the bulk of workers in the new service economy. Half of all workers in restaurants, grocery stores, and department stores are under 24. As one journalist recently put it, "hundreds of thousands of young people are spending hours making decaf lattes, folding jeans, grilling burgers, or unpacking boxes of books and records for minimum wage." And their poverty rates are twice the national average.

Since these jobs are so plentiful, many young people don't feel the need to commit to a career right out of college. And because so many of the entry-level "real" jobs pay almost as badly, and are almost as mind-numbing, they are even less motivated to do so. The young have been raised in a culture that promises instant gratification; the idea of working hard for future rewards just doesn't resonate with them. They don't have their eyes on the prize; it's really more like their "eyes on the fries," as a recent documentary film put it. The increased instability of their long-term employment prospects, coupled with their sense that jobs must be emotionally and financially fulfilling, leads to a volatile career trajectory. Many experience the "two-month itch" and switch jobs as casually as they change romantic partners. They take "stop-gap jobs," engaging in what I like to call "serial jobogamy." Listen to Jon, a 1992 Rutgers grad, who told a journalist about his career cluelessness:

I had absolutely no idea what I wanted to do right out of college. I fell blindly into a couple of dead-end jobs, which were just there for me to make money and figure out what I wanted to do. When I had no idea what I wanted to do, I couldn't even picture myself doing anything because I was so clueless about what was out there. I had so little direction. I was hanging on to these completely dead-end jobs thinking that maybe something would turn up. I was unhappy about the situation, and the only thing that made it better was that all of my friends out of college were in the same boat. We would all come home and complain about our jobs together. We were all still drunks back then.

Many young adults feel they are just treading water, waiting for the right job, the right person, the right situation, to reveal itself. "I'm just sitting around waiting for my life to begin, while it's all just slippin' away," sings Bruce Springsteen on "Better Days."

Most guys do grow out of this phase, eventually. They get tired of living four-to-a-room, tired of dead-end jobs that leave them broke and exhausted, tired of answering to their parents if they live at home, and they begin to reconsider career paths that they once dismissed as being "too boring." Some go on to graduate school; others accept those entry-level jobs that, they hope, will lead to something better. But in our increasingly competitive economy, where the cost of living is rising and the availability of well-paying jobs is shrinking, they're facing a tougher time of it than ever. When their first real job requires that they work late every night, yet only pays enough to cover the rent if they share a two-bedroom apartment with four other people, it's no wonder guys are reluctant to grow up.

Education for What?

Young people today are the most highly educated group of young people in our history. At the turn of the last century, only a small fraction of male teens attended secondary schools. Most lived with their families and made considerable financial contributions to the family income. In fact, for many working-class families, the family's most prosperous years were the years their children were living at home with them.

Now, the vast majority of teens attend secondary school. In 2000, over 88 percent of all people 25 to 29 had completed high school and nearly 30 percent (29.1 percent, to be precise) had a BA—up from 17 percent only thirty years ago.

Although more are going to college, it's taking them longer to finish. Four years after high school, 15 percent of the high-school graduating class of 1972 had obtained their degree. Ten years later, the percentage had been cut to less than 7 percent, and today it's closer to 4 percent four years out.

They also leave college with huge debts. Two-thirds of all college graduates owe more than $10,000 when they graduate; the average debt is nearly $20,000, and 5 percent owe more than $100,000. Recent college graduates owe 85 percent more in student loans alone than graduates a decade ago according to the Center for Economic and Policy Research. (The amount you are allowed to borrow has steadily increased as well, enabling more students to stay in school, yet increasing their repayment burdens when they leave.) And this doesn't begin to touch the credit card debt amassed by this age group, which has more than doubled between 1992 and 2001. Bombarded daily with promotional offers from credit card companies, many rack up debt like I used to collect baseball cards.

The twentieth century has seen these kids move from being productive citizens to being dependent on their families, the educational system, and the state. Less than one-third of this age group are employed enough to make them potentially financially independent. Those who live with their parents make virtually no contribution to family income. The opposite is true, and for a lot longer time. More than one-third of youth aged 18 to 34 receive cash from their parents, and nearly half receive what sociologists call "time-help" from their parents in any given year—that is significant contributions of time helping kids with their daily lives, from cooking, to cleaning, to doing laundry—averaging about $3,410 in cash and about 367 hours of help.

No wonder two-thirds of all young people 18 to 24 live with their parents or other relatives, and one-fifth of all 25-year-old Americans still live at home. And no wonder that 40 percent of all college graduates return to live with their parents for at least some period of time in that age span. Forget the empty nest syndrome—for one in five American families it's still a "full nest."

One reality that makes this possible is that we live in a culture of privilege. Many parents today can afford to a greater extent than ever before to let their children take advantage of this situation. They have large homes, larger disposable incomes, and are more receptive to the idea of kids coming back to the nest. This is not necessarily a bad trend, but it certainly helps explain why young people are taking so much longer to reach adulthood.

What the Experts Say—and Don't Say

Others have surely noticed that something is happening, that there is a difference from the way previous generations passed from adolescence to adulthood. A front-page story in *USA Today* in September 2004 was followed a few months later by a cover story in *Time* calling them "twixters"—neither kids nor adults, but betwixt and between. But the subsequent letters the magazine published offer a glimpse into our national confusion. The twixters themselves wrote eloquently about their situations. One moved back home after college because she couldn't find a job that paid enough to live on her own—only to find that ". . . the majority of my high school class had done the same thing." But, she insisted, ". . . we are not lazy. We want to work and make our way in the world." Another pointed out that her generation is ". . . overwhelmed by indecision. We have the necessary tools, but now have too many options and not enough options at the same time. We are stuck."

By contrast to the twixters themselves adult letter writers were uniformly unsympathetic. They blamed the kids, as if the disastrous economy, sky-high housing costs, and high aspirations with no ways to fulfill them were somehow the fault of job seekers, not job-suppliers—namely the adults themselves. "If only their parents had cut the golden apron strings and left them to their own devices, they would have learned to be more independent," wrote one. "There's not a single thing wrong with the young adults who live off their parents that a stint in the U.S. Marine Corps couldn't fix," wrote another. "Why do we need to come up with a new label for kids who stay home with their parents while figuring out what to do?" asked another, before reminding us that "we've had a name for that for years: moocher."

Ironically, all of the twixter letters were from women, and all of the adult respondents were male. And though *Time* did not comment on this interesting gender difference, it is an important element in our conversation: It is fathers—far more than mothers—who deeply resent the return of their college-graduate children. Mothers may, for a time, mourn the absence of their children, as if their world has suddenly lost its center of gravity and spins aimlessly off its axis. Fathers, by contrast, often celebrate their new freedom from child-care responsibilities: They buy new golf clubs, load up on Viagra, and talk about this being, finally, their "turn." Mothers may be ambivalent about the "full nest" syndrome, but their husbands seem to be universally unhappy about it.

Developmental psychologists and sociologists have also tried to map this newly emerging stage of life. Sociologist James Cote, at the University of Western Ontario, calls the period "youthhood," while Terri Apter, a social psychologist in Cambridge, England, calls them "thresholders," who suffer from the neglect and scorn from parents who mistake their need for support and guidance as irresponsibility and immaturity.

Perhaps the most ambitious effort to map this post-adolescent *terra incognita* has been psychologist Jeffrey Arnett's studies of what he calls "emerging adulthood." Like Erickson a half-century ago, Arnett sees emerging adulthood as a time for the gradual unfolding of a life plan, a "time for serious self-reflection, for thinking about what kind of life you want to live and what your Plan should be for your life." It's a period of increased independence—including independence from the preordained roles that they inherited from their elders. They are moving deliberately if unevenly toward intimate relationships, a steady and stable career path, and family lives, and along the way they are developing closer friendships with their parents, since the old issues of adolescent rebellion have been resolved by time and experience.

In an ideal world, this might be a dream trajectory. Yet Arnett's view of this stage of life is so sanguine, so sanitized, it's hardly recognizable. It's hard to square such serious self-reflection with the bacchanalian atmosphere of a college weekend; increasing autonomy and a decreasing reliance on peer groups with the fraternity initiations, athletic hazing, and various forms of sexual predation that often fill exposés of campus life.

Perhaps the chief characteristic of this stage of life is its indeterminacy. There's a massive mismatch between the ambitions of this group and their accomplishments. They graduate from college filled with ideas about changing the world, making their contribution, and making lots of money, and they enter a job market at the bottom, where work is utterly unfulfilling, boring, and badly paid. "It concerns me that of the many gifted people I went to school with, so few of them are actually doing what they really want to do," said one. This was a generation that was told from the get-go that each of them was special, in which their self-esteem was so inflated they became light-headed, in which they were rewarded for every normal developmental milestone as if they were Mozart.

Extremely other-directed, they perform to please grownups—parents, teachers—but exhibit little capacity for self-reflection or internal motivation. They have high self-esteem, but often little self-awareness. Many suspect that their self-esteem, so disconnected from actual achievement, is a bit of a fraud. Many lack a moral compass to help negotiate their way in the world.

For these young people, the world is unstable and uncertain. They drink more than they think they should, take more drugs, and probably get involved in more hookups and bad relationships than they think they should. And they also get more down on themselves, because at this stage they also think they should know better. Their suicide rate is the highest for any age group except men over 70.

They're also more disconnected from society. They have less confidence in social, economic, and political institutions. They are less likely to read a newspaper, attend church, belong to a religion or a union, vote for a president, or identify with a political party than any other age group, according to the General Social Survey. They're more cynical or negative about other people and less trusting. They are less likely to believe that people are basically trustworthy, helpful, fair, or that human beings are naturally good.

Adulthood Is an Attitude

If the demographic markers of adulthood are now scattered across a decade or more, young people today are turning to more attitudinal indicators of when they become adults. Arnett found that the traditional demographic markers held little sway in determining whether or not a student felt like an adult. On the other hand, psychological criteria received much higher endorsements. "Accept responsibility for the consequences of your actions" led the list. Being able to "decide on personal beliefs and values independently of parents or other influences" was next, tied with being "less self-oriented, develop[ing] greater consideration for others."

So, today people become adults when they *feel* like adults. They experience a "situational maturity." Sometimes they want to be treated like adults, sometimes they want to be treated like children. (And their parents invariably guess wrong!) "You don't get lectures about what life is like after college," comments a guy named Brandon to journalist Alexandra Robbins in her book, *Quarterlife Crisis*. "You don't have a textbook that tells you what you need to do to find success." "People have to invent their own road map," commented another.

And they don't experience a calamitous break with their childhoods, since there is no one time when all five transitional indicators are achieved. By spreading them out, adulthood becomes a gradual process, a series of smaller decisions. One looks back suddenly and realizes one is actually an adult. The General Social Survey found that most people believe the transition to adulthood should be completed by age 26, a number that seems to rise every year.

One young man recently wrote to me that, a year after graduating from college and moving across the country, his father had come to visit him. And the father stayed at the son's apartment. "I'm starting to feel like a real adult," he wrote. "I mean, when you live in a different city from your parents and when they visit, they stay with you, well . . . you're an adult!"

Gender: The Missing Conversation

One reason Jeffrey Arnett and his colleagues can be so sanguine about emerging adulthood is because there is nary a word about gender in their work. But how can one possibly discuss the age group 16 to 26 and not talk about gender? It's the most gendered stage of a person's development. Sociologists James Cote and Anton Allahar call it "gender intensification"—the assertion of "exaggerated notions associated with the different roles that still hold many men and women in separate spheres of endeavor." This stage is when the struggle to prove manhood becomes even more intense, in part because it's no longer as easy to differentiate between men and women as it was in the past. The traditional markers of manhood—being the head of a household, having a steady job, and providing for the material needs of a family—are obsolete. The days when "girls were girls and men were men," are long gone. What once marked manhood today marks adulthood—for both sexes. So what does it mean to be a man? That's something most guys are still trying to figure out.

Today's young men are coming of age in an era with no road maps, no blueprints, and no primers to tell them what a man is or how to become one. And that's why none of the terms given to this stage of development—"emerging adulthood," "transition to adulthood," "twixters," "thresholders"—has any resonance whatever with the young men I have spoken to on college campuses and in workplaces around the country. Almost all of them call themselves—and call each other—"guys." It's a generic catch-all term that demarcates this age group, setting it apart from "kids" and "grownups."

Understanding exactly what guys are up against is vital and urgent—for the young men, for those who love them, and for our society. Young men need more than the often volatile combination of anomie and entitlement that can come to characterize Guyland. They need guidance. They need the adults who orbit their world—their parents, teachers, counselors, bosses, coaches, administrators—to understand what is happening in their lives, the pressure they feel to live up to unattainable ideals of masculinity, and the feelings of doubt, anxiety, and shame that often accompany that quest. And they need—and deserve—a larger public conversation about the world they inhabit, to enable them to better navigate its more hazardous shoals.

Even *with* a map, it is a difficult passage to chart. After all, part of the definition of masculinity is to act as if one knows exactly where one is going. If men have a difficult time asking for directions when they get lost driving their cars, imagine what it feels like to feel lost and adrift on the highway of life! One must act as if one knows where one is going, even if it isn't true. And it's this posture, and the underlying sense that one is a fraud, that leaves young men most vulnerable to manipulation by the media and by their peers. It's as if they're saying, "If I just follow along and don't ask any questions, everyone will assume I have it all together—and I won't be exposed."

Guyland thus becomes the arena in which young men so relentlessly seem to act out, seem to take the greatest risks, and do some of the stupidest things. Directionless and often clueless, they rely increasingly on their peers to usher them into adulthood and validate their masculinity. And their peers often have some interesting plans for what they will have to endure to prove that they are real men.

They feel incomplete and insecure, terrified that they will fail as grownups, that they will be exposed as fraudulent men. "Every man's armor is borrowed and ten sizes too big and beneath it, he's naked and insecure and hoping you won't see," is how journalist Norah Vincent put it in her cross-dressing memoir, *Self-Made Man.* Caught between being "real boys" and real men, they have all the entitlement and none of the power. No wonder that, to guys, boyhood is a safe and secure retreat—it's a regression with a mission.

Guyland is a volatile stage, when one has access to all the tools of adulthood with few of the moral and familial constraints that urge sober conformity. These "almost men" struggle to live up to a definition of masculinity they feel they had no part in creating, and yet from which they feel powerless to escape. Individually, a guy often feels that if there is a playbook everyone else has read it—except him. That playbook is called "The Guy Code."

3 | "BROS BEFORE HOS": THE GUY CODE

Whenever I ask young women what they think it means to be a woman, they look at me puzzled, and say, basically, "Whatever I want." "It doesn't mean anything at all to me," says Nicole, a junior at Colby College in Maine. "I can be Mia Hamm, I can be Britney Spears, I can be Madame Curie or Madonna. Nobody can tell me what it means to be a woman anymore."

For men, the question is still meaningful—and powerful. In countless workshops on college campuses and in high-school assemblies, I've asked young men what it means to be a man. I've asked guys from every state in the nation, as well as about fifteen other countries, what sorts of phrases and words come to mind when they hear someone say, "Be a man!"

The responses are rather predictable. The first thing someone usually says is "Don't cry," then other similar phrases and ideas—never show your feelings, never ask for directions, never give up, never give in, be strong, be aggressive, show no fear, show no mercy, get rich, get even, get laid, win—follow easily after that.

Here's what guys say, summarized into a set of current epigrams. Think of it as a "Real Guy's Top Ten List."

1. "Boys Don't Cry"
2. "It's Better to be Mad than Sad"
3. "Don't Get Mad—Get Even"
4. "Take It Like a Man"
5. "He Who has the Most Toys When he Dies, Wins"
6. "Just Do It," or "Ride or Die"
7. "Size Matters"
8. "I Don't Stop to Ask for Directions"
9. "Nice Guys Finish Last"
10. "It's All Good"

The unifying emotional subtext of all these aphorisms involves never showing emotions or admitting to weakness. The face you must show to the world insists that everything is going just fine, that everything is under control, that there's nothing to be concerned about (a contemporary version of Alfred E. Neuman of *MAD* Magazine's "What, me worry?"). Winning is crucial, especially when the victory is over other men who have less amazing or smaller toys. Kindness is not an option, nor is compassion. Those sentiments are taboo.

This is "The Guy Code," the collection of attitudes, values, and traits that together composes what it means to be a man. These are the rules that govern behavior in Guyland, the criteria that will be used to evaluate whether any particular guy measures up. The Guy Code revisits what psychologist William Pollack called "the boy code" in his bestselling book *Real Boys*—just a couple of years older and with a lot more at stake. And just as Pollack and others have explored the dynamics of boyhood so well, we now need to extend the reach of that analysis to include late adolescence and young adulthood.

In 1976, social psychologist Robert Brannon summarized the four basic rules of masculinity:

1. "No Sissy Stuff!" Being a man means not being a sissy, not being perceived as weak, effeminate, or gay. Masculinity is the relentless repudiation of the feminine.
2. "Be a Big Wheel." This rule refers to the centrality of success

and power in the definition of masculinity. Masculinity is measured more by wealth, power, and status than by any particular body part.

3. "Be a Sturdy Oak." What makes a man is that he is reliable in a crisis. And what makes him so reliable in a crisis is not that he is able to respond fully and appropriately to the situation at hand, but rather that he resembles an inanimate object. A rock, a pillar, a species of tree.

4. "Give 'em Hell." Exude an aura of daring and aggression. Live life out on the edge. Take risks. Go for it. Pay no attention to what others think.

Amazingly, these four rules have changed very little among successive generations of high-school and college-age men. James O'Neil, a developmental psychologist at the University of Connecticut, and Joseph Pleck, a social psychologist at the University of Illinois, have each been conducting studies of this normative definition of masculinity for decades. "One of the most surprising findings," O'Neil told me, "is how little these rules have changed."

Being a Man Among Men

Where do young men get these ideas? "Oh, definitely, my dad," says Mike, a 20-year-old sophomore at Wake Forest. "He was always riding my ass, telling me I had to be tough and strong to make it in this world."

"My older brothers were always on my case," says Drew, a 24-year-old University of Massachusetts grad. "They were like, always ragging on me, calling me a pussy, if I didn't want to play football or wrestle. If I just wanted to hang out and like play my Xbox, they were constantly in my face."

"It was subtle, sometimes," says Warren, a 21-year-old at Towson, "and other times really out front. In school, it was the male teachers, saying stuff about how explorers or scientists were so courageous and braving the elements and all that. Then, other times, it was phys-ed class, and everyone was all over everyone else talking about 'He's so gay' and 'He's a wuss.' "

"The first thing I think of is my coach," says Don, a 26-year-old former football player at Lehigh. "Any fatigue, any weakness, any sign that being hit actually hurt and he was like 'Waah! [fake crying] Widdle Donny got a boo boo. Should we kiss it guys?' He'd completely humiliate us for showing anything but complete toughness. I'm sure he thought he was building up our strength and ability to play, but it wore me out trying to pretend all the time, to suck it up and just take it."

The response was consistent: Guys hear the voices of the men in their lives—fathers, coaches, brothers, grandfathers, uncles, priests—to inform their ideas of masculinity.

This is no longer surprising to me. One of the more startling things I found when I researched the history of the idea of masculinity in America for a previous book was that men subscribe to these ideals not because they want to impress women, let alone any inner drive or desire to test themselves against some abstract standards. They do it because they want to be positively evaluated by other men. American men want to be a "man among men," an Arnold Schwarzenegger-like "man's man," not a Fabio-like "ladies' man." Masculinity is largely a "homosocial" experience: performed for, and judged by, other men.

Noted playwright David Mamet explains why women don't even enter the mix. "Women have, in men's minds, such a low place on the social ladder of this country that it's useless to define yourself in terms of a woman. What men need is men's approval." While women often become a kind of currency by which men negotiate their status with other men, women are for possessing, not for emulating.

The Gender Police

Other guys constantly watch how well we perform. Our peers are a kind of "gender police," always waiting for us to screw up so they can give us a ticket for crossing the well-drawn boundaries of manhood. As young men, we become relentless cowboys, riding the fences, checking the boundary line between masculinity and femininity, making sure that nothing slips over. The possibilities of being unmasked are everywhere. Even the most seemingly insignificant misstep can pose a threat or activate that haunting terror that we will be found out.

On the day the students in my class "Sociology of Masculinity" were scheduled to discuss homophobia, one student provided an honest and revealing anecdote. Noting that it was a beautiful day, the first day of spring after a particularly brutal Northeast winter, he decided to wear shorts to class. "I had this really nice pair of new Madras shorts," he recounted. "But then I thought to myself, these shorts have lavender and pink in them. Today's class topic is homophobia. Maybe today is not the best day to wear these shorts." Nods all around.

Our efforts to maintain a manly front cover everything we do. What we wear. How we talk. How we walk. What we eat (like the recent flap over "manwiches"—those artery-clogging massive burgers, dripping with extras). Every mannerism, every movement contains a coded gender language. What happens if you refuse or resist? What happens if you step outside the definition of masculinity? Consider the words that would be used to describe you. In workshops it generally takes less than a minute to get a list of about twenty terms that are at the tip of everyone's tongues: wimp, faggot, dork, pussy, loser, wuss, nerd, queer, homo, girl, gay, skirt, Mama's boy, pussy-whipped. This list is so effortlessly generated, so consistent, that it composes a national well from which to draw epithets and put-downs.

Ask any teenager in America what is the most common put-down in middle school or high school? The answer: "That's so gay." It's said about anything and everything—their clothes, their books, the music or TV shows they like, the sports figures they admire. "That's so gay" has become a free-floating put-down, meaning bad, dumb, stupid, wrong. It's the generic bad thing.

Listen to one of America's most observant analysts of masculinity, Eminem. Asked in an MTV interview in 2001 why he constantly used "faggot" in every one of his raps to put down other guys, Eminem told the interviewer, Kurt Loder,

The lowest degrading thing you can say to a man when you're battling him is to call him a faggot and try to take away his manhood. Call him a sissy, call him a punk. "Faggot" to me doesn't necessarily mean gay people. "Faggot" to me just means taking away your manhood.

But does it mean homosexuality? Does it really suggest that you suspect the object of the epithet might actually be attracted to another guy? Think, for example, of how you would answer this question: If you see a man walking down the street, or meet him at a party, how do you "know" if he is homosexual? (Assume that he is not wearing a T-shirt with a big pink triangle on it, and that he's not already holding hands with another man.)

When I ask this question in classes or workshops, respondents invariably provide a standard list of stereotypically effeminate behaviors. He walks a certain way, talks a certain way, acts a certain way. He's well dressed, sensitive, and emotionally expressive. He has certain tastes in art and music—indeed, he has *any* taste in art and music! Men tend to focus on the physical attributes, women on the emotional. Women say they "suspect" a man might be gay if he's interested in what she's talking about, knows something about what she's talking about, or is sensitive and a good listener. One recently said, "I suspect he might be gay if he's looking at my eyes, and not down my blouse." Another said she suspects he might be gay if he shows no sexual interest in her, if he doesn't immediately come on to her.

Once I've established what makes a guy "suspect," I ask the men in the room if any of them would want to be thought of as gay. Rarely does a hand go up—despite the fact that this list of attributes is actually far preferable to the restrictive one that stands in the "Be a Man" box. So, what do straight men do to make sure that no one gets the wrong idea about them?

Everything that is perceived as gay goes into what we might call the Negative Playbook of Guyland. Avoid everything in it and you'll be all right. Just make sure that you walk, talk, and act in a different way from the gay stereotype; dress terribly; show no taste in art or music; show no emotions at all. Never listen to a thing a woman is saying, but express immediate and unquenchable sexual interest. Presto, you're a real man, back in the "Be a Man" box. Homophobia—the fear that people might *misperceive* you as gay—is the animating fear of American guys' masculinity. It's what lies underneath the crazy risk-taking behaviors practiced by boys of all ages, what drives the fear that other guys will see you as weak, unmanly, frightened. The single cardinal rule of manhood, the one from which all the other characteristics—wealth, power, status, strength, physicality—are derived is to offer constant proof that you are not gay.

Homophobia is even deeper than this. It's the fear *of* other men—that other men will perceive you as a failure, as a fraud. It's a fear that others will see you as weak, unmanly, frightened. This is how John Steinbeck put it in his novel *Of Mice and Men*:

> "Funny thing," [Curley's wife] said. "If I catch any one man, and he's alone, I get along fine with him. But just let two of the guys get together an' you won't talk. Jus' nothin' but mad." She dropped her fingers and put her hands on her hips. "You're all scared of each other, that's what. Ever'one of you's scared the rest is goin' to get something on you."

In that sense, homosexuality becomes a kind of shorthand for "unmanliness"—and the homophobia that defines and animates the daily conversations of Guyland is at least as much about masculinity as it is about sexuality.

But what would happen to a young man if he were to refuse such limiting parameters on who he is and how he's permitted to act? "It's not like I want to stay in that box," says Jeff, a first-year Cornell student at my workshop. "But as soon as you step outside it, even for a second, all the other guys are like, 'What are you, dude, a fag?' It's not very safe out there on your own. I suppose as I get older, I'll get more secure, and feel like I couldn't care less what other guys say. But now, in my fraternity, on this campus, man, I'd lose everything."

The consistency of responses is as arresting as the list is disturbing: "I would lose my friends." "Get beat up." "I'd be ostracized." "Lose my self-esteem." Some say they'd take drugs or drink. Become withdrawn, sullen, a loner, depressed. "Kill myself," says one guy. "Kill them," responds another. Everyone laughs, nervously. Some say they'd get mad. And some say they'd get even. "I dunno," replied Mike, a sophomore at Portland State University. "I'd probably pull a Columbine. I'd show them that they couldn't get away with calling me that shit."

Guys know that they risk everything—their friendships, their sense of self, maybe even their lives—if they fail to conform. Since the stakes are so enormous, young men take huge chances to prove their manhood, exposing themselves to health risks, workplace hazards, and stress-related illnesses. Here's a revealing factoid. Men ages 19 to 29 are three times less likely to wear seat belts than women the same age. Before they turn nineteen though, young men are actually *more* likely to wear seat belts. It's as if they suddenly get the idea that as long as they're driving the car, they're completely in control, and therefore safe. Ninety percent of all driving offenses, excluding parking violations, are committed by men, and 93 percent of road ragers are male. Safety is emasculating! So they drink too much, drive too fast, and play chicken in a multitude of dangerous venues.

The comments above provide a telling riposte to all those theories of biology that claim that this definition of masculinity is "hard-wired," the result of millennia of evolutionary adaptation or the behavioral response to waves of aggression-producing testosterone, and therefore inevitable. What these theories fail to account for is the way that masculinity is coerced and policed relentlessly by other guys. If it were biological, it would be as natural as breathing or blinking. In truth, the Guy Code fits as comfortably as a straightjacket.

Boys' Psychological Development: Where the Guy Code Begins

Masculinity is a constant test—always up for grabs, always needing to be proved. And the testing starts early. Recently, I was speaking with a young black mother, a social worker, who was concerned about a conversation she had had with her husband a few nights earlier. It seems that her husband had taken their son to the barber, which, she explained to me, is a central social institution in the African-American community. As the barber prepared the boy's hair for treatment, using, apparently some heat and some painful burning chemicals, the boy began to cry. The barber turned to the boy's father and pronounced, "This boy is a wimp!" He went on, "This boy has been spending too much time with his mama! Man, you need to put your foot down. You have got to get this boy away from his mother!"

That evening the father came home, visibly shaken by the episode, and announced to his wife that from that moment on the boy would not be spending as much time with her, but instead would do more sports and other activities with him, "to make sure he doesn't become a sissy."

After telling me this story, the mother asked what I thought she should do. "Gee," I said, "I understand the pressures that dads feel to 'toughen up' their sons. But how old is your boy, anyway?"

"Three and a half," she said.

I tried to remind her, of course, that crying is the natural human response to pain, and that her son was behaving appropriately. But her story reminded me of how early this pressure starts to affect an emotionally impervious manly stoicism.

Ever since Freud, we've believed that the key to boys' development is separation, that the boy must switch his identification from mother to father in order to "become" a man. He achieves his masculinity by repudiation, dissociation, and then identification. It is a perilous path, but a necessary one, even though there is nothing inevitable about it—and nothing biological either. Throw in an overdominant mother, or an absent father, and we start worrying that the boy will not succeed in his masculine quest.

Boys learn that their connection to mother will emasculate them, turn them into Mama's Boys. And so they learn to act *as if* they have made that leap by pushing away from their mothers. Along the way they suppress all the feelings they associate with the maternal—compassion, nurturance, vulnerability, dependency. This suppression and repudiation is the origin of the Boy Code. It's what turns those happy, energetic, playful, and emotionally expressive 5-year-olds into sullen, withdrawn, and despondent 9-year-olds. In the recent spate of bestselling books about boys' development, psychologists like William Pollack, James Garbarino, Michael Thompson, Dan Kindlon, and others, argue that from an early age boys are taught to refrain from crying, to suppress their emotions, never to display vulnerability. As a result, boys feel effeminate not only if they *express* their emotions, but even if they *feel* them. In their bestseller, *Raising Cain,* Kindlon and Thompson describe a "culture of cruelty" in which peers force other boys to deny their emotional needs and disguise their feelings. It's no wonder that so many boys end up feeling emotionally isolated.

These books about boys map the inner despair that comes from such emotional numbness and fear of vulnerability. Pollack calls it the "mask of masculinity," the fake front of impervious, unemotional independence, a swaggering posture that boys believe will help them to present a stoic front. "Ruffled in a manly pose," the great Irish poet William Butler Yeats put it in his poem "Coole Park" (1929), "For all his timid heart."

The ruffling starts often by age 4 or 5, when he enters kindergarten, and it gets a second jolt when he hits adolescence. Think of the messages boys get: Stand on your own two feet! Don't cry! Don't be a sissy! As one boy in Pollack's book summarizes it: "Shut up and take it, or you'll be sorry." When I asked my 9-year-old son, Zachary, what he thought of when I said "be a man" he said that one of his friends said something about "taking it like a man. So," he explained, "I think it means acting tougher than you actually are."

Recently a colleague told me about a problem he was having. It seems his 7-year-old son, James, was being bullied by another boy on his way home from school. His wife, the boy's mother, strategized with her son about how to handle such situations in the future. She suggested he find an alternate route home, tell a teacher, or perhaps even tell the boy's parents. And she offered the standard "use your words, not your fists" conflict-reducer. "How can I get my wife to stop treating James like a baby?" my colleague asked. "How will he ever learn to stand up for himself if she turns him into a wimp?"

The Boy Code leaves boys disconnected from a wide range of emotions and prohibited from sharing those feelings with others. As they grow older, they feel disconnected from adults, as well, unable to experience the guidance towards maturity that adults can bring. When they turn to anger and violence it is because these, they believe, perhaps rightly, are the only acceptable forms of emotional expression allowed them. Just as the Boy Code shuts boys down, the Guy Code reinforces those messages, suppressing what was left of boyhood exuberance and turning it into sullen indifference.

No wonder boys are more prone to depression, suicidal behavior, and various other forms of out-of-control or out-of-touch behaviors than girls are. No wonder boys drop out of school and are diagnosed as emotionally disturbed four times more often as girls, get into fights twice as often, and are six times more likely than girls to be diagnosed with Attention Deficit and Hyperactivity Disorder (ADHD).

The Pressure to Conform

I often ask my students to imagine two American men—one, 75 years old, black, and gay, who lives in downtown Chicago, and the other, a 19-year-old white heterosexual farm boy living 100 miles south of Chicago. How might their ideas about masculinity differ? And what ideas about masculinity might they have in common, ideas that transcend class, race, age, and sexual or regional differences?

While the Guy Code isn't everywhere exactly the same, and while there are some variations by class or race or age or sexuality, the pressure to conform is so powerful a centripetal force that it minimizes differences, pushing guys into a homogenous, ill-fitting uniform. The sociologist Erving Goffman once described the dominant image of masculinity like this:

> In an important sense there is only one complete unblushing male in America: a young, married, white, urban, northern, heterosexual, Protestant, father, of college education, fully employed, of good complexion, weight, and height, and a recent record in sports . . . Any male who fails to qualify in any one of these ways is likely to view himself—during moments at least—as unworthy, incomplete, and inferior.

This dynamic is critical. Every single man will, at some point in his life, "fail to qualify." That is, every single one of us will feel, at least at moments, "unworthy, incomplete, and inferior." It is from those feelings of inadequacy and inferiority that we often act recklessly—taking foolish risks, engaging in violence—all as an attempt to repair, restore, or reclaim our place in the sacred box of manhood.

It's equally true that guys express the Guy Code differently at different times of their lives. Even at different times of day! Even if he believes that to be a man is to always be in charge, to be aggressive and powerful, he is unlikely to express that around his coaches or teachers, let alone his parents. There are times when even the most manly of men must accept authority, obey orders, and shut up and listen.

This is especially true in Guyland, because this intermediate moment, poised between adolescence and adulthood, enables young men to be somewhat strategic in their expression of masculinity. They can be men when it suits them, when they want to be taken seriously by the world around them, and they can also be boys when it suits them, when they don't want to be held to account as adults for their actions, but simply want to get away with it.

Violence as Restoration

The Guy Code, and the Boy Code before it, demands a lot—that boys and young men shut down emotionally, that they suppress compassion, and inflate ambition. And it extracts compliance with coercion and fear. But it also promises so much as well. Part of what makes the Guy Code so seductive are the rewards guys think will be theirs if they only walk the line. If they embrace the Code, they will finally be in charge and feel powerful. And so, having dutifully subscribed, young men often feel cheated—and pissed off—when the rewards associated with power are not immediately forthcoming.

Violence is how they express all that disappointment. Rage is the way to displace the feelings of humiliation, to restore the entitlement. "The emotion of shame is the primary or ultimate cause of all violence," writes psychiatrist James Gilligan. "The purpose of violence is to diminish the intensity of shame and replace it as far as possible with its opposite, pride, thus preventing the individual from being overwhelmed by the feeling of shame." "It's better to be mad than sad," writes psychologist James Garbarino.

Virtually every male in America understands something about violence. We know how it works, we know how to use it, and we know that if we are perceived as weak or unmanly, it will be used against us. Each of us cuts his own deal with it.

It's as American as apple pie. Resorting to violence to restore one's honor from perceived humiliations has been around ever since one caveman chided another on the size of his club, but few modern societies have made violence such a cultural and psychological foundation. Cultural historian Richard Slotkin's history of the American frontier claims that our understanding of violence is regenerative: It enables us to grow. The great anthropologist Margaret Mead once commented that what made American violence stand out was our nearly obsessive need to legitimate the use of violence; ours is an aggression, she wrote, "which can never be shown except when the other fellow starts it" and which is "so unsure of itself that it had to be proved." Americans like to think that we don't start wars, we just finish them.

And what's true on the battlefield is also true on the playground. Watch two boys squaring off sometime. "You wanna start something?" one yells. "No, but if you start it, I'll finish it!" shouts the other. Adolescent male violence is so restorative that it's even been prescribed by generations of dads to enable their boys to stand up for themselves. And they've had plenty of support from experts, like J. Alfred Puffer, author of *The Boy and His Gang*, a child-rearing manual from the early twentieth century which offered this counsel:

There are times when every boy must defend his own rights if he is not to become a coward and lose the road to independence and true manhood . . . The strong willed boy needs no inspiration to combat, but often a good deal of guidance and restraint. If he fights more than, let us say, a half dozen times a week—except, of course, during his first week at a new school—he is probably over-quarrelsome and needs to curb. The sensitive, retiring boy, on the other hand, needs encouragement to stand his ground and fight.

In this bestseller, boys were encouraged to fight once a day, except during the first week at a new school, when it was presumed they would fight more often!

The contemporary Guy Code also descends from older notions of honor—a man had to be ready to fight to prove himself in the eyes of others. In the early nineteenth century, Southern whites called it "honor"; by the turn of the century it was called "reputation." Later in the century, "having a chip on your shoulder"—walking around mad, ready to rumble—were installed as fighting words in the American South, as a generation of boys were desperate to prove their manhood after the humiliating defeat in the Civil War. By the 1950s, blacks in the northern ghettos spoke of "respect," which has now been transformed again into not showing "disrespect," or "dissing." It's the same code, the same daring. And today that postbellum "chip on your shoulder" has morphed into what one gang member calls the "accidental bump," when you're walking down the street, "with your chest out, bumping into people and hoping they'll give you a bad time so you can pounce on them and beat 'em into the goddamn concrete."

Violence, or the threat of violence, is a main element of the Guy Code: Its use, legitimacy, and effectiveness are all well understood by most adolescent guys. They use violence when necessary to test and prove their manhood, and when others don't measure up, they make them pay.

The Three Cultures of Guyland

Practically every week we can read about a horrible hazing incident on campus, or an alcohol-related driving accident following a high-school prom, or allegations of a date rape at a party the previous weekend. Bullying is ubiquitous in middle schools and high schools across America, and not infrequently a case of bullying is so outrageous it becomes newsworthy. Rape on campus occurs with such alarming frequency that most colleges now incorporate sexual awareness training into their freshman orientation practices (apparently students not only must learn how to find their way around campus and how to use a library, but they must also learn how not to rape their classmates).

Every single emergency room in every single hospital adjoining or near a college campus stocks extra supplies on Thursday nights—rape kits for the sexual assault victims, IV fluids for those who are dehydrated from alcohol-induced vomiting, blood for drunk driving accidents. On many campuses, at least one party gets "out of hand" each week, and someone is seriously injured: A group of guys stage a "train" or a "ledge party," or someone gets so sick from drinking that they need to be hospitalized. And that's just the more "routine" weekend events. Newspaper and magazine stories, alarmist television exposés, and campus crusaders typically focus on the extreme cases—the fatal drunk driving accidents, the murder-by-hazing.

Though it may not be possible to read these headlines without a shudder of horror, most adults among us, particularly those of us with sons and daughters who live in Guyland, are nonetheless often able to convince ourselves that these stories are not about *our* kids. We might even think the media is a bit hysterical. Our sons aren't rapists. They don't tie cinderblocks to each other's penises and then throw those blocks off the roof, for crying out loud. They don't drink and drive, or get in fistfights, or paint swastikas on each other's passed-out drunken bodies. They're good kids. We believe these stories are anomalies, that the perpetrators are deviants, bad apples who otherwise don't represent the majority of guys. We look to psychology to explain these rare occurrences: bad parenting, most likely, or the cumulative negative effects of media consumption. We treat these as individual cases, not as a social and cultural phenomenon that impacts all guys, including the ones we know and love.

And, as I've argued, for the most part that's true. Most guys *are* good guys, but that doesn't lessen the reality of the violence that surrounds them, or the ways that they, and we, collaborate by turning a blind eye. If we really want to help guide our sons to manhood, it's imperative that we, as a society, look at their world with eyes wide open. We must be willing to ask the hard questions. How do such events happen? And what do such extreme cases tell us about the dynamics of Guyland, the operations of the Guy Code in action?

Guyland rests on three distinct cultural dynamics: a culture of entitlement, a culture of silence, and a culture of protection. Taken together, these cultures do more than make these more extreme cases the actions of a small group of predatory thugs. They suggest the ways in which we, too, are implicated. Why? Because if we really want to help these guys, then we must know the world they live in.

The Culture of Entitlement

Many young men today have a shockingly strong sense of male superiority and a diminished capacity for empathy. They believe that the capacity for empathy and compassion has to be suppressed, early on, in the name of achieving masculinity. That this is true despite the progress of the women's movement, parents who are psychologically aware and moral, stunning opportunities for men and women, is disappointing at best. But there is no way around it: Most young men who engage in acts of violence—or who watch them and do nothing, or who joke about them with their friends—fully subscribe to traditional ideologies about masculinity. The problem isn't psychological; these guys aren't deviants. If anything, they are overconforming to the hyperbolic expressions of masculinity that still inform American culture.

This culture of entitlement is the reward for subscribing to the Guy Code. As boys they may have felt powerless as they struggled heroically to live up to impossible conventions of masculinity. As William Pollack argues, "it's still a man's world, but it's not a boys' world." But *someday it would be.* Someday, if I play my cards right, if I follow all the rules, the world will be mine. Having worked so hard and sacrificed so much to become a man—it'll be my turn. Payback. I'm entitled.

It's facile to argue about whether or not young men "have" power: Some do, some don't. Some are powerful in some settings, but not in others. Besides, power isn't a possession, it's a relationship. It's about the ability to do what you want in the world. Few *people* feel that sort of power even as adults: Most of us "have to" work, we are weighed down by family and workplace obligations. But even when they feel powerless, unlike women, men feel *entitled* to power.

This sense of entitlement is crucial for understanding Guyland—and the lives of young men as they pass into adulthood. Here is another example. Not long ago, I appeared on a television talk show opposite three "angry white males" who felt they had been the victims of workplace discrimination. They were in their late twenties and early thirties—just on the other side of the Guyland divide. The show's title, no doubt to entice a large potential audience was "A Black Woman Stole My Job." Each of the men described how he was passed over for jobs or promotions for which all believed themselves qualified. Then it was my turn to respond. I said I had one question about one word in the title of the show. I asked them about the word "my." Where did they get the idea it was "their" job? Why wasn't the show called "A Black Woman Got *a* Job," or "A Black Woman Got *the* Job"? These men felt the job was "theirs" because they felt entitled to it, and when some "other" person—black, female—got the job, that person was really taking what was "rightfully" theirs.

Another example of entitlement appeared in an Anna Quindlen column in the *New York Times*. "It seems like if you're a white male you don't have a chance," commented a young man who attended a college where 5 percent of his classmates were black. By way of explanation, Quindlen commented

> What the kid really meant is that he no longer has the edge, that the rules of a system that may have served his father will have changed. It is one of those good-old-days constructs to believe it was a system based purely on merit, but we know that's not true. It is a system that once favored him, and others like him. Now sometimes—just sometimes—it favors someone different.

Young men feel like Esau, that sad character in the Bible who sold his birthright for a bowl of lentils and never felt whole again. From that moment, everything belonged to Jacob, and we never hear of Esau again. And, like Esau, young men often feel that they've been tricked out of it, in Esau's case by a pair of hairy arms offered to his blind father, and in the case of guys today, by equally blind fathers who have failed to pass down to them what was "rightfully" supposed to be theirs.

The Culture of Silence

If thwarted entitlement is the underlying cause of so much of the violence in Guyland, and if violence is so intimately woven into the fabric of the Guy Code as to be one of its core elements, how come no one says anything about it?

Because they're afraid. They're afraid of being outcast, marginalized, shunned. Or they're afraid that the violence just might be turned against them if they voice their opposition too vehemently. So they learn to keep their mouths shut, even when what they're seeing goes against everything they know to be good. The Guy Code imposes a "code of silence on boys, requiring them to suffer without speaking of it and to be silent witnesses to acts of cruelty to others," write Dan Kindlon and Michael Thompson. Boys and men learn to be silent in the face of other men's violence. Silence is one of the ways boys *become* men.

They learn not to say anything when guys make sexist comments to girls. They learn not to say anything when guys taunt or tease another guy, or start fights, or bully or torment a classmate or a friend. They scurry silently if they're walking down the street and some guys at a construction site—or, for that matter, in business suits—start harassing a woman. They learn not to tell anyone about the homoerotic sadism that is practiced on new kids when they join a high-school or college ath-letic team, or the school band, or a fraternity. Or when they hear that a bunch of guys gang raped a classmate. They tell no parents, no teachers, no administrators. They don't tell the police. And they certainly don't confront the perpetrators.

A friend recently wrote to me about his experience leading a work-shop for high-school kids in the frozen Yukon Territories of Canada. From the stories of their teachers, it was clear that the school had a tough and aggressive boy culture. He was surprised, then, when the boys opened up, and spoke with candor and honesty. During a break, though, he heard them talking about the fighting that went on each week at their school. A circle would form around a fight as it began. And the boys would cheer with glee.

He was taken aback. Suddenly these same boys, who minutes earlier had been earnest and caring, were now gleefully recounting blow-by-blow descriptions of the fights. Apparently without effort, they had shifted into masculine performance mode, each trying to outdo the other with shows of verbal bravado.

He interrupted them. "Wait a minute," he said. "I've spent the past day and a half with you guys, hearing you talk about your lives. I know you don't like that fighting. I know you don't like having to prove you're a real man. So how come you're going on about how great these fights are? Why do you stand in that circle and cheer the others on?"

The group went deadly silent. No one met his eyes. No one smirked or glanced that conspiratorial look that young people often share when an adult is challenging them. Finally, one boy looked up.

"So why do you cheer the fights?" my friend asked.

"Because if you don't, they'll turn on you. Because if you don't, you'll be the next one inside the ring."

If they're quiet, they believe, if they hide in the mass, if they disappear, maybe the bullies will ignore them, pick on someone else.

The silence is not limited to boys. Girls, too, know about the Guy Code, know how weaker guys are targeted, bullied, battered, and they keep quiet also. "We know that it's wrong," Ellen, a sophomore at the University of Illinois told me. "But we know that if we go along with it, the cool guys will like us. No big deal. It isn't like they're hitting *us*, is it?"

That silence, though, is what gives the perpetrators and the victims the idea that everyone supports the Guy Code. It's what gives everyone a mark of shame. And it's what keeps it going—even when so many guys are aching to change it, or eliminate it altogether. The first rule of the Guy Code is that you can express no doubts, no fears, no vulnerabilities. No questions even. As they might say in Las Vegas: What happens in Guyland stays in Guyland.

The Culture of Protection

By upholding the culture of silence, guys implicitly support the criminals in their midst who take that silence as tacit approval. And not only does that silence support them, it also protects them. It ensures that there will be no whistleblowers and, as we'll see, that there will be no witnesses when, and if, the victims themselves come forward. Nobody knows anything, nobody saw anything, nobody remembers anything.

Yet it's one thing for the guys themselves to protect one another— as we've seen, there's a tremendous amount at stake for them, and the pressure is high to conform—it's another thing entirely when the entire community that surrounds these guys also protects them. When the parents, teachers, girlfriends, school administrators, and city officials make the decision to look the other way, to dismiss these acts of violence as "poor judgment" or "things getting a little out of hand." I call this protective bubble of community support that surrounds Guyland the *culture of protection*. Communities rally around "their" guys, protecting the criminals and demeaning their victims. This shields the participants from taking full responsibility for their actions and often provides a cushion of support between those who feel entitled and the rest of the world.

It's natural for parents to want to protect their children. Parents work hard to keep their children safe—we immunize them, try to get them into the best schools, and intercede on their behalf if they are victimized or bullied. But sometimes this natural instinct to protect children may also infantalize them, may keep them from accepting responsibility for their actions, or confronting the negative consequences of their mistakes. And sometimes, parents' efforts to protect and defend their young adults may actually enable them to transgress again, or even to escalate the severity of their actions to the point where they are trying to get away with something truly criminal.

Not only do parents' responses characterize this culture of protection, but the entire community's response may shield them as well. From teachers, coaches, and school administrators who look the other way, as long as it didn't happen on school property, to the community determined to maintain the illusion that theirs is an ideal community in which to live and raise children, it's often neighbors and friends who exacerbate the problem by siding with the perpetrators against the victims.

The culture of silence and the culture of protection sustain many of guys' other excessive behaviors—from Justin Volpe and his police friends who sodomized Abner Louima, to the military brass who looked the other way when cadets at the Air Force Academy were routinely sexually assaulting female cadets, to the codes of silence on campus following any number of hazing deaths. And those who do stand up and challenge the culture of male entitlement—the whistleblowers—are often so vilified, ostracized from their communities, and threatened with retaliation that they might as well join the Witness Protection Program. Parents who stick up for their victimized kids can find themselves shunned by their neighbors and former friends; administrators who try and discipline perpetrators often face a wall of opposition and lawsuits—especially if the perpetrators happen to be athletes on winning teams.

"Our Guys"

A startling—and extreme—example of how these three cultures play out in Guyland is the infamous sexual assault in Glen Ridge, New Jersey, in 1989. It is well documented in the bestselling book *Our Guys* by Bernard Lefkowitz and also in a made-for-TV movie. I use this example, and others like it, not because the crime itself is typical—thankfully it is not—but because the cultural dynamics that enable the most extreme and egregious offenses in Guyland are equally present even in the more everyday aspects of guys' lives. We need to take a close look at the kind of culture that allows this to happen even once. Sociologists often point to extreme examples of phenomena, as if to say: If we can see such processes at work even here, then surely we can see them at work in more quotidian events. And, indeed, the response—by the criminals, their peers, and the larger community—was typical of the social dynamics that sustain and support Guyland as a whole.

In the spring of 1989, thirteen high-status athletes at Glen Ridge

High School lured a 17-year-old "slightly retarded" girl into one of the guys' basement. Chairs had been arranged, theater style, around a sofa in the middle of the room. Most of the boys arranged themselves on the chairs, while a few led the girl to the sofa and got her to perform oral sex on one of the highest-status boys.

As the event began to unfold, one sophomore noticed "puzzlement and confusion" in the girl's eyes, and turned to his friend and said, "Let's get out of here." Another senior baseball player, age 17, said he started to "feel queasy" and thought to himself, "I don't belong here." He and another baseball player got up to leave. On the way out, he said to another guy, "It's wrong. C'mon with me." But the other guy stayed. In all, six of the young men left the scene, while seven others—six seniors and one junior—remained in the basement. All of them were 17 or 18 years old.

As the girl was forced to continue giving oral sex to the boy, the other boys laughed, yelled encouragement to their friends, and derisively shouted, "You whore!" One guy got a baseball bat, which he forced into her vagina. As he did this (and followed with a broom handle), the girl heard one boy say, "Stop. You're hurting her." But another voice chimed in, "Do it more."

Later, the girl remembered that the boys were all laughing, while she was crying. When they finished, they warned her not to tell anyone and she left the house. The event concluded with an athletic ritual of togetherness as the boys stood in a circle, clasping "one hand on top of the other," Lefkowtiz writes, "all their hands together, like a basketball team on the sidelines at the end of a time-out."

In the eyes of their friends, their parents, and their community, these guys were not pathological deviants. They were all high-status athletes, well respected in their schools and in their communities. They were not crazed psychotics, they were regular guys. Our guys.

So, too, were the football players at Wellington C. Mepham High School, a well-funded, well-heeled high school in a relatively affluent Long Island neighborhood, who participated in another extreme example. When students returned from vacation in the fall of 2004, they were confronted by rumors of a terrifying hazing incident that had taken place during the summer. While away at a training camp in Pennsylvania in August, three varsity members of Mepham's football team sexually abused three young teammates in a hazing ritual. According to the police report, the boys were sodomized with pine cones, broom handles, and golf balls, all of which had been coated with Mineral Ice, a Ben-Gay–like cream that produces intense menthol-induced coolness, and is typically used to treat sore muscles. When applied to moist or broken skin, or used internally, it causes severe pain. Thirteen other players watched, but did nothing.

Once again, the perpetrators were respected members of the community—good boys, Boy Scouts, pillars of the tight-knit community. Just regular guys.

When I've described the sexual assaults in Glen Ridge to young men around the country, they instantly and steadfastly agree: those guys who actually did it are thugs, and their behavior is indefensible. "C'mon, man," said one, "they should be charged with criminal assault and go to jail. QED." And they show equal contempt for the guys who stayed, watched, and did nothing. "What is up with that?" another said. "It's just wrong."

When we consider the guys who left, many of the guys I've spoken with assure me that they too would have left at the first sign of the assault. Self-congratulation comes easily and quickly. "No way am I staying there," one guy said. "At the first sign of trouble, I'm gone," said another. Other guys readily agree. All seem to identify with the guys who left, who refused to participate. And they're all feeling pretty good about it until a female student invariably asks, "Yeah, but did they call the police? Did they tell anybody?"

No. No one called the police. No one told a teacher or an administrator. No one told their parents. No one told *anybody*.

And the next day, *everyone* at Glen Ridge High School knew what had happened. Everyone knew, that is, that a bunch of guys had "had sex with" that particular girl and other guys had watched. And she let them! And that next day not one student told their parents, their teachers, their administrators. Not one student—male or female—called the police to report the assault.

In fact, it wasn't until two weeks later that the girl herself finally told her parents what had happened to her, and why she was crying all the time, unable to sleep and eat, and why she was so bruised and sore "down there."

In the Mepham case, the assault was perpetrated by three guys while thirteen other players watched. They did not intervene to stop this cruel and horrific assault on their teammates. They did not tell the coaches, their parents, school administrators, or the police. They did nothing. "Of course, we heard about it instantly," one Mepham graduate told me. "Everybody did. Man, it was like the only thing everyone was talking about the next day. 'Hey, did you hear what went down at the football camp?'"

It's those *other* guys who illustrate the second cultural dynamic of Guyland—the *culture of silence.* And not only did none of the bystanders in Glen Ridge or Mepham intervene, but none told a parent or a teacher, or reported the assault to the police. As the case played out in Glen Ridge for six whole years the guys consistently refused to "turn" on their friends and provide incriminating evidence.

The motto of Guyland is "Bros Before Hos." One remains steadfastly loyal to your guy friends, your bros, and one never even considers siding with women, the hos, against a brother. It is the guys to whom your primary allegiance must always be offered, and for many that may even extend to abetting a crime. Anything less is a betrayal of Guyland.

No one is immune to the culture of silence. Every single kid is culpable. If you still don't think this has anything to do with you, ask yourself what you would have done. If you think this has nothing to do with your son, ask him what he would do if he heard about such a thing. Then ask him when was the last time he actually *did* hear about such a thing.

The culture of silence is the culture of complicity. The bystanders may think that they withdraw their support—by turning away, leaving the scene, or just standing stoically by—but their silence reinforces the behaviors anyway. It's as strong an unwritten code as the police department's famed "blue wall of silence," or the Mafia's infamous rule of "omerta," or the secret rituals of the Masons. Breaking the silence is treason, worse, perhaps, than the activities themselves.

The relationship between perpetrators and bystanders is crucial in Guyland. Peer loyalty shields the perpetrators, and helps us explain the question of numbers. Despite the fact that the overwhelming majority of guys do not sexually assault their teammates, gang rape college women at fraternity parties, or indulge in acts of unspeakable cruelty, they also do nothing to stop it.

Most bystanders are relatively decent guys. But they are anything but "innocent." The bystander comforts himself with the illusion "this isn't about me. I've never bullied anyone." This is similar to the reaction of white people when confronted with discussions of racism or sexism on campus. "It's not about me! My family didn't own slaves." Or "I never raped anyone. These discussions about sexual violence are not about me."

It *is* about them. The perpetrators could not do what they do without the amoral avoidance and silence of the bystanders. In a way, the violence is done *for* them—and so it is most definitely *about* them.

When the story about the Mepham football hazing broke, and the national media descended on sleepy Bellmore, Long Island, the community reacted as one—it defended the players and the coaches who denied any responsibility. Parents of the boys who had been abused were threatened with death if they pressed charges. "It's simple," read one letter to a victim's parents. "Keep your mouth shut and nothing will happen to your family." Campus rallies were held for the team, both the coaches and the players.

When the school administration took the drastic (and courageous) step of canceling the entire football season, Mepham students felt that *they* had been victimized by an overzealous superintendent. "I don't see why we should all be penalized for the actions of a few football players," commented one girl.

Not everyone participates in this culture of protection, of course. Recall the case of Spur Posse a few years ago. The Southern California clique of young men kept tallies of the girls they had had sex with (many of the girls, some as young as 11, had been coerced). When the boys were exposed as sexual predators and rapists, their fathers seemed almost proud. "That's my boy!" said one. "If these girls are going to give it away, my boy is going to take it," said another. The mothers, however, were surprised, even shocked. They wanted to talk to their sons, find out how such a thing was possible. So the culture of protection is not uniform; there are gender gaps—and these gaps between mothers and fathers will form a crucial part of our discussion of what we, as a society, can do to make Guyland a more hospitable place.

The Guy Code keeps young men from venturing beyond the borders of Guyland. The good guys are silenced and the predators and bullies are encouraged. What we need, of course, is exactly the reverse—to empower the silent guys to disable the predators, to facilitate young men's entry into an adulthood propelled by both energy and ethics, and animated by both courage and compassion.

N ow that we have a sense of the philosophical principles that underlie Guyland, we need to see the way the Guy Code operates in the lives of young men in America today. The next few chapters will explore the spaces they call home much as an anthropologist might explore a different culture—examining its terrain, its economy, its rites and rituals, its belief systems and cultural practices, and the behaviors and attitudes that support and sustain it.

4 | HIGH SCHOOL: BOOT CAMP FOR GUYLAND

By the time most boys enter high school, the Boy Code is so firmly in place that it morphs effortlessly into the Guy Code. But suddenly the stakes seem higher—the potential for failure greater, the punishment for that failure more severe.

The hormonal changes that boys experience during puberty are bewildering enough, and high school adds a new overlay of expectations about proving masculinity, deciphering a pecking order that seems to have its own internal and impenetrable logic, and navigating the relentless domination of jock culture. Add to this the sudden importance of girls and it's easy to understand how boys often lose their way.

And all this takes place just as parents begin to withdraw in the name of facilitating greater autonomy in their children's lives, and school administrators and teachers shift into a more rigorous academic mode to facilitate college admissions.

New problems, greater pressure, less supervision—high school is a perfect storm. It's a moment of intense insecurity coupled with an equally intense injunction to prove one's self and to establish one's place in the hierarchy. Guys are vulnerable, they're impressionable, and most of them are searching for a way to be that will leave them feeling in control. It's a massive identity project, one that will take each of them a lifetime to complete.

The "War Against Boys"?

Some of the clearest evidence of this vulnerability is the current "boy crisis" in schools. The evidence is overwhelming that boys of all ages are having trouble in school. They are underachieving academically, acting out behaviorally, and disengaging psychologically. Many are failing to develop those honorable traits we often associate with masculinity—responsibility, thoughtfulness, discipline. Boys drop out of school, are diagnosed as emotionally disturbed and commit suicide four times more often as girls; they get into fights twice as often. Boys are six times more likely to be diagnosed with Attention Deficit and Hyperactivity Disorder (ADHD). They score consistently below girls on tests of reading and verbal skills, and have lower class rank and fewer honors than girls.

Yet while everyone agrees that boys are in trouble, we don't necessarily agree on the source of the crisis, and thus we strongly disagree about its remedies. To hear some tell it, the source of boys' problems is, in a word, girls, who have eclipsed boys in school achievement and honors, college admissions and attendance. This is not the fault of the girls themselves, others argue, but the fault of "misguided" feminists who, in their zeal to help girls get ahead, have so transformed elementary and secondary education as to make it a hostile environment for boys.

Boys seem to have "lost out" to girl power, and now "the wrong sex may be getting all the attention in school." Pop psychologist Michael Gurian claims schools "feminize" boys, forcing active, healthy, and naturally rambunctious boys to conform to a regime of obedience, giving them the message, he says, that "boyhood is defective." Another pundit writes that "school is a terrible place for boys. In school they are trapped by 'The Matriarchy' and are dominated by women who cannot accept boys as they are. The women teachers mainly wish to control and to suppress boys."

By far the most sustained fusillade against feminism as the cause of boys' woes comes from Christina Hoff Sommers, formerly a philosophy professor and now a resident anti-feminist pundit at the American Enterprise Institute. In her 2000 book, *The War Against Boys*, Sommers claims that schools are an "inhospitable" environment for boys, where their natural propensities for rough and tumble play, competition, aggression, and rambunctious violence are cast as social problems in the making. Efforts to transform boys, to constrain or curtail them, threaten time-tested and beneficial elements of masculinity and run counter to nature's plan. These differences, she argues, are "natural, healthy, and, by implication, best left alone." The last four words of her book are "boys will be boys"—to my mind, the four most depressing words in educational policy discussions today. They imply such abject resignation: Boys are such wild, predatory, aggressive animals that there is simply no point in trying to control them.

The idea that feminist reforms have led to the decline of boyhood is both educationally unsound and politically untenable. It creates a false opposition between girls and boys, assuming that the educational reforms undertaken to enhance girls' educational opportunities have actually hindered boys' educational development. But these reforms—new initiatives, classroom reconfigurations, teacher training, increased attentiveness to students' processes and individual learning styles—actually enable larger numbers of *students* to get a better education, boys as well as girls. Further, "gender stereotypes, particularly those related to education," hurt both girls and boys, and so challenging those stereotypes and expressing less tolerance for school violence and bullying, and increased attention to violence at home, actually enables both girls *and* boys to feel safer at school.

What's more, the numbers themselves may be deceiving. First, more *people*—both male and female—are enrolling in college than ever before. Female rates are going up faster than male rates, but both are increasing. Second, while it's true that more women than men are enrolling in college, that discrepancy has more to do with race than gender. Among middle- and upper-income white students there is virtually no gender gap at all in college enrollments, which suggests that boys' suffering—

at least the suffering of the boys these pundits are talking about—isn't as widespread a disaster as they predict. According to Jacqueline King at the American Council on Education, half of all middle- and upper-income white high-school graduates going to college this year are male. What accounts for the gender gap are the statistics regarding working class, black, and Latino college students: In all three groups, women are far more likely than men to go to college.

And although girls are catching up to boys in science and math, and far outdistancing them in English and languages, the cause is neither the disappearance of some putative math gene nor the machinations of some feminist science cabal. It has to do with the ways in which boys and girls experience masculinity and femininity. Again, it's about *gender*—about the Guy Code, and that means the only way that parents and teachers are going to be able to meet this new wrinkle in our educational institutions is by paying attention to gender.

Let's take the science and math side of the equation first. Much of the work of developmental psychologists suggests that when girls hit adolescence these once-assertive, confident, and proud young girls "lose their voice," as psychologist Carol Gilligan so memorably put it. At a slightly earlier age, as William Pollack and others have found, when the Boy Code kicks in, boys seem to become *more* confident, even beyond their abilities. You might even say that boys *find* their voices, but it is the inauthentic voice of bravado, of constant posturing, of foolish risk-taking, and gratuitous violence. The Boy Code teaches them that they are supposed to be in power, and thus they begin to act like it.

That is to say: At adolescence, *girls suppress ambition, boys inflate it.* Girls are more likely to undervalue their abilities, especially in the more traditionally "masculine" educational arenas such as math and science. As a result, only the most able and most secure girls take such courses. The few girls whose abilities and self-esteem are sufficient to enable them to "trespass" into a male domain skew female data upward. By contrast, too many boys who overvalue their abilities remain in difficult math and science courses longer than they should; they pull the boys' mean scores down.

Readers who wonder about this might reflect on what happens in those first-year science courses like organic chemistry or biochemistry that are required for pre-med students. At many universities, the mandate to the professor is to make sure that only about half the class passes the course and goes on to the major. Otherwise, the reasoning goes, too many "unqualified" students will think they have what it takes to become doctors. Once their ambitions are deflated, they drift away.

What is interesting is that although females now outnumber males in the entering classes at medical schools across the country, males far outnumber females in those entry-level courses. Again, having underestimated their abilities, the women self-select before they ever get to the class; the men, by contrast, having overestimated their abilities, need someone to tell them.

A parallel process is at work in English and foreign languages, where girls' test scores far outpace boys. But this is hardly the result of "reverse discrimination"; rather, it is because the boys bump up against the Guy Code. While boys tend to regard any sort of academic success as feminizing—notice how they pick on the nerds or the geeks—English is seen as especially "feminine." Boys who study literature are seen as "effeminate, enfeebled bookworms." Ethnographic research has consistently found that boys profess disinterest in English because of what it might say about their (inauthentic) masculine pose. "Most guys who like English are faggots," commented one boy. The traditional liberal arts curriculum is seen as feminizing. Unlike math and science, where there is little room for opinion and conjecture, the language arts and social sciences are about human experience, and so studying them requires that you discuss human experience—something that leaves many guys feeling uncomfortable.

Boys tend to hate English and foreign languages for the same reasons that girls love them. There are no hard and fast rules, but rather one expresses one's opinion about the topic and everyone's opinion is equally valued. "The answer can be a variety of things, you're never really wrong," observed one boy. "It's not like math and science where there is one set answer to everything." Another boy noted:

I find English hard. It's because there are no set rules for reading texts . . . English isn't like math where you have rules on how to do things and where there are right and wrong answers. In English you have to write down how you feel and that's what I don't like.

Compare this to the comments of girls in the same study:

I feel motivated to study English because . . . you have freedom in English—unlike subjects such as math and science—and your view isn't necessarily wrong. There is no definite right or wrong answer and you have the freedom to say what you feel is right without it being rejected as a wrong answer.

Interestingly, girls assume they'll be wrong—they like subjects where their answers are "not necessarily wrong," while boys assume they'll be right, so they like subjects where there is no gray area. Girls like English because it's harder to be wrong; guys hate it because it's harder to be right. In that sense, it is not the school experience that "feminizes" boys, but rather the ideology of traditional masculinity that keeps boys from wanting to succeed.

The pressure on boys and young guys to conform, first to the Boy Code and then to the Guy Code, is intense and unforgiving. Might that constant pressure actually be what lies behind the problems boys are having in school? And the fear of failure—of being seen as a geek or a sissy, of becoming a target, or of the shame that attends being a passive bystander—is not only what lies behind guys' poor performance academically, but also what lies behind so much of the behavior that baffles the adults in their lives, and leaves so many young guys with knots in their stomachs every time they eat in the cafeteria, go to the bathroom, stand by their locker, walk out onto the playground, change their clothes in the locker room, or even walk from one class to the next. For so many boys, only by shutting down completely, becoming stoic, expressionless robots, can they navigate those public spaces. Is it any wonder that boys are having trouble in school? Could it be that the very aggression and rambunctiousness—that is, the norms of the Guy Code—are what get in boys' way in school?

Ubiquitous Bullying

Many of America's high schools have become gauntlets through which students must pass every day. Bullies roam the halls, targeting the most vulnerable or isolated, beating them up, destroying their homework, shoving them into lockers, dunking their heads in toilets, or just relentlessly mocking them. It's all done in public: on playgrounds, in bathrooms, hallways, even in class. And the other kids laugh and encourage it, or they scurry to the walls, hoping to remain invisible so that they won't become the next target. For many, just being noticed for being "uncool" or "weird" is a great fear.

Why are some students targeted? Well, because they're gay, if they are. Or because they "seem" gay, which may be just as disastrous for a teenaged guy. After all, the most common put-down in American high schools today is "that's so gay," or calling someone a "fag." It refers to anything and everything: what kind of sneakers you have on, what you're eating for lunch, some comment you made in class, who your friends are, or what sports team you like. The average high-school student in Des Moines, Iowa, hears an anti-gay comment every seven minutes—and teachers intervene only about 3 percent of the time. After spending a year in a California high school, one sociologist titled her ethnographic account "Dude, You're a Fag."

It's true that gays and lesbians are far more often the target of hostility than their straight peers. A CBS poll in 1999 found that one-third of eleventh graders knew of incidents of harassment of gay or lesbian students. Almost as many admitted to making anti-gay remarks themselves. But the anti-gay sentiments are only partly related to sexual orientation. Calling someone gay or a fag has become so universal that it's become synonymous with dumb, stupid, or "wrong."

But to dig a little deeper, it's "dumb" because it isn't *masculine* enough. To the "that's so gay" chorus, homosexuality is about gender nonconformity, not being a "real man," and so anti-gay sentiments become a shorthand method of gender policing. One survey found that most American boys would rather be punched in the face than called gay. Tell a guy that what he is doing or wearing is "gay," and the gender police have just written him a ticket. If he persists, they might have to lock him up.

It's because of what guys think being gay means: It means not being a guy. That's the choice: gay or guy. In a study by Human Rights Watch, heterosexual students consistently reported that the targets were simply boys who were unathletic, dressed nicely, or were bookish and shy, and girls who *were* athletic, assertive, or "had an attitude." Recall what Eminem said: Calling someone a faggot doesn't mean you think he's gay, but that you think he's not a real man. And those are fighting words.

Take the case of Jesse Montgomery. Daily, Jesse was treated to verbal taunts about being a "faggot, queer, homo, gay, girl, princess, fairy, freak, bitch, pansy" and more. It was "severe and unrelenting." He was regularly punched, kicked, tripped in the halls. His classmates used superglue to stick him to his seat, threw things at him, and stole his books and notebooks. Some of the torment was directly sexual:

> One of the students grabbed his own genitals while squeezing [Jesse's] buttocks and on other occasions would stand behind [him] and grind his penis in [Jesse's] backside. The same student once threw him to the ground and pretended to rape him anally, and on another occasion sat on [Jesse's] lap and bounced while pretending to have intercourse with him.

Other students watched and laughed. Jesse Montgomery is straight.

So, too, was Dylan Theno, an eighteen-year-old former student at Tonganoxie High School in Kansas. Beginning in the seventh grade, he was consistently taunted as a "flamer," "faggot," and "masturbator boy" and harassed daily in the lunchroom and on the playground. Teachers looked the other way, or laughed along with the harassers. Why? "Because I was a different kid, you know, I wasn't the alpha male. I didn't . . . you know, I had different hair than everybody else; I wore earrings," he said. "I did *tae kwon do*. I didn't play football through high school. . . . I wasn't a big-time sports guy at school."

Over a four-year period, he complained to principals, school board members, and the superintendent, all to no avail. At one point, Dylan told me, the principal announced that the word "fag" would be prohibited at school—a new rule that everyone, legitimately, blamed on Dylan. The harassment escalated, and he dropped out, got a GED, and sued the school. For their part, the administrators claimed that the harassment was his "own fault," and that Theno's "own conduct . . . constitute[ed] intervening causes." In August 2005, the court found that the school acted "in willful disregard of [Theno's] safety and created an opportunity and atmosphere in which students felt they could harass [him] openly and with impunity." The court awarded him $250,000.

Of course, if you actually *are* gay, the harassment is relentless—and often dismissed entirely by the adults in charge, or, worse, considered appropriate.

In most respects, Jamie Nabozny was a typical high-school kid. Born and raised in the middle-American small town of Ashland (population 8,600) on Lake Superior in the northern tip of Wisconsin, Nabozny was tall and lanky, a bit gawky, shy and quiet, a good student. And gay.

When he came out at age 11, his parents hoped it was simply a "phase" he would pass through. But he was their son, and they accepted him as he said he was. His classmates were not as tolerant. Beginning in seventh grade, first at Ashland Middle School and later at Ashland High School, attending classes became a daily torment. Jamie was harassed, spit on, mock-raped while at least twenty other students looked on and laughed, urinated on, called a "fag" by a teacher, and kicked and beaten by other kids. Each time he complained to school administrators; each time his parents backed him up. And each time the school principals and teachers shrugged off his complaints, telling Jamie that he should "expect" this sort of treatment if he's gay, and that, well, "Boys will be boys." The one guidance counselor who did support him was replaced.

Jamie was so frightened he got sick. "Every day I had stomach aches. I lived in fear every day I got on that bus," he recalled. "I started walking to school . . . I had to live every day trying to avoid being harassed." He began to come to school extremely early, so he could get to the library before the other kids arrived. "I had to use the bathrooms usually used by teachers to avoid the kids in the bathrooms." Twice, Jamie attempted suicide. Then a few other boys nearly killed him. Then, this:

> One morning when Nabozny arrived early to school, he went to the library to study. The library was not yet open so Nabozny sat down in the hallway. Minutes later he was met by a group of eight students led by Stephen Huntley [one of the ringleaders of the constant assaults]. Huntley began kicking Nabozny in the stomach, and continued to do so for five or ten minutes while the other students looked on laughing. [Again] Nabozny reported the incident to . . . the school official in charge of disciplining, [who] laughed and told Nabozny that he deserved such treatment because he is gay. Weeks later, Nabozny collapsed from internal bleeding that resulted from Huntley's beating.

Several operations and hospitalizations later, Nabozny withdrew from school, moved to Minneapolis, was diagnosed with Post-Traumatic Stress Disorder, and completed high school through a GED.

This description of Nabozny's torment doesn't come from Jamie Nabozny himself, or from his parents, or from some mythical purveyors of a gay agenda. It comes from the statements of fact in the decision rendered by the U.S. Court of Appeals for the Seventh Circuit in 1996, after Nabozny successfully sued the school district and the principals of both the middle school and the high school, who paid out close to $1 million in damages.

Nabozny's lawsuit, coupled with the 1996 Supreme Court decision *Davis* v. *Monroe*, opened a door for those who are the targets of bullying and harassment in school. School districts and administrators may be held liable if they do not intervene effectively to stop the abuse. What's amazing is not that they have to intervene, but that it took the courts until the mid-1990s to figure out that boys might also need protection from such harassment and abuse.

Yes, one might say, it's terrible what happened to Jamie Nabozny. No one should have to endure such torture. And surely the school adminis-tration was criminally negligent not to intervene, since every child, gay or straight, has the right to be safe in his school. It is easy to feel out-raged and indignant when the case is as clear-cut as Jamie Nabozny's. But what about when the bullying doesn't extend to physical assault? What if Nabozny had only been teased? Teasing and bullying are just part of the social life of teenagers. Right? Some of us might even remem-ber our own high-school days. After all, bullies have been around since slate boards and chalk. One of life's lessons is learning how to deal with them. Maybe bullies don't require active intervention by teachers and administrators. Maybe, say the fathers, our sons have to learn to fight back, to "stand up for themselves." Or, maybe, say the mothers, they need to have the inner strength to walk away. These might be viable options for some kids, but they cannot be the only recipe for dealing with such harassment.

Imagine, for a moment, that instead of being gay, Jamie Nabozny was black, and his assailants white. Or that he was Jewish and his tor-mentors used anti-Semitic slurs as they beat him up. The issues would have been far clearer. Most Americans find such explicit racist and anti-Semitic behavior unacceptable, an affront to their moral sensibili-ties. Racism and anti-Semitism are out of bounds even when they don't become physical, and most of us believe that those who openly express those sentiments should be severely punished. Why is the same not true of gay-bashing?

The New Normal: Pervasive Predation

School violence has become so utterly commonplace that many parents and administrators assume it's a false problem created by hysterical overreacting parents, or some nameless forces of political correctness who want to throw a wet blanket over all naturally rambunctious male play, turning us into a nation of wimps. But the evidence of bullying's ubiquity alone is quite convincing. In one study of middle- and high-school students in Midwestern towns, 88 percent reported having observed bullying and 77 percent reported being a victim of bullying at some point during their school years. "If all the girls who have ever been sexually harassed reported the guys who did it, there would no longer be any boys in school," commented one teenage girl to the author of a study in *Seventeen* magazine.

A 2005 survey of 3,450 students in middle and high school conducted by the Harris Poll found that almost two out of three students said they had been verbally or physically harassed or assaulted *during the past year.* And why? Because of their perceived or actual appearance, gender, sexual orientation, gender expression, race/ethnicity, disability, or religion. And the teachers know about it; more than half describe bullying and harassment as a serious problem in their schools.

The latest wrinkle in bullying is neither physical nor even verbal; it's virtual. Schools are increasingly reporting cases of "cyber-bullying" in which some kids are targeted for hateful email messages, or hateful and humiliating comments are posted on cyber-bulletin boards and school chat rooms. A survey of 5,500 teens found that 72 percent said that online bullying was just as distressing as the face-to-face kind.

Most teachers and administrators see only the physical bullying, and most schools have rules prohibiting physical aggression. But what about the constant verbal torment, or the sexual harassment? A recent survey in Long Island found that only 7 percent of high-school students said "physical harm" was the primary weapon of bullies; 65 percent said teasing. And this is where the gender of bullying appears to break down. The overwhelming majority of the physical bullying is done by boys, but there is also a significant amount of verbal bullying by girls, as recent bestsellers such as *Odd Girl Out* and *Queen Bees & Wannabes* first revealed.

Yet this increasing gender parity in nonphysical aggression may be deceptive. While it is certainly the case that girls can be and frequently are as verbally aggressive as boys, it is also useful to ask who benefits from the aggression. Here the answers are equally revealing. Boys do it, of course, to establish and then maintain their place in the male pecking order; the bullying makes sure that those at the top stay there, and it reinforces their belief that they are entitled to be there. But many girls use verbal aggression to impress those boys at the top, believing that their efforts at humiliating other girls, or even revictimizing the boys who have already been targeted, will win them the attention of the top males. Girls' aggression may end up sustaining the hierarchy, which is, itself, an expression of gender inequality.

Of course, just because a behavior is common doesn't mean it is without consequences. For many of the victims of this daily torture, their lives are transformed into waking nightmares. They lose sleep, lose status, lose friends. Some become depressed or despondent. Some self-medicate with drugs or alcohol. They feel sick more often, and stay home from school. Every day, according to the National Association of School Psychologists, 160,000 American youths skip school fearing they will be the targets of bullies.

Their friends fade away because they are frightened off. "When I was in high school," recounts Jake, now a 23-year-old graduate student in California, "I was constantly harassed because people assumed I was gay. My friends were scared to be seen with me, because they would get hassled too. It was like the bullies made it appear I was contagious or something. If anyone was nice to me, or hung out with me, they'd get hassled the next day. There was only one guy who stuck with me, because he didn't care what they said. I lost all my other friends when I became a target."

The bullies, though, don't fare so well either. While it's true that bullies often enjoy high prestige in school, it is also true that their experience of entitlement leads them to overestimate the degree to which that entitlement carries over to life outside school. As a result, bullies grow up deficient in social coping and negotiating skills and are more likely to engage in substance abuse, according to William Coleman, a pediatrics professor at the University of North Carolina School of Medicine.

"Bullying should not be considered a normative aspect of youth development," concluded the authors of an article in the *Archives of Pediatrics & Adolescent Medicine*. "But rather a marker for more serious violent behaviors." Bullies are four times more likely to have engaged in criminal activity before age 24; and a full 25 percent have criminal records before they turn 30.

These behaviors are not a sign of boys being boys; they serve as evidence that some kids are predators. Saying "Boys will be boys" is worse than letting them off the hook. It encourages them.

High-School Hazing and the Rites of Passage

While joining an athletic team or an extracurricular club or organization may be somewhat palliative against being targeted for random bullying in the hallways or cafeteria, it doesn't guarantee that kids will be safe. One of the most insidious behaviors in these organizations is hazing. Bullying is about teaching you to stay in your place. Hazing is more organized, more systematic, and is used as a condition of membership in the organization. Hazing is a rite of passage; it is the way you *earn* a place that is different from the one you currently occupy.

Hazing is "any activity expected of someone joining a group that humiliates, degrades, abuses or endangers, regardless of the person's willingness to participate," according to researchers at Alfred University, who conducted the most comprehensive study of hazing ever. About 1.5 million high-school students are hazed every year. In the Alfred study, close to half of all high-school students who belong to organized groups reported being subjected to hazing activities. Forty-three percent reported being subjected to humiliating activities, and thirty percent said that they had done something illegal as part of their initiation. About one-fifth described something dangerous, or involving substance abuse. It's hard to know if the amount and severity of hazing has increased in the past few decades, but certainly the rituals have become more creative and involve increasingly sexually humiliating events. Nowhere is this more evident than among high-school athletes.

Of course, rookies on athletic teams, military recruits, and fraternity pledges have always been hazed. (I'll return to these issues in the next chapter.) But now it's also true for the kids who join the band, debate club, or the cheerleading squad. Almost every type of high-school group had significantly high levels of hazing in the Alfred study, even groups ordinarily considered "safe." Twenty-four percent of students involved in church groups were subjected to hazing activities, and more than a third said they wouldn't tell anyone about it because "there is no one to tell" or "adults won't handle it right."

Hazing activities are voluntary and consensual, which often leads adults and the public to dismiss them as inconsequential. Yet the consensuality itself needs to be questioned. When membership in a group has such conditions attached, can it really be deemed entirely consensual? If you can't opt out of the hazing, it isn't a choice, but a requirement.

Brian Seamons was a member of the Sky View High School football team in Utah. One day, after practice, four of his teammates grabbed him as he left the shower, forcibly held him down, and used athletic adhesive tape to tie up his genitals, and then left him, naked, tied to a towel rack in the locker room. They then brought in a girl Seamons had dated so she could see what had been done to him.

Brian immediately told the school administrators and the police. They apparently informed the coach of Brian's allegations, because the coach called a team meeting. There, one of the team captains, who had been one of Brian's assailants, accused Brian of betraying the team by going public with his accusations. The coach then demanded that Brian apologize to the team for doing so, and informed him that unless he did apologize, he would never again play for the team. After an agonizing night, during which Brian's father offered his son a lot of support, Brian decided he would not apologize. The coach replied that he was "sick of Brian's attitude, sick of Brian's father's attitude" and that he was off the team. The next day, the school district administration canceled the last game of the season.

Brian sued in federal court, arguing that the coach and the school violated his rights of free speech in removing him from the team for reporting the incident. The court awarded him $250,000. And the coach, whom I would probably nominate as the "Coach I Would Least Like My Own Son to Play For," got transferred to another school in the district—and is still coaching football.

Strong and athletic, as a senior Jeff expected to letter in three sports in his Iowa high school: football, baseball, and track. But what he didn't expect was the brutality meted out by the other players on the rookies—brutality that was known not only to the coaches, but also encouraged by them:

I couldn't believe that the coaches actually wanted to have the rookies beat up and tortured like that. Ben Gay in their jockstraps, used tampons in their lockers, and all the punching and shoving. It was constant. And, man, if you screwed up and made a bad play, then they'd really go after you.

Somehow, though, Jeff got through his first year in all three sports. It was when he was expected to do the same to the next year's rookies that he balked.

I just couldn't do that to them, man. I just couldn't. I knew it wasn't right when they were doing it to me, and some of the things they wanted to do, like shoving a lacrosse stick up the guy's butt, well, it was gross. So I just tried to, like, not be around when it happened.

His teammates noticed, and confronted him. When he refused to participate, they started harassing him. And when one of his teammates told the coach that Jeff wasn't helping "initiate" his teammates, his coach reprimanded Jeff—for breaking the bonds of the team. His coach offered him a choice: either participate in activities Jeff knew to be both illegal and immoral, or quit the team. He quit.

In Trumbull, Connecticut, nine wrestlers were charged with felonious assault in 2000 when they bound a 15-year-old first-year teammate with tape, rolled him up in a wrestling mat, threw the mat against the wall, and pounded it. Afterward, they raped him with the handle of a plastic knife.

That's another difference between bullying and hazing. Bullying is universally condemned, though it's often tolerated as a nuisance, or, at best, an object lesson for boys to learn to assert themselves. Hazing, by contrast, is often supported—by the very people who are supposed to be supervising our children and keeping them safe. Coaches often look the other way, assuming that these rituals heighten team spirit and bonding. Some fathers even defend the practice, because, "Well, that's what happened when I was in high school and I turned out pretty well." This is a fallacy of misattribution. Maybe these fathers turned out all right *despite* their being tortured instead of *because* of it?

As in prison, sexual humiliation and rape invokes terror and reinforces hierarchy. Art Taylor, a psychologist at the Center for the Study of Sport in Society at Northeastern University, argues that such "humiliating hazing rituals are more likely to tear people apart, destroy trust, and cause feelings of hatred." To defend such activities in the name of team building or male bonding is at best perverse and at worst criminally insane.

Make no mistake: Girls haze also. But they, too, do it to sustain the male hierarchy. That is, girls hazing girls ultimately reflects and sustains the dominance of guys. Lizzie Murtie, a 14-year-old freshman gymnast in Essex, Vermont, was hazed along with the other team rookies by being forced to perform mock fellatio on several boys in a parking lot—in front of a large crowd of other kids. (Each girl had to kneel in front of the boy, facing away from the crowd, so they couldn't see what was actually happening, and eat a banana that protruded from his zipper.) Totally humiliated, Lizzie subsequently became clinically depressed, couldn't concentrate, and avoided her friends. Her grades dropped. When she finally told her parents and they complained, the school board sentenced the seniors to some community service—which some failed to perform. They graduated with their class and went on to college.

What's important here is not so much that girls can haze other girls—of course they can. It's that the hazing is so clearly about humiliating girls through subservience to boys. That the girls were ordered to perform mock fellatio—and, I'm told, in some cases, penises replaced bananas—reinforces the fact that the girls are, to some degree, hazing each other in the service of a larger mission: impressing the boys. Imagine the contrasting case: A group of rookie boys are ordered to simulate cunnilingus on an older girl. Doesn't quite have the same humiliating resonance, does it? In fact, what would be far more likely is that the boys would also be ordered to perform mock fellatio on an older boy. It's the subservience to the boy, the "servicing" of the older boy, which is the source of humiliation—whether it's done to girls or boys, and whether it's done by girls or boys.

Don't Get Mad—Get Even

The dynamics of boy culture and the impact of the emergent Guy Code can turn high school into a terrifying torment of bullying, gay-bashing, and violence. Few guys make it through those hostile hallways (and playgrounds, locker rooms, and bathrooms) entirely unscathed. Most do make it through relatively intact, of course, but many will carry their wounds with them for the rest of their lives. And a few will turn their pain into self-hating depression or explosive rage.

For some targets of bullying, the relentless torture and the humiliation are simply too much to bear. Some will self-medicate; a desire to get numb underlies much of teen drug and alcohol consumption, especially when they're drinking or getting stoned by themselves. A few may try and take their own lives. Close to 85 percent of all teen suicides are by boys. And some even take matters into their own hands. That's certainly the case for the overwhelming majority of boys who show up at school one day, armed to the teeth, and open fire on their classmates. In what have become known as rampage school shootings, a young white boy or boys bring a small arsenal of assault weapons and rifles to school and open fire, seemingly at random, killing or wounding many in the melee. Often the massacre ends when they turn the guns on themselves.

For the past five years, I've conducted a research study of all the cases of random school shootings in the United States. I examined a sample of media accounts of these events with interviews with parents, teachers, and other students at some of the communities that have experienced these tragic shootings. One factor seems to stand out: Nearly all the boys who committed these tragic acts have stories of being constantly bullied, beaten up, and gay-baited. Nearly all have stories of being mercilessly and constantly teased, picked on, and threatened. Not because they were gay, but because they were *different* from the other boys. Theirs are stories of "cultural marginalization" based on criteria for adequate gender performance—specifically the enactment of codes of masculinity. Even a study by the United States Secret Service found that two-thirds of the school shooters had been bullied at school and that revenge was one of their motives.

High-school students understand this. In a national survey, nearly nine of ten teenagers said they believed that the school shootings were motivated by a desire "to get back at those who have hurt them" and that "other kids picking on them, making fun of them, or bullying them" were the immediate causes. "If it's anyone it'll be the kids that are ostracized, picked on, and constantly made fun of," commented one boy.

Luke Woodham, an overweight 16-year-old honor student in Pearl, Mississippi, was part of a little group that studied Latin and read Nietzsche. Students teased him constantly for being overweight and a nerd, taunted him as "gay" or "fag." Even his mother called him fat, stupid, and lazy. On October 1, 1997, Woodham stabbed his mother to death in her bed before he left for school. He then drove her car to school, carrying a rifle under his coat. He opened fire in the school's common area, killing two students and wounding seven others. After being subdued, he told the assistant principal, "The world has wronged me." Later, in a psychiatric interview, he said, "I am not insane. I am angry . . . I am not spoiled or lazy, for murder is not weak and slow-witted; murder is gutsy and daring. I killed because people like me are mistreated every day. I am malicious because I am miserable."

Fourteen-year-old Michael Carneal was a shy and frail freshman at Heath High School in Paducah, Kentucky, barely 5 feet tall, weighing 110 pounds. He wore thick glasses and played in the high-school band. He felt alienated, pushed around, picked on. Boys stole his lunch, constantly teased him. He was so hypersensitive and afraid that others would see him naked that he covered the air vents in the bathroom. He was devastated when students called him a "faggot" and almost cried when the school gossip sheet labeled him as "gay." On Thanksgiving, 1997, he stole two shotguns, two semiautomatic rifles, a pistol, and 700 rounds of ammunition, and after a weekend of showing them off to his classmates, brought them to school hoping that they would bring him some instant recognition. "I just wanted the guys to think I was cool," he said. When the cool guys ignored him, he opened fire on a morning prayer circle, killing three classmates and wounding five others. Now serving a life sentence in prison, Carneal told psychiatrists weighing his sanity that, "People respect me now."

Columbine High School has become the touchstone case, the case to which all observers must eventually refer. And even here, the connection between being socially marginalized, picked on, and bullied propelled Eric Harris and Dylan Klebold deeper into their video-game-inspired fantasies of a vengeful bloodbath. Athletes taunted them: "Nice dress" they'd say. They would throw rocks and bottles at them from moving cars. The school newspaper had recently published a rumor that Harris and Klebold were lovers. Here's the way one of their friends described his experience with the jock culture that ruled the school:

> Almost on a daily basis, finding death threats in my locker . . . It was bad. People . . . who I never even met, never had a class with, don't know who they were to this day. I didn't drive at the time I was in high school; I always walked home. And every day when they'd drive by, they'd throw trash out their window at me, glass bottles. I'm sorry, you get hit with a glass bottle that's going forty miles an hour, that hurts pretty bad. Like I said, I never even knew these people, so didn't even know what their motivation was. But this is something I had to put up with nearly every day for four years.

On April 20, 1999, Harris and Klebold brought an arsenal of weapons to their high school and proceeded to walk through the school, shooting whomever they could find. The entire school was held under siege until the police secured the building. In all, twenty-three students and faculty were injured, and fifteen died, including one teacher and the perpetrators.

To this day, Americans remain shocked and horrified by the tragic shooting at Columbine. In a way, it defies explanation. At the same time, it demands it. Efforts by those who would preserve the bully culture—to make the story of Harris and Klebold a case of psychologically unhinged but rational and conscious moral actors—fall sadly short. New psychiatric analysis offers a more complex portrait of Klebold, a depressed and troubled boy, and Harris, a coldblooded, remorseless psychopath. But the effort to substitute an image of evil or "simple" psychopathology for an image of aggrieved entitlement of the victims of bullying and relentless torture reveals a psychological myopia that could only come from one who had never experienced it. If Harris was indeed so deranged, then it begs the question of why no one in the entire school ever seems to have noticed.

School shooters are malicious because they are miserable and angry. Tormented by their peers and marginalized from the mainstream culture, they use violence as a way to restore their manhood which has been challenged. Though certainly psychologically troubled, even insane, many of the rampage school shooters carry their sense of aggrieved entitlement like a badge of honor. They are fervent subscribers to the Guy Code, particularly the belief that real men don't get mad, they get even. In fact, of all the students at Columbine High School on that sunny morning in April 1999, it's possible that none was a more passionate true believer in the Guy Code than were Klebold and Harris.

So What Is the Answer?

The issues we face are serious: Boys are underperforming in school, bullying and hazing are ubiquitous, and violence is a daily reality of many boys' lives. And when you factor in the suicide attempts, the self-medication, the violent outbursts, or the sullen withdrawals, it's clear that we must devise strategies to enable all sorts of boys to feel safe enough to go to school, and secure enough to know that they will be valued for who they are.

This isn't simply a problem of isolating the bad apples and throwing them out of school. It is a flaw in the system, and were it to happen in our workplaces, someone would recognize the incredible inappropriateness of this kind of behavior. Unfortunately, many of the anti-bullying programs that are currently being promoted are too syrupy sweet, too loaded with feel-good bromides to be effective. High-school kids see right through some earnest guitar-strumming ex-hippie singing about smiling on our brother and loving one another right now. On the other hand, school environments must facilitate intellectual and emotional growth, not stifle it. "I don't feel like adolescents should have to go to school in survival mode," says Leon, from Long Beach, California.

To make schools safe enough for our children to take the emotional and intellectual risks that good education requires demands that we look closely at what we now know, and what we need to find out.

1. First, we need good, accurate information. The school climate feels different to teachers and administrators than it does to the students. We need data. Anonymous student questionnaires are necessary, so kids can respond freely. Just the simple act of surveying the school sends a message to students that the administration is paying attention.

2. Each school must establish a well-developed anti-bullying policy, using enforceable guidelines and consequences that are consistently meted out.

3. We need to be sure that these policies are well publicized to both kids and parents.

4. We need to develop a pedagogy of resilience. While resilience can be nurtured among individuals, we need to develop strategies to break the circles of fear and anxiety that strangle bystanders into cowed silence. Developing a safe place for those who have seen something they know is wrong, giving them a way to develop positive supports for intervention, empowers guys to do the right thing. They may decide to collectively confront the bullies, or they can report it collectively—and thus dilute the fear that each individual guy will be the "one who told."

5. Staff members—including coaches as well as teachers and administrators—must be trained to intervene. Research by Shepard Kellum at The Johns Hopkins University reveals how classrooms, teachers, and school settings create the conditions for high or low levels of violence. Kellum did a follow-up study of aggressive first-grade boys in a class with a weak teacher, who allowed high levels of chaos and the formation of aggressive peer groups and bullying cliques. By the sixth grade, those same boys were about 20 times more aggressive than a comparison control group.

6. Teachers need to be trained to respect each other. If teachers are to be role models, they need to pay attention to what they are modeling. Some male teachers put down their female colleagues, or support or ignore the teasing or bullying in their own classrooms as a way to enhance their own credibility with their male students. This unethical betrayal of their students needs to be challenged. Teachers also need to be trained to spot the signs of potential abuse and neglect at home.

7. We need to pay attention to nonclassroom space. Since most bullying behaviors take place in the hallways, cafeterias, playgrounds, locker rooms, or bathrooms, these are the places where supervision may be more necessary. One school decided simply to have the teachers walk in the halls during the time between classes. Usually teachers stay in their classrooms, so halls may become sites of harassment. Psychologist Michael Thompson reports that in the schools where adult supervision is high and visible, the boys are grateful that adults step into a potentially threatening situation. "It is as if they say 'Thank you for saving us from what we were about to do to each other.'"

8. A student who reports bullying or hazing must be taken seriously. We often treat whistleblowers as criminals—they're "snitches" who "rat" on their "friends"—when we should treat them as heroes. Remember that in over 80 percent of all rampage school shootings, at least one other person knew the attacker was planning something.

9. There must be adequate counseling services for both bully and victim.

10. Parents must get involved—collectively. Of course, parents need to remain in dialogue with their children about their experiences, watching for signs of distress, withdrawal, depression. But they must also act in concert, demanding that administrators make and keep schools safe for their children, and take bullying as seriously as they take rates of

college admissions or football championships. Parents need to demand that school boards pay attention, and, if they fail to act decisively, run a slate of parents against them in the next school board election.

11. Government must get involved. California, Minnesota, and New Jersey have passed laws that protect students from dis crimination and harassment because of gender identity and ex pression. Five more states (Connecticut, Massachusetts, Ver mont, Washington, and Wisconsin) and Washington D.C. pro tect gay and lesbian students from harassment. And a dozen more (Arizona, Arkansas, Colorado, Georgia, Indiana, Oklahoma, Oregon, Illinois, New Hampshire, Rhode Island, Tennessee, West Virginia) have general statewide anti-bullying laws. High schools aren't supposed to be heaven; but they needn't be hell.

Some two centuries ago, William Wordsworth lamented the passing of "the coarser pleasures of my boyish days" with all "their glad animal movements." Today, those glad animal movements might be labeled date rape, bullying, or sexual harassment. Have we gone too far, have we made it impossible for boys to . . . well, be boys? Not at all. We're doing what we've always done—reshaping and redefining what it means to be a man in a culture that is constantly changing. Many of the skills and values that a man will need in the twenty-first century are the same ones that men have always needed—constancy, a sense of purpose, honor, and caring discipline. And many are skills and values that we thought we would never associate with the ideal of masculinity—compassion, patience, nurturing, and disciplined caring.

A year after Jamie Nabozny filed his lawsuit, another student at the same high school found himself the target of incessant bullying and gay-baiting. He called Jamie one night and stammered a few hesitant words before he panicked and hung up. A few weeks later, the boy killed himself.

If we shrug our collective shoulders and say resignedly "boys will be boys"—as the middle-school principal told Jamie Nabozny, and as so many pundits and pop psychologists seem to be saying—we do them a great disservice. We abandon boys to be half-men. They will never grow up to be the kind of men they are capable of becoming. And when they go off to college, where the Guy Code is of a completely different magnitude, they'll lack any ambition to become men.

5 | THE RITES OF ALMOST-MEN: BINGE DRINKING, FRATERNITY HAZING, AND THE ELEPHANT WALK

The cab meets the foursome outside of Nick's house at 11:45 p.m. In fifteen minutes, he will turn 21, and Tempe, Arizona's Mill Avenue is waiting for him and his crew. Mill Avenue looks like a lot of avenues near college campuses across the country: a string of bars with names like Fat Tuesday, Margarita Rocks, and The Library. (That way if your parents call you can tell them that you are going to "The Library" and not be lying.) "Let's start out at Fat Tuesday and then go from there," Nick says as the cab drops them off. Tonight is Nick's "power hour," a college ritual where the birthday boy goes out on the eve of his twenty-first birthday to have as much fun as possible (read: drunkenness) between midnight and the closing of the bars. The practice goes by many names on many campuses, but a common theme always emerges: You walk into a bar and stumble out of it.

Nick starts his night by ingesting some vile concoction invented solely for the enjoyment of the onlookers. Tonight the drink of choice is a "Three Wise Men," a shot composed of equal parts Jim Beam, Jack

Daniels, and Johnnie Walker. Other variations include the more ethnically diverse (substitute Jose Cuervo for the Johnnie Walker), or the truly vomit-inducing (add a little half-and-half and just a splash of Tabasco). The next drink comes at him fast, a Mind Eraser, another classic of the power hour. It's like a Long Island Iced Tea except more potent, and it is drunk through a straw as quickly as possible. Shot after shot after shot is taken, the guys become all the more loud and obnoxious, and the bar manager brings a trash can over to Nick's side, just in case.

Not surprisingly, the trash can comes in handy. Nick's body finally relents as closing time approaches. He spews out a stream of vomit and the other guys know it's time to go. Fun was had, memories were made, but most importantly . . . he puked. His friends can rest easy; a job well done.

Jason, a freshman at the University of Georgia, has been waiting all semester for this night. He's put up with a lot of humiliating abuse from the brothers, done mountains of their laundry, made their beds, and even written a paper for the pledgemaster. He's mopped up vomit-stained bathrooms at the fraternity house on the morning after parties, done stupid things, and drank a bit more—okay, a lot more—than he ever did in high school. One more night and he's sure he'll be in.

The pledges gather in the rec room at about 10 p.m. Dressed, as instructed, in old T-shirts and jeans, they were told to bring flip flops, a change of clothes, and a jockstrap. (A jockstrap?) An anxious frivolity permeates the room, as brothers drink beer with the pledges. After everyone seems good and drunk the brothers swarm over the pledges, yelling their demands to recite the fraternity's mission statement, rituals, and membership information. Screw it up, the brothers yell, and you might not make it.

Calisthenics, of a sort, follow. Push-ups, then chugging some beers. Sit-ups, and more chugging. Most of the pledges are ready to puke. They are then told to strip naked and stand in a straight line, one behind the other (which is hard enough given how much they have had to drink). Each pledge is ordered to reach his right hand between his legs to the pledge standing behind him and grab that guy's penis, then place his left hand on the shoulder of the guy in front of him. (You have to bend over to make this work.) Forming a circle, they walk around the basement for several minutes, in what is known as the "elephant walk." By now it is nearly 2 a.m. "Okay, you worthless pieces of shit," the pledgemaster screams. "Now let's see if you're willing to give it all for the brotherhood!"

Still naked, the pledges stumble to the second-floor balcony of the house. The brothers measure out lengths of rope, and a cinderblock is tied to the end of each, so that it almost—but not quite—touches the ground. The pledges are blindfolded as the other ends of the ropes are tied to the base of each pledge's penis. "You better have a big enough dick, pledge," the pledgemaster shouts. "If your dick isn't big enough, you aren't getting into this house. This block is gonna rip it the fuck off your body! How do you like that, you little weenies? Our dicks made it! Is yours big enough?"

Each pledge feels a little tug on his rope, and then hears the cinderblocks being lifted up to the edge of the balcony. The next thing he knows, he feels a sharp tug and hears the cinderblock being pushed off the edge and crashing to the ground below. One guy screams and starts to cry. Another pisses. Blindfolds are removed and the brothers are laughing their heads off. Turns out the ropes were not really tied to those blocks after all. They embrace their new "brothers," and it is over: Jason has made it.

These snapshots capture typical events that are taking place at colleges and universities across America. Binge drinking is epidemic, and nowhere near as innocuous as many of us would like to believe. Hazing rituals span the range from the ridiculous to the truly criminal, occasionally becoming lethal as well. There is an impulse—among parents, college administrators, alumni, and the guys themselves—to chalk it all up to harmless fun. College is supposed to be the best years of your life. Yet stories like those above also suggest something important about Guyland that lurks beneath the surface of all that "fun": its chronic insecurity, its desperate need for validation, and the sometimes sadistic cruelty with which that validation is withheld and then conferred.

Here's what guys know. They know that every move, every utterance, every gesture is being carefully monitored by the self-appointed gender police, ensuring that everyone constantly complies with the Guy Code—even if they don't want to. They know that if you do go along, you'll have friends for life, you'll get laid, you'll feel like you belong. And if you don't, you won't. If you're lucky, you'll just be ignored. If you're not, you'll be ostracized, targeted, bullied. The stakes are so high, the costs of failure enormous. Many guys—perhaps most—suspect that they might not have what it takes. They feel unable to live up to the Guy Code, yet their fear compels them to keep trying. And so many of the other guys seem to do it so effortlessly.

And so the initiations begin—initiations that are designed to prove misguided notions of masculinity, with legitimacy conferred by those who have no real legitimacy to confer it. No wonder the rituals become increasingly barbaric, the hazing increasingly cruel. And at the same time the initiations serve another purpose, perhaps less clear than the first. They also reassure the guys that they are not yet men, not yet part of the adult world, and that there's still time to have a little fun before they have to find their way in the real world.

Initiation: Replacing Mother

Initiation is about transition, a moving from one status to another. Its power rests on the instability of one's current identity. A person undergoes initiation in order to stabilize a new permanent identity.

Initiations are centerpieces of many of the world's religions. Sometimes the rituals are arduous, other times they are relatively benign. In Judaism and Islam, circumcision is practiced as a rite of passage that marks the boy's membership in the community. In Judaism, it is performed at birth, signifying the covenant of God with Abraham—that Abraham was willing to sacrifice his only son to his belief in God. In Islam, circumcision takes place at different times, depending on the sect. In Turkey, for example, the *sunnet* takes place at 13, roughly the onset of puberty, and is a certifiable rite of passage to manhood.

In Christianity, ritual circumcision is not required but we can consider Christian baptism as an initiation ritual. In the baptism, the old self is symbolically, ritually, destroyed—drowned—and the new self is reborn into the community of the Church. And though baptism is not gender-specific, as both males and females are baptized, it is nonetheless a meditation about gender. (After all, the original baptisms were for men only.) The old "feminized self," born of a woman, is destroyed and the priest, always a man, brings the new self to life. In a sense, then, the male priest has given birth to the new man. The mother may have given birth, but the child does not become a member of the community until the priest confers that status. Women are pushed aside, and men appropriate their reproductive power.

Freud made such a moment the centerpiece of his theory of child development. Before the Oedipal crisis, Freud argued, the child, male or female, identifies with mother, the source of love, food, and nurturing. To become a man, a boy must leave his mother behind, and come over to his father's side. The successful resolution of the Oedipal complex is identification with the masculine and "dis-identification" with the feminine. Whether or not one subscribes to Freudian theory, all theories of initiation pivot on uncertainty, anxiety, indeterminancy. It is an unstable moment, what anthropologist Victor Turner called a "liminal" stage—a stage of in-between-ness, "neither here nor there; they are betwixt and between the positions assigned and arrayed by law, custom, convention, and ceremony."

Initiations in Guyland are about the passage from boyhood to manhood. Boyhood is the world of women—Mama's boys, wimps, wusses, and losers—or the world of men who are considered women—gays, fags, homos, queers. Or babies. One guy told me of the "Baby Dinner" at his fraternity house at a large public university in the Northeast. Pledges dressed in diapers, with little white bonnets on their heads. The pledgemaster would put gross previously chewed food on their heads, simulating pabulum, and the pledges would scoop it off with their fingers and eat it. Many fraternities have equally infantalizing rituals. If initiation is going to validate your manhood, first you have to regress to babyhood.

Initiations, then, are all about masculinity—testing it and proving it. It's not that women don't initiate girls into womanhood. But rarely does becoming a woman involve danger, or threats, or testing. A girl might be inducted into womanhood when her mother explains menstruation at puberty. Or she might be briefed by her friends about the hows and whys of sex, or by her roommates about how to navigate the world of men. But a woman doesn't typically feel the need to prove she is a "real woman." In fact, if she feels a need to prove anything, it's usually some misguided notion of being equal to the guys. Katie, a 22-year-old junior at Hobart and William Smith Colleges, explained:

> A "real woman"? Hmmm. Yeah, I had to prove it, had to prove I was a real woman. I hooked up with a guy I didn't know after drinking several guys under the table. That sort of showed them. You know, sort of a "anything you can do I can do better" sort of thing. And you know what? They haven't bothered me about it since.

"But," I asked, "how does drinking to excess and having sex with someone you don't know prove your femininity?"

"Uh, I guess it doesn't," she said after a pause. "It meant I was equal to the guys. That's sort of proving it, isn't it?"

Who Does the Validating?

In the United States, proving masculinity appears to be a lifelong project, endless and unrelenting. Daily, grown men call each other out, challenging one another's manhood. And it works most of the time. You can pretty much guarantee starting a fight virtually anywhere in America by questioning someone's manhood. But why must guys test and prove their masculinity so obsessively? Why are the stakes so high? Why so different here than elsewhere? In part it's because the transitional moment itself is so ill-defined. We, as a culture, lack any coherent ritual that might demarcate the passage from childhood to adulthood for men or women. Not surprisingly, it also remains unclear who, exactly, has the authority to do the validating.

In non-Western cultures, it is the adult men of the community whose collective responsibility it is to ensure the safe ritual passage of boys into manhood. The older men devise the rituals, they perform the ceremonies, and they confer adult male status as only adults can. They have already passed over to adulthood—as husbands, workers, and fathers, often of the very boys they are initiating. As legitimate adults, they can authentically validate the boys' manhood.

As a result, once initiated, men no longer have identity crises, wondering who they are, if they can measure up, or if they are man enough. It's over, a done deal. There's nothing left to prove.

Not so in Guyland.

In the 1990s, the poet Robert Bly and many other men wondered about how the current generation of elders might initiate young men into manhood. Among the "mythopoetic" men's gatherings of the 1990s, older men, in their forties and fifties and sixties, bemoaned the loss of that ritualized initiation in America, and feared the consequences for the next generation of men. "Only men can initiate men, as only women can initiate women," Bly wrote in his bestselling book, *Iron John*. "Women can change the embryo to a boy, but only men can change the boy to a man. Initiators say that boys need a second birth, this time a birth from men."

Instead of criticizing their own abdication of responsibility, as they rushed from careers to affairs to divorces, many of these mythopoetic men seemed angry at the boys themselves for failing to seek their guidance and request their mentorship. The retreats were populated by hundreds of mentors, but with few young men to whom they could impart their wisdom.

Bly may have been right. But in Guyland, it is not men who are initiating boys into manhood. It is boys playing at initiating other boys into something they, themselves, do not even possess—that they *cannot* even possess. In America's fraternities, military boot camps, and military schools, and on athletic teams, it's always peers who are initiating peers. In fact, initiation and hazing are required to take place when adults are not there, *because* adults are not there—not the coaches, nor the professors, nor the administrators. In some cases, this is because the adults want to have "plausible deniability." They want to be able to claim that they didn't know—couldn't have known—what was happening. But they do, of course; odds are that they went through it themselves, and feel powerless or unwilling to stop it. They may even believe in it.

Perhaps that is why initiations in Guyland are so perilous—and so pointless. Maybe it doesn't work because it can't work. Since peers cannot really initiate peers into a new status, the initiations must be made ever more arduous. And because they are trying to prove what cannot be proved, each generation raises the ante, indulges in more cruelty, and extracts greater pain.

The very mechanisms of initiation in Guyland are so distorted that they can never produce a real man—sensible, sober, responsible, a decent father, partner, husband. Initiations in Guyland have nothing to do with integrity, morality, doing the right thing, swimming against the tide, or standing up for what is right despite the odds. In fact, initiations in Guyland are about drifting with the tide, going along with peer pressure even though you know it's both stupid and cruel, enabling or performing sometimes sadistic assaults against those who have entrusted their novice/initiate status into your hands. The process makes initiation into fraternities or athletic teams or the military closer to a cult than a band of brothers.

"Proof-ing it" All Night

Drinking to excess is the lubricant of initiations—but it can be an initiation itself. As we saw with Nick earlier, power hours are a birthday celebration, a rite of passage, and an initiation all rolled into one. Ever since Congress passed the Uniform Drinking Age Act of 1984, turning 21 has become a national birthday party, in every state, in every community. "You go out, hang out with your friends, you drink a shitload, and you throw up," says one 21-year-old. "And if you don't throw up, then your friends didn't do their job."

For most college students, by the time they turn 21, they've already had ample opportunity to work on their tolerance. A recent survey in Montana (a heavy drinking state across all age groups) found that 38 percent of high schoolers had binged in the previous thirty days—higher than the national average of 28 percent. (Yet that national average is pretty significant itself!) Binge drinking—drinking several times during the week and throughout the weekend—has become a staple of college life. Two out of five college students are binge drinkers according to a survey by Henry Wechsler, a professor of public health at Harvard. Among fraternity and sorority members the rate balloons to 80 percent. Wechsler defines binging as consuming five or more drinks in one session for males and four or more in a row for females, at least once in the past two weeks. By Wechsler's count, 6 percent of college students would qualify as alcoholic and nearly one-third would be given a diagnosis of "alcohol abuser." Almost half—44 percent—reported at least one symptom of either abuse or dependence.

This holds for girls, too. Historically, as Helen Lefkowitz Horowitz reminds us in her history of the American college campus, ". . . relatively few coeds joined college men in drinking, and both men and women college students generally disapproved of their doing so." Today, however, when women do drink—and boy, do they ever!—guys set the terms and women often face an impossible choice. She might be praised for "keeping up with the guys" or "drinking like a man," or just as easily criticized for the same behavior. Here's Jesse, a junior at Arizona:

> Omigod! There were like these two girls who used to go here, and they were like friends with one of the brothers, and they could, I swear, drink any guy under the table. They were amazing. I know a lot of guys thought they were like pigs or something, because they drank as much as we did, but I thought they were totally cool. And I will tell you nobody ever got over on them.

On the other hand, if she is responsible and prudent in her alcohol consumption she may be publicly praised for acting like a lady, but she also won't get invited to many parties. Guys in Guyland want girls to be their "near-equals." If they don't play at all, they threaten the legitimacy of Guyland; if they play the game better than the guys, the same threat holds true.

While binge drinking is found nearly everywhere in Guyland, that doesn't mean that it is spread evenly across every campus, college town, and neighborhood. Even if two of five students are binge drinkers, three out of five are not. Sixty percent drink responsibly—or not at all.

Nor is it everywhere the same. In my conversations with students all over the country, I heard far more tales of binge drinking on large state university campuses, especially those located in what are colloquially called "college towns," where the local economy revolves around the campus. Towns like Bloomington, Indiana, and Lawrence, Kansas; Norman, Oklahoma and Boulder, Colorado. Towns where bars line the streets leading from campus in virtually every direction, or where students can walk easily from party to party, and where big-time sports give people an excuse to party every weekend. A downtown where you can stagger out of a bar, plastered to within an inch of consciousness, and be reasonably certain you won't get mugged or stabbed, run over, or left on the side of the road, where someone will sort of recognize you and make sure you are okay—at least most of the time.

In other words, drinking "dangerously" requires a significant amount of safety. You may not know everyone you're partying with, but you know that the people you are with are very likely to know people you know. You don't "lose control" without having a large set of "controls" already built into the system. (As we'll see later, the same is true of hooking up.) Students at large urban campuses like Temple or Columbia, where personal safety is less of a given, don't report such high levels of binge drinking.

Binging is also not evenly distributed across campuses. Fraternities and sororities, according to Wechsler, are ". . . awash in a sea of alcohol." Three-fourths of all Greeks are binge drinkers (80 percent of males and 69 percent of females). It's also a white thing: The vast majority of black, Hispanic, and Asian students do not binge drink.

Unhealthy Hangovers

Of course, college campuses have been drenched in alcohol for a very long time. University presidents have constantly complained about drunk students since, well, since there were students. Henry Adams recalled that his mid–nineteenth-century Harvard classmates drank so much that they had bouts of delirium tremens. F. Scott Fitzgerald felt obliged to add a drunk driving accident in *This Side of Paradise* (1920), his debut novel, about his eating club days at Princeton.

More recently, though, it's become ubiquitous. A 1949 study found that 17 percent of college men and 6 percent of college women reported drinking more than once a week. A 1979 survey at four universities in Florida found that 80 percent of the students drank, 40 percent specifically "to get high" and 13 percent drank "to excess." These days, the percentage who are drinking at all is about the same four out of five, but those who drink more than once a week is even higher—more than one-fourth of males (26 percent) and more than one in five females (21 percent).

Getting drunk beyond consciousness may be a way of proving yourself to your friends, your fraternity brothers, or sorority sisters, of showing your teammates that you'd take one for the team. The number of athletic teams that use alcohol as a ritualized form of hazing is astonishingly high. It's usually an easy initiation: You drink, you puke, you sleep it off. Nobody gets hurt. In fact, it may be so popular because it's so easy.

But let's not kid ourselves. Binge drinking can also be dangerous. Experiments on laboratory rats found that after significant abstinence, binge drinkers are able to learn effectively—but they cannot relearn quickly or effectively. According to Fulton T. Crews, director of the Bowles Center for Alcohol Studies at the University of North Carolina, when faced with a new situation, binge drinkers become disoriented and cannot adjust. They continue to show toxicity in their brains long after they stopped drinking. And drinking both hampers the development of new nerve cells and destroys older ones.

What's true in rats seems to be equally true in humans. According to psychiatrist Paul Steinberg, binge drinking "clearly damages the adolescent brain more than the adult brain," especially in the orbitofrontal cortex, which uses associative information to envision future outcomes. Binging "can lead to diminished control over cravings for alcohol and to poor decision making. One can easily fail to recognize the ultimate consequences of one's actions."

Binging can even be lethal. Jason Kirsinas, a Presidential Scholar at Cal State, Long Beach, lapsed into a coma and died after a night of drinking on his twenty-first birthday. Jason Reinhardt, a student at Moorehead State in Minnesota, had sixteen of the "required" twenty-one drinks in one hour on his twenty-first birthday and died at a fraternity house a few hours later with a blood alcohol level of 0.36 percent (more than four times the legal limit of .08 percent).

Every year, according to a 2002 report from the National Institute on Alcohol Abuse and Alcoholism, 1,400 college students aged 18 to 24 are killed as a result of drinking; nearly half a million suffer some sort of injury. Most deaths and injuries are the result of drunk driving accidents. Hospitalizations for alcohol overdose or alcohol poisoning are a regular feature of campus life. To put it in perspective, 4,039 American servicemen and women have died in the Iraq war since the invasion began in March 2003, more than five years ago. Every two years, American college campuses lose the same number as perished in the terrorist attacks on the World Trade Center.

The campus papers reporting these deaths invariably list the students' ages, and they are almost always 21 or around 18. In fact, the 21-year-olds are often exactly 21; indeed, it is during their birthday celebration that they drink themselves to death. The 18-year-olds are first-year students, and theirs are the result of binge drinking at a level they had never even approached in high school.

Every weekend hospital emergency rooms in college towns are crammed with students, campus infirmaries offer extended hours, and every residence hall advisor needs special training on responding to alcohol-induced trauma or injury. One report found that in fraternities on campus ". . . exclusive drinking to the point of vomiting was tolerated and even celebrated." In the 1980s, the number of claims from binge drinking and hazing had become so enormous that the National Association of Insurance Commissioners ranked fraternities and sororities as the sixth worst risk for insurance companies—right behind hazardous waste disposal companies and asbestos contractors. Some insurance companies began to refuse to cover fraternities. Even the Arizona Supreme Court weighed in: A 1994 court ruling found that ". . . we are hard pressed to find a setting where the risk of an alcohol-related injury is more likely than from under-age drinking at a university fraternity party the first week of the new college year."

The scope of campus drinking has seeped into virtually every crevice of the academic edifice. Campus parties are alcoholic soak zones. Every weekend, dorm bathrooms are clogged with students worshipping at the porcelain God. Partying 'til you puke is hardly deviant; it's the norm. College students spend $5.5 billion a year on alcohol—more than they spend on soft drinks, tea, milk, juice, coffee, and schoolbooks combined.

But while it's clear that college students today are drinking more than ever, the reason behind all that drinking isn't as clear. There are several factors at play, all of which relate. Once, drinking was one of a range of recreational activities. In my college years, one was a beer drinker or a pot head, and the campus seemed evenly split between the two. There were also more serious drinkers and druggies, but hard liquor and psychedelic drugs were hardly the norm. Today drinking is not only the norm, it often feels like the only thing going. "My roommate freshman year didn't drink at all," said David, a recent graduate of the University of Wisconsin at Madison. "And I felt sorry for him. He was a loser, a total zero. He had no friends. I mean, everybody drank. Everyone who was cool."

We usually think alcoholism runs in the family—that kids become heavy drinkers when they see their parents drinking a lot. But it turns out not to be the case in Guyland. Psychologist Mark Fondacaro found that having family members who were heavy drinkers was actually *negatively* related to students drinking. Drinking behavior was instead overwhelmingly related to peers—alcohol abuse runs across friendship networks rather than intergenerationally.

That is a most important finding. Students do not, typically, binge alone, but rather in a network of drinking buddies, what sociologists call a "risky network." "The bonds of friendship," writes Wechsler, "always tighten when they are wet." Or, as the kids say, "Friends who sway together stay together." The more drinking buddies you have in your network of friends, the more you will likely drink.

Closely related to this is the misperception that all the other kids are drinking just as much, if not more, than you are. Research consistently finds that college students dramatically overestimate the amount that other students drink—and then that they drink to keep up. This misreading of others' behaviors may lead to a distorted self-marinating "keeping up with the Joneses," but it also serves as an entry point to discussions with young people, as the awareness of what people are *actually* doing may be a way to set a different gauge for one's own behavior.

And even when guys do recognize the blossoming of alcoholism among their friends, the culture of silence ensures that they won't intervene in any meaningful way.

"I'd say I know maybe three or four guys who, well, who might meet the legal definition of the term alcoholic," says Matt, who is all of 22 and a senior at Kansas. "I mean, they don't just drink at night or on weekends like I do. I mean they pretty much drink all the time. Like in the afternoon. Sometimes in the morning to help with a hangover. And like pretty much every day."

"Why," I ask him, "don't you do something about it?"

"Well, I don't think they'd take too kindly to that. I mean, everyone is entitled to act like they want in college, right? Our fraternity has a sort of 'live and let live' attitude. And besides, they're cool guys and everybody likes them."

Jeff, his 21-year-old fraternity brother walks by our conversation and joins in.

"It's not like nobody cares. I do, really, but I do it like quietly. Once, I tried to talk to Billy about it. He told me he was fine, completely under control, and that I shouldn't worry about him. I backed off, but like now I sort of keep an eye on him. Like if we were somewhere and he was wasted, I would definitely not let him drive. But it's cool here; he won't get hurt or anything. So I watch him on campus."

For the parents of college-aged guys, all this extreme drinking is often incomprehensible. It's a waste of time, a waste of money, alarmingly dangerous, and their own hindsight insists that it isn't even actually *fun*. What's fun about vomiting? What they might not understand is that drinking for these guys involves a lot more than just getting drunk. It's also about freedom—or what they think freedom means. It's about being a man.

By the time most young men go off to college, they've been living under the watchful eyes of their parents their entire lives. It is their parents who oversee the college admissions process, their parents who make sure their homework is done before they're allowed to hang out with their friends, their parents who make sure they're home by midnight. In middle-class America, parenting is a full-time job, and it's taken seriously. And this is not necessarily a bad thing. Yet one of the unintended results of overinvolvement is that the child never learns to develop his own internal compass regarding what constitutes appropriate behavior. All his guidelines are imposed from outside. If you get drunk, you'll get in trouble. If you don't do your homework, you'll get in trouble. All their lives they've tested the limits, gone to the edges, only to have their parents say the final "No," or bail them out if they've gone too far.

Then they go off to college. Their parents drop them off, say their tearful goodbyes, and leave—and they are transformed from overinvolved helicopter parents to absentee parents in the space of one afternoon.

As a result, for these guys, freedom is equated with a lack of accountability—not having to answer to anyone—and so being irresponsible becomes a way of declaring your freedom and, hence, your adulthood. And they've never had so much freedom. They are accountable to no one, and as long as they maintain a reasonable GPA, they're free to do as they like. It might not exactly be adulthood, but they certainly aren't kids anymore.

At the same time, college is considered the last hurrah before the real demands of adulthood begin. Most know that when they graduate they'll be expected to get jobs, support themselves, be responsible. As they see it, they've only got four more years of boyhood left, and they're going to make the best of it. And perhaps this is why binge drinking is so attractive. It allows them to prove their manhood and hold onto their boyhood all at the same time. All the freedom and none of the responsibility.

This also explains why the binging usually doesn't last forever. Guys who binge drink in college don't necessarily binge drink through the remainder of their twenties, let alone their thirties and forties. That's not to say that guys in their late twenties and early thirties don't get together in bars and clubs, drink to excess on occasion, and have raucous parties. Of course they do. But the steady practice of binging—drinking copious amounts to get as drunk as possible in the shortest amount of time— seems largely confined to the college years. The demands of adult life simply won't allow it. Eventually, those ubiquitous red plastic cups give way to stemware and martini glasses, beer goggles replaced by reading glasses. Here's Ted, 26, now living in Chicago:

> Oh sure, we go out and party, go have some beers in the local bar after work or on weekends. But Christ, I have to get up in the morning. I have to go to work, and I have to do at least a minimally competent job.

Richie, 25, agrees:

> Those days were wild. We would drink 'til we passed out, or until we could get some girl drunk enough to score, or just drink and laugh together and do stupid crazy shit all night. But who can do any of that now? I mean, I'm in law school, I have a girlfriend, I gotta stay sober.

He pauses, a cross between embarrassed and nostalgic. "Listen to me! I'm beginning to sound like my father. Holy shit, I'm a fucking grownup."

Uncivil Rites

Binge drinking is both ritualized—the expected norm for parties in Guyland—and a specific ritual, often tied to initiation into a club or organization like a fraternity or an athletic team. There it may be coupled with other activities that fall under the heading "hazing."

Hazing takes place everywhere men gather on campus, whether on athletic teams, in fraternity houses, secret societies, or even in clubs and organizations. (Indeed, the very first mention of President George W. Bush in the *New York Times* came on November 8, 1967, when, as a Yale senior, he was asked about a story in the *Yale Daily News* reporting that his fraternity, Delta Kappa Epsilon, was ritually branding its pledges with a hot coat hanger. The newspaper called the practice "sadistic and obscene," but Bush defended it, saying that the resulting wound was "only a cigarette burn.")

Hazing is a broad term, describing behavior that ranges from dumb pranks or silly skits to seriously dangerous and even potentially lethal activities. It can involve things that you are forced to do, from memorizing arcane trivia about your fraternity chapter or singing pornographic songs to doing people's laundry or fetching their mail, from drinking contests to participation in ridiculous, humiliating, or degrading rituals. Or it can involve things being done to you, from being subject to verbal taunts and humiliating yelling to physical assault, sexual assault, branding, torture, and ritual scarification.

On campus today, the overwhelming majority of the nearly half-million men who belong to collegiate fraternities have undergone some form of hazing. Most of the quarter-million women who belong to sororities have as well.

The most recent study of collegiate hazing, released in March 2008, surveyed more than 11,000 students at 53 institutions. Survey directors, University of Maine professors Elizabeth Allan and Mary Madden found that more than half of students who belonged to campus organizations—from fraternities to the glee club—had experienced some forms of hazing. It was most common on varsity athletic teams (74 percent) and fraternities and sororities (73 percent) but 56 percent of all members of performing arts organizations, 28 percent of academic clubs, and 20 percent of honor societies also reported being hazed. For 31 percent of the men and 23 percent of the women hazing included drinking games; 17 percent of the men and 9 percent of the women drank until they passed out. About one-fourth believe that their coach or advisor knew about it.

Most hazing rituals are just plain stupid. Lots of vulgar references to body parts, symphonies of farting, belching, and gagging. "The truth is, most of it is just plain dumb," says Jake, a twenty-four-year-old and former pledgemaster at his Michigan State fraternity house:

> We'd line 'em up at all hours, yell at them for a while, quiz 'em on chapter history, lore, and make sure they memorized all the brothers' names, hometowns, majors, and favorite beers. Like who cares, really? Dumb shit like that.

"Oh," he adds as an afterthought, "we'd make 'em drink. A lot." Now he smiles for a moment, remembering. "A real lot."

Often, these hazing rituals result in a sort of cat-and-mouse game between the pledges and the brothers. Jared, 20, tells me about his experience as a pledge at Duke:

> The brothers were always calling us to do stuff at weird hours, or drinking until we passed out or puked or something. But who can do that shit all the time? I mean, I'm pre-med, and I can't be like staggering into my organic chemistry lab with a blinding hangover, can I? So the pledges would do all sorts of things to sort of get out of it. We'd fake being plastered, I mean so drunk that they'd stop making us drink. Or we'd conveniently miss a lineup the night before a test. One time, I went to the infirmary and said I had a bad stomach ache because I just knew they were going to call us at like 2 a.m.

Yet at least some hazing rituals are sufficiently degrading or humiliating—and dangerous—that they qualify as physical or sexual assaults.

At first glance, one might be tempted to see these sexualized rituals such as the elephant walk as homoerotic. (Indeed, it would be difficult not to see them that way.) But they are also about the sexual humiliation of presumed heterosexual males—and part of that degradation is homophobic taunting. Perhaps the more obviously homoerotic the ritual, the more overtly homophobic must be the accompanying narrative. But it also has everything to do with women. Initiation rituals are more rigorous and significant in societies that are highly patriarchal—in fact, the greater the level of gender inequality in a society, the more centrally important is their initiation ritual. These rituals demarcate the line between men's space and women's space.

The rituals are often sexually humiliating, sometimes violent, and always about manhood. Take, for example, "teabagging," named after the visual similarities between a tea bag and a scrotum. In this ritual, a brother opens his pants and squats over the face of a sleeping pledge, then rubs his scrotum on the pledge's face. Awakening, the pledge is greeted by someone's genitals dangling in his face. Or take egg races, in which all the pledges shove a peeled hard-boiled egg up their rectums and then have to either walk or run around to the delight of the brothers. Or the wedgie, involving the forced removal of another brother's underwear while he is still wearing them—without taking off his pants. To administer the wedgie properly, one guy told an anthropologist, ". . . several brothers wrestle the victim to the ground and reach inside his pants and grab the elastic portion of the underwear and pull until they are ripped off the victim." A brother described this process as a very painful experience and added, "When I go to a party, I either don't wear any underwear or I wear an old pair that would be easily ripped off. They did it to me once in front of a date I brought and it was embarrassing. She thought we were real immature."

Other hazing rituals are unmistakably homoerotic, like "Ookie Cookie," which depends first on another homosocial ritual, the Circle Jerk. In the Ookie Cookie, a group of guys masturbate together and ejaculate on a cookie, which the pledges are then required to eat.

Such rituals provide ample evidence that hazing is less about younger males trying to impress their elders, and far more about the sense of entitlement that the older males have to exact such gratuitously violent and degrading behaviors from those more vulnerable than they. Hazing is brutal because brotherhood cannot be cemented by words—by oaths or declarations. The cement of the brotherhood is blood, sweat, and tears—and, apparently, vomit and semen.

What is driving the initiation rights? What are they really about?

The groups proclaim that the point of the rituals is to test the commitment of the prospective members. Yet closer examination reveals something far more subtle at work. The rituals may be proving manhood, but it is the manhood of the members themselves rather than of the initiates that is on the line. Inflicting such punishment confirms the *members'* legitimacy. It is a way for them to reassure themselves that they belong to a group so worthy that other guys are willing to suffer just to join them.

And that means that ending the brutal assaults that constitute hazing cannot only be about instilling some sense of morality or compassion among the brothers—that is, it can't only be about appealing to their better selves. Efforts to confront hazing must also confront the sense of worthlessness that these brutal rituals are designed to mute.

Black Brothers in White Guyland

Fraternities are historically white groups; indeed, the Greek system really became entrenched in the United States during the late nineteenth century, when large land-grant universities, like Wisconsin and Minnesota and Michigan, were required to admit women, newly arrived immigrants, and freed blacks who had migrated north. Fraternities were an answer to the question: Where can a white guy go where he won't have to be around all these women, minorities, and immigrants?

I recall my own experience of freshman rush in the late 1960s, when I was politely told that one fraternity wouldn't be interested in me because in the oath of membership one had to solemnly swear to uphold "the Anglo-Saxon heritage"—something that I, a Jew, couldn't hope to do. Nor could a Catholic, or a black, Latino, or Asian student.

Predictably, these groups responded to racial and gender exclusion by establishing their own sororities and fraternities. Today, fraternities are nearly as dominant on historically black campuses like Morehouse and Howard as they are at some predominantly white universities. And sadly, contemporary black fraternities have embraced many of the same hazing rituals as the white ones. One hears some rather harrowing tales of initiation, including branding and whipping that might make white fraternities sound tame. No one could have predicted that more than a century after slaves were routinely branded by their owners that black fraternities would actually be branding their pledges. In one 1993 incident, pledges in one black fraternity at the University of Maryland were ". . . punched, kicked, whipped, and beaten with paddles, brushes and belts over a two-month period. All of the recruits sustained serious injuries, some of which required hospitalization. . . ."

Whipped and branded? Perhaps, as one anthropology professor commented, it is a ". . . . way of taking the symbol of horrible oppression and turning it into something positive. . . . It's the African-American male seizing command of his body and conveying the message to white America—'I'm taking command of my body.'" Or, as another said, it's an ". . . attempt by a fragmented, victimized, and marginalized group to seize agency, create space, and become men." Or that branding expresses ". . . a sense of commitment and permanence in an uncertain and impermanent world."

This is what the culture of protection sounds like. This is what it sounds like when grown men so heavily identify with the younger men they are supposed to be supervising, monitoring, and mentoring toward adulthood. Failing to condemn such practices is a sign not of solidarity but of cowardice.

Why Do Guys Put Up with It?

Why do guys participate in ceremonial degradation? Part of it is simply because they want to be liked, want to be accepted, want to be one of the cool guys, the in crowd, aligned with the alpha males. "I went along with all that [hazing] because I wanted to be liked and couldn't figure out a way to accomplish that except to be all things to all people. In trying to be something I could not be I prostituted myself," one former pledge told journalist Hank Nuwer.

"By the end of freshman orientation you pretty much know that the fraternities rule here," said Chuck, 21, a junior at the University of Oregon. "This isn't like Reed or Santa Cruz, where everything is hippy dippy. This is fucking rah-rah college. The frats have all the parties, get all the hot girls, and have all the cool guys. You want to hang around with the athletes and the hot girls, right? Well, they are the only game in town. I joined even though they seemed sort of stupid and definitely seemed sort of smug and arrogant, you know. But they were *it*. There wasn't anything else. And I wanted a social life."

Dave, 26, recalls his first week in the dorm at Cornell:

> From the second you arrive on campus, the frat guys are everywhere. During freshman orientation, in the evenings, they come around the guys' floors, like selling stuff, like school spirit sort of stuff, like beer mugs, and college jackets and stuff. They're like the concession guys at the ball park. They come in, socialize a bit, show you what they're selling. But really, they're selling being frat guys. And all the freshman guys wanted to buy that.

"Not to be in a fraternity or sorority was widely regarded as being nothing at all," writes Larry Lockridge recalling his father's experience in a fraternity at Indiana in the 1930s.

Part of it is the Guy Code—the desperate desire to feel worth, to feel powerful, to be validated as a man. Somehow these almost-men seduce themselves into believing that these guys, a year older and so much cooler, hold the magical key that will open the door to a feeling of confident manhood with nothing left to prove. As Jackson, a senior at Lehigh explained:

> I knew from the moment I accepted a bid to pledge Beta that my fate was sealed. I would be a cool guy. I would be one of them. No, I mean, I would be one of *us*. It was a really special feeling. Like I could do anything, because the other guys would always have my back. And *we* could do anything because, well, because we were Betas, and on this campus, Betas rule. No one—and I mean Greek types, administrators, other guys, and, yeah, well, even you professors—would ever be able to touch us.

In reality, of course, going through the torture of hazing doesn't make you a man. In a sense, fraternity hazing is the distorted mirror image of cultural rituals of initiation, where boys actually do become men in the eyes of their culture. In the collegiate fraternity something else is happening. Just at the moment when your entire culture tells you that it's time to grow up—be a man, step up to sober adult responsibilities, declare a professional ambition, pair up romantically, settle down and get married to the person with whom you will spend your entire life "forsaking all others," have kids, a mortgage, a responsible job, bills to pay—just at that sad, depressing moment of the actual transition to adulthood here is a group of slightly older peers who collectively scream "No!" Not so fast. No need to grow up just yet. Be our brother. Remain a boy. Irresponsible and carefree. "[I]t's a damn shame it's got to end. The fraternity and everything," wrote William F. Buckley Jr. fondly recalling his days in a secret society, and imagining the plight of a young man facing a world entirely infiltrated by women. "Someday we should build us all a fraternity house that wouldn't end. And we could initiate our friends and go off and drink like freshmen and never graduate. Hell! Why build a fraternity house! Let's build a gigantic fraternity system!"

As we've seen, the ability *not* to grow up, *not* to become a man, is Guyland's definition of freedom. And guys believe that it's certainly worth undergoing some humiliating rituals, doing gross and stupid things, and even getting sick over. In fact, doing that gross and stupid stuff is what convinces you that you have not crossed over the threshold of adulthood, that you are still just a guy. It's a man's world, all right. It can wait.

Defending the Cavemen

In the mid–1970s, Hank Nuwer was a graduate student at the University of Nevada, Reno, and witnessed a few initiations near his home. Then he heard about another in which a student was killed and another experienced serious brain damage. Since that time, he's been on a virtual one-man crusade to eliminate hazing. Nuwer is now a journalism professor, and his book *Wrongs of Passage* is a chilling compendium of hazing-related deaths and injuries on America's campuses. "With at least one death every year between 1970 and 2007, it seems incredible that this collision of deadly and bizarre behavior can continue to exist, let alone flourish, on as many campuses as it does," he told me.

Since the 1970s, there has been at least one student fatality every year involving hazing. Most have a similar trajectory: The pledges are forced to drink massive amounts of alcohol in a short amount of time while the brothers, if they are watching at all, are usually hurling epithets at the pledges. One guy blacks out and can't be revived, or he begins to lose consciousness as he throws up, suffocating on his own vomit. By the time any of his utterly wasted brothers or the other pledges notice anything, it's too late.

Lynn Gordon Bailey, known to his friends as Gordie, was captain of his high-school football team at Deerfield Academy and member of the drama club. On September 16, 2004, this 18-year-old from Dallas, Texas, was enjoying his first night as a pledge of Chi Psi fraternity on the University of Colorado's Boulder campus. By the next morning, he was dead of alcohol poisoning, having consumed seventeen shots of whiskey in about thirty minutes in a hazing ritual. His blood alcohol level was 0.328.

Here is where the dynamics of Guyland kick into high gear. While fraternity members refused to speak to reporters, other Colorado students were distraught, and spoke publicly about it. Some came forward to talk to reporters about their own participation in alcohol-sodden parties and drinking rituals at what was being trumpeted as America's #1 party school. The response of the administrators was to send threatening letters to those students who spoke with reporters. The Vice Chancellor wrote, "I hope you realize how your portrayal in the newspaper negatively impacts so many CU students."

Again, that's the culture of protection. Don't do it, but when you do, for God's sake, please don't tell anyone about it because it makes us look bad. And don't post it on Facebook, MySpace, or any other website where some activist can bust us! Less than two weeks later, a 19-year-old CU student was arrested for the drunken sexual assault of a sorority member in the restroom of a swanky downtown hotel during a fraternity party.

While hazing and forced binging are common in Guyland, the adults who are supposed to be in charge are often running for cover. They know what is happening, even if they profess shock and dismay when they hear about another fraternity hazing death or the death of a 21-year-old at a power hour. Certainly coaches, deans of students, residence hall advisors, and the heads of Greek organizations on campus know what's happening. Even though it takes place off their watch, they know. They just pass the buck.

Or perhaps the culture of protection is actually a bit more pernicious than we think. To be sure, administrators are often hamstrung between complicitous silence from the hazers and indignant bribery by some of the wealthy alumni on whom the administrators depend. But perhaps they also believe in the hazing and the binging and the rest of it. They may even identify with these guys.

Some colleges and universities actually seem to promote the very alcohol soaked environments they are simultaneously trying to police. Henry Wechsler suggests that one can easily measure the alcohol-friendliness of the administration. It's a simple equation: the higher the number of bars within walking distance of campus and the greater the amount of alcohol sold at sporting events, then the higher the number of students who report that they are both drinkers and binge drinkers. In the case of the University of Colorado, the biggest liquor store, with the closest proximity to campus, was owned by the Director of Athletics.

Hazing and binging certainly have their defenders. Every time a university president decides it's time to reign in the fraternities, monitor the athletic teams, or try and restrict underage drinking on campus, howls of derisive protest go up—from current students for whom college is one nonstop party, to alumni who threaten to withdraw their financial support if the administration or Board of Trustees displaces one metaphoric hair on the college's head or interferes in any way with the autonomy of the fraternities. This is especially true at private colleges and universities, where alumni financial support is the lifeblood of the institution. Every time, it seems, there is a campus investigation, alumni threaten to stop donating, sue the college, and otherwise make life miserable for any reformist administration.

Alumni successfully blocked former Dartmouth president James O. Freedman from disbanding the fraternity system even after the film

Animal House, written by former Dartmouth frat guys, exposed the college to disastrous publicity. Currently, the administration at Colgate is under constant fire from alumni who fear that disbanding the fraternities will emasculate the university—this from a school that has been coed for nearly forty years, currently enrolls more women than men, and has a female president.

And these administrators are stymied from within. "Investigators of hazing deaths and injuries are often stymied in their attempt to get facts because members of secret societies believe that breaking their code of silence is disloyal," writes hazing expert Hank Nuwer. What's more, insurance carriers "instruct fraternities never to admit liability when faced with a potential claim."

Many a university president has been hounded by the righteous anger of alums, who recall their own beer-sodden college days with a mixture of fondness and pain, and believe that today's battalions of political correctness have siphoned all the fun out of the college experience. Alumni have been claiming forever that they had it far tougher—and they turned out all right, didn't they? At the turn of the twentieth century, for example, the Board of Regents and the administration at the University of Kansas outlawed the fist fights that had become commonplace on campus. Most undergraduates supported the administration, finding the "tradition" silly and dangerous. Not the alums. One, class of 1896, taunted the younger KU men:

> What's the matter with K.U.? The May Pole scrap is gone, or emasculated into "Ring Around the Rosy"; the junior prom and the senior reception are as tame as a pink tea in an Old Ladies Home . . . and the authorities seem to think that the University is a school for namby-pambies and Lizzie boys.

Today, when alumni suggest that the ritual torture they experienced as frat guys is what made them the men they are today they make two mistakes. First, they engage in what psychologists call "attribution error." That is, they attribute some consequence (having a great time in college, becoming a man) to the wrong cause (drinking oneself into unconsciousness, being sexually ridiculed and humiliated). Actually, this is the way many of us respond to trauma: we believe it has had some healing or strengthening quality and our passage through it is an indication of our successfully overcoming the trauma.

Second, it's bad history. Every generation thinks they had it tougher than the one that comes after them. Asking "Is it worse today?" is the wrong question. Even if it was worse back then, which it probably wasn't, so what? A lot of things were different. Back then, drivers didn't wear seat belts, hockey goalies didn't wear face masks, kids didn't sit in car seats, or wear bike helmets. Back then, doctors didn't do genetic screening for diseases, MRIs, or colonoscopies. Back then, most Americans believed that women shouldn't vote because they were too delicate and fragile. Just because it might have been worse in the past doesn't absolve us in the present.

The point is, of course, that standards change. Today we insist on greater safety for our children. We demand to know what's in the food we eat. We believe in equality, in individual dignity, in protecting those who have no voice, in leveling the playing field. Timeless universal truths turn out to be flexible in light of new information. Change isn't necessarily bad or good. It just is.

As we'll see, there are some positive signs coming from the nation's campuses about how to deal with hazing, binging, and other assorted activities of Guyland. Some schools are returning to a more active monitoring of the students under their charge, and some fraternities are going dry, eliminating hazing altogether, or building some positive bonding experiences into the brotherhood equation.

And while the overtly sexualized hazing rituals are evident in many noncampus groups as well—workplaces, military barracks, sports teams, essentially, wherever guys of a certain age gather—it's equally true that eventually guys grow out of it. Binging, hazing, and the like virtually disappear by the late twenties; few corporate law firms or manufacturing plants rely on such sexualized graphic humiliation as a way for men over age 30 to prove themselves. It may be that these institutions have simply developed other ways to extract that commitment or indulge the sadistic pleasure in humiliating others, or it may simply be that the potential initiate has other arenas—as husband or father, perhaps—in which his masculinity is now demonstrated, and so there may simply be less on the line.

And yet, as these stories continually remind us, the stakes are enormous. The February 2005 hazing death of 21-year-old Cal State, Chico junior Matt Carrington led to indictments of several of his fraternity brothers. Carrington did not die of alcohol poisoning, but of "water intoxication." He and another pledge were left in a cold wet basement doing calisthenics for hours with their feet in raw sewage while fans blasted icy air at their wet bodies. They were ordered to drink from a five-gallon jug of water that was continually filled.

The pledges urinated and vomited on themselves and each other. But then Carrington began having a seizure. Fraternity brothers didn't call an ambulance, perhaps for fear their hazing activities would be exposed. By the time they did call, it was too late. Carrington's heart stopped beating, his brain and lungs swollen beyond recognition from the water.

As they were sentenced to six months to a year in prison for their part in Carrington's death, his fraternity brothers expressed remorse instead of defiant silence. "I did what I did out of a misguided sense of building brotherhood, and instead I lost a brother. I will live with the consequences of hazing for the rest of my life," said Gabriel Maestretti, a former altar boy and volunteer coach who was a leader of the fraternity. "My actions killed a good person, and I will be a felon for the rest of my life. . . . Hazing isn't funny, it's not cute. It's stupid, dangerous. It's not about brotherhood, it's about power and control."

Here is the beginning of the conversation that should be happening across the country.

6 | SPORTS CRAZY

My son Zachary and I were returning by subway from a Mets game last season when a group of about eight black teenaged boys got into our subway car. They were talking loudly to each other as they stood near us. Some of the other riders became visibly anxious; a few moved away in the car, a few others got out at the next station to change cars. But Zachary was listening to them as they nearly shouted at each other in mock anger. Gradually it dawned on him (and me) that they were constructing the best starting five in NBA history, yelling back and forth, pulling players in and out. As is typical, they were dramatically overrepresenting current players—at least to my Baby Boomer ears. I mean, Dwayne Wade is good, but. . . .

Zachary looked up at one guy and said, "But Magic Johnson was the best passer ever, and he could shoot from outside and drive the lane. You have to have Magic!"

The guy looked down at Zachary. Stared at him. So did his friend standing next to him. And another. A few seconds passed. Then, the guy closest to us smiled broadly, put his hand out to high-five Zachary, and claimed Magic as his own choice. Zachary looked at me. "Dad," he leaned in close and asked, "who was the guy you said was the best shot blocker ever?" "Bill Russell," I replied. Zachary offered Russell over Shaquille O'Neal, which began another round of discussion—one in which he was now included. When the guys left, each walked past Zachary and high-fived him. And, having been accepted by kids who were both older and more knowledgeable, Zachary practically floated home on that train.

Walk into any dorm on any campus where there are guys sitting around watching TV—or into any fraternity house, or apartment shared by a group of single guys, or bar, or even, these days, many restaurants. You will be surrounded by sports, bombarded by sports. It's everywhere. Guys are sports crazy.

And we've been crazy about sports for more than a hundred years, ever since modern spectator sports—baseball, football, and later basketball and ice hockey—were first introduced at the turn of the last century. In the first decades of the twentieth century, the baseball diamond was the only place in America where rural and urban men bumped into each other, so separate were their worlds. And the stands were just about the only places where factory workers and office bureaucrats rubbed shoulders. Sports—playing them, watching them, exulting in victories, despairing over defeats—was one of the great equalizers of American democracy (except if you happened to be black; those barriers took another half-century to fall).

For more than a century, men have known that playing sports provided physical fitness, a healthy competition, and lots of fun. Watching has always instilled civic pride as we root for our home teams, bond across class boundaries, and experience the tonic freshness of bucolic splendor in the gritty city.

These days, American guys are possibly more sports crazy off the field than on it. They read the sports page, check out sports magazines online, listen to sports radio, watch sports on TV, and watch shows about sports on TV. They go to restaurants and bars that tune into several sports events at once. They wear more team and player-branded jerseys than ever before, and there is more bonding through athletic wear than through shared interests. They play fantasy baseball, football, basketball, and hockey, in which they select and manage their own teams through an entire season. They participate in countless endless arguments about the relative merits of players.

Sports is so ubiquitous in Guyland that it often seems to crowd out other forms of social life. Guys live for sports, and live through sports. It serves so many purposes—validating our manhood; bridging generational, racial, and class divides; cementing the bonds among men; and more clearly demarcating the boundaries between Guyland and Herland. Here are a few snapshots.

It's 10 o'clock on a Tuesday night at Goodfellas, a bar in downtown Wilmington frequented by college guys from the local campus of the University of North Carolina. The music is loud, the noise level high, and all eyes are glued to the large flat-screen TVs hanging from the walls, showing three different baseball games. Guys comment to each other about each game, and small cheers go up whenever something happens on any of the screens. (The guys also check out the few unattached women at the bar and the men's room is plastered with soft-core pornographic pictures, but the focus seems to be on a different type of scoring.)

At 6 p.m., when Nate comes home from work to the Philadelphia apartment he shares with three other guys, he grabs a beer and sits down with his pals to watch *SportsCenter* on ESPN and catch up on the days' sports news. They'll watch again at 11, when the rest of the country might tune into their local news show. And those who can't sleep will simply leave the TV tuned to ESPN and watch whatever is on late into the night.

At lunch, Walter, 24, joins about seven other stockbrokers and bond traders at Delmonico's, the famous steakhouse that has been serving the up-and-coming Masters of the Universe on Wall Street since it was founded in 1837. In the lounge, next to the dark wood paneling, TVs don't just have stock tickers in a constant stream, but also games, highlights, and *SportsCenter*. And if that's not enough, you can always go downmarket to Ryan's Sports Bar, a few blocks away, where TVs ring the bar, all with sports.

Every evening during his commute from work, Jim, 26, joins nearly a million other guys as he tunes into WFAN ("The Fan") radio in New

York, and listens to "Mike and the Mad Dog"—a five-and-one-half-hour call-in sports talk show that he listens to on his computer during slow moments, and then all the way back to the Long Island suburban house he shares with his wife and their 2-year-old daughter. "I love listening to Mike and the Mad Dog," he tells me.

> The guys who call are great, really knowledgeable, and Mike always steers the conversation away from nasty comments about women or about athletes' private lives. You know, I mean sex lives. I think that's why the athletes themselves go on the show, because they know he respects them. I've even called in a couple of times, you know. Once, I pulled over on the fucking L.I.E. to mouth off about the Jets or the Mets. And he completely agreed with me.

Make no mistake: There is nothing "wrong" with any of this. Some of my fondest moments as a child were arguing about who was the best centerfielder in New York—Mickey Mantle, Duke Snider, or Willie Mays. I love reading the sports page with Zachary, and I love discussing how our various teams have fared. I'm never happier than when I'm coaching his Little League baseball team, or his soccer team, or when we play roller hockey in the park as training for the ice hockey season. I love being a Hockey Dad and a Soccer Dad and I always smile as I listen to him argue with his friends about whether José Reyes or Derek Jeter is the best shortstop in baseball.

I say all this to be clear: *I love sports.* They have always been an integral part of my life. I play them, watch them, talk about them. Through sports I have felt connected to my family, my community (the Brooklyn of the Dodgers), and my friends.

But we need to ask some questions about what sports mean to us, to think about the place sports occupy in our lives. We need to talk about talking about sports. Talking about sports creates a female-free zone where guys can be guys. It mutes differences among men by race or class or age—differences that made others on that subway ride with Zachary visibly uncomfortable. Sports talk provides a temporary respite from having to think about our differences and the complexities of life all the damned time. And not the least of these complexities involves women.

Once, of course, the entire public sphere was a man's world. Today, everywhere you look—the corporate boardroom, the classroom, the military squad, the athletic field—there are women. Is it so surprising that guys today rely more on talking about sports, playing fantasy sports, and living and breathing sports 24/7? Sports talk has become the reconstituted clubhouse, the last "pure" all-male space in America.

Loving Sports

I asked guys across the country about sports—what they like and don't like, what they watch and play, and what they talk about. Their voices rang like a nationally dispersed chorus that all sang the same song. But while they knew all the words, and were familiar with the melody, I had a hard time getting anyone to risk a solo and actually be articulate about the place of sports in their lives. They'd waffle between a sort of incoherent mumbling—tinged, at times, with an edgy defensiveness— and a vague but seemingly deep nostalgia.

Said Rick, a junior at Emory, "Uh, I dunno. It's fun, it's, it's cool, it's like, well, it's what guys *do*. I don't think I understand the question. I mean, why do I like sports? Because I'm a guy."

Jeff, a senior at Bowdoin, was no more helpful. "Why do I like sports? What's not to like? It's just what guys do."

Ted, a former track star at Auburn, stressed the physical exertion:

There's something so exhilarating about training hard, working your body, pushing it to its limits, and then competing against guys who have trained just as hard. Can you do it, can you take it up one more notch, can you find one more spurt in there?

And Justin, a sophomore at Penn, echoed these sentiments:

I grew up playing sports, watching sports. It was the only way to be a guy in my school. I mean, you could be smart, but you'd better not show it. You could be, like, talented or artistic or whatever, but you better not show it. Everyone was always going around saying "that's so gay" and "this is so gay." And the one thing they never said that about was sports. The guys who never got bullied or teased were the guys who were into sports. So, like, sports was not only a way to be a guy, it was the single most important way to prove you weren't, like, you know, like gay.

Guys like sports because it's the easiest way to choose "guy" over "gay"—and make sure everyone gets the right idea about them. It's reassuring, especially during a time of adolescent turmoil and inevitable doubts and questions when nothing is as clear as they wish it were. The novelist Zane Grey once wrote "All boys love baseball. If they don't they're not real boys." Guys also believe the converse: If they do love sports, they *are* real boys.

Guys also like following sports because it's a way to talk with other guys without having to talk about your feelings. It's a certain conversation starter in any uncertain social situation—walk into a party, a bar, a classroom, and say "How 'bout them Mets?" Instant bonding. Sports talk clears a path for easy entry. Even when guys say it self-consciously, ironically, at a lull in the conversation, their recourse to it underscores its value as a sort of cynical currency.

Among the funniest scenes in the film *Birdcage* occurs when Armand (played by Robin Williams) is trying to teach his partner Albert (a drag queen played by Nathan Lane) how to pass as a "real man." After teaching him to walk like John Wayne, Williams positions himself under a tree and instructs Lane to shake his hand forcefully and break the ice with a sure-fire conversation starter.

"How do you feel about those Dolphins? I mean 4th and 2 and they go for it . . ."

To which Lane responds as only a gay man—i.e. a "failed" man— possibly could. "How do you think I feel? Betrayed, bewildered." The audience howls because Lane missed the cue. Williams didn't really want to know how he was *feeling*!

The Crying Game

There is something else in the mix of men and emotions. Men use sports to both hide their feelings and to *express* their feelings. Sports legitimize our emotions, and enable us to express a fuller range of emotions than we ordinarily do in our everyday lives. They allow men to experience ecstasy. Watch guys' faces when their team scores—pure joy. The emotions of sports are simple and uncomplicated: the thrill of victory and the agony of defeat.

But perhaps the most important thing is that sports let men cry. We cry without getting stares that say we're not real men. We cry from pain, from defeat, from the joy of winning a championship, from the intensely emotional feelings we have for our teammates.

A couple of years ago, my family took a Canadian friend to a base-ball game at Yankee Stadium. August 13, 2005 was "Mickey Mantle Memorial Day"—ten years since Mantle had died. It was to be the day his plaque was unveiled in Memorial Park, part of the outfield (now behind the wall) that had been a pilgrimage site for Yankee fans for half a century. The ceremony, emceed by Billy Crystal and includ-ing former Yankee players and a few survivors of Mantle's family, was interminable—an hour-long sob-fest. All around us, men my age and older were weeping unashamedly. My wife was so stunned by the cloy-ing bathos in which the entire event was drenched that she pronounced it "a chick flick for guys." My son fidgeted and wondered when the game would begin. But my friend and I, neither of us Yankee fans in our youth, were deeply moved by such public displays of affection for a frag-ile idol, especially coming from men who would do almost anything to toughen up their sons.

Sports enables men to defy the cardinal rule of masculinity—"Don't Cry." It enables men to access their emotions and get in touch with their "inner boy." Men may not cry—but boys do. Sports are about a return to boyhood. They offer the pleasures of regression. Playing and following sports is a way for men to postpone adulthood indefinitely.

We may age (here I include myself) but the players we watch, they're still 22 years old, and we still often feel like wide-eyed 12-year-olds watching them, idolizing them, wanting to grow up to be like them—even if we are old enough to be their fathers. Sports enable us to fantasize that we are still the boys of summer, even as we age into the autumn of our lives.

Like fraternity initiations and binge drinking, sports are sometimes another activity that almost-men engage in to prolong childhood and avoid becoming men—which we think means being sober, responsible, serious fathers and workers, unable to have fun. Sports recall the bucolic American past, unhurried by the drive of the corporate clock. They remind us of the purity and innocence of play. And there is nothing intrinsically wrong with this—except that in Guyland, many men never seem to leave the stadium. For them sports aren't a time-out; they're the endgame.

Like so many parts of Guyland, the continuum runs from harmless and even positive experiences of emotional expressiveness, friendship, and connection through the vaguely silly or gross, toward the other pole on which such positive experiences may be based on dominance, exclusion, and anger. Sports may provide a safe haven for guys to express their emotions, to connect with each other, to reach back to their childhood. And as a place of emotional vulnerability and expressiveness, love of sports can be easily manipulated and abused. A safe haven for guys cannot be based on making women feel unsafe.

Make Room for Daddy

Our love of sports may also be about connecting with one person in particular—the one person who has the power to validate your manhood or dissolve it in an instant: Dad.

It's my story too. My father caught my first pitches, was the umpire at my Little League games, the coach of my Pony League team. He'd take ten minutes in between patients (his office was attached to our house) when I'd come home from school to play catch with me, to ask me how my day was. He took me fishing. He taught me how to shoot a rifle, set up a BB gun range in our basement, and took me hunting. We learned to ski together, to ice skate together. We'd wake up at 5 o'clock on Saturday mornings to play golf together, teeing off at 7 and arriving home just as the rest of the family was waking up. It was our time together, and I cherished it. He was the teacher, I his avid student.

My father taught me how to love a baseball team. For us, it was the Brooklyn Dodgers. A Brooklyn-based chiropractor, my dad counted several Dodger pitchers as patients. And, of course, like many a Dodger fan, my father taught me how to have your heart broken by your team. It wasn't just that they lost; it was that they left. My father cried the day the Dodgers announced their move to Los Angeles. We packed up and moved to the suburbs. He never watched a Dodger game again.

Watching sports with my father was one of the joys of my childhood. Reading about it in the paper, talking about our teams, cemented our bonds. Sports, guys told me constantly, was a crucial way to bond with their fathers. Sometimes, it was the only way they ever spent time together. Some guys waxed nostalgic, recalling moments of connection with fathers who had now grown more distant, who had drifted away after divorce, or who had broken those intimate bonds in some other way.

"My father wasn't around a lot," says Mike, 24, a recent Brown graduate who now lives in Brooklyn. "He traveled a lot, worked really hard, and then he and my mom got a divorce. But every weekend we'd go play ball together. You know, I think . . ." his voice trails off and Mike gets a faraway look in his eyes. "You know," he says, "I think the most intimate memory of my dad was when he reached around me and showed me how to hold a bat. I remember that every time I pick up a bat today."

I met Mike on the baseball field near my home where I was having a catch with my son. What is striking is that Zachary and I had known Mike for a grand total of about five minutes and his emotions—deep, tender—were so readily accessible to him. At least as long as we were all playing ball.

"When I was little, my dad was so much a part of my life," recalls Albert, a 25-year-old graphic designer in Boston. "Every day growing up, I could count on some things—playing ball, talking with him about the Sox or the Bruins, or the Celtics. Even the Patriots. I think that was the only way he knew to be close to me, the only thing we could actually talk about. I still feel bad. He died in 2003, and he never saw the Red Sox win it all. Never." His eyes get a little watery.

Other guys wince at the memories, recoiling still from judgmental tyrants, Great Santiniesque fathers who pushed and pushed their sons to perform in sports, fathers who let them know that they had to work incessantly, and that still they would never be satisfied. Fathers whose competitive anger at their sons was a way to pretend that they themselves weren't getting old.

"It was the only way I was going to get my dad to pay any attention to me at all," said Jeff, now 27. "He was so critical, all the time, he just never let up. But I nearly killed myself, playing with injuries, screwing up my knees, pushing myself beyond everything, just to get his approval. Which, when I think about it, I think I almost did."

For decades, I've been hearing stories like this from middle-aged men—either the misty nostalgia of rare moments of connection or the wrenching struggle to perform well enough athletically to try to please an implacably tyrannical judge. But I didn't expect to hear it from younger men, from the guys who are, after all, our sons. I had thought we, the men of my generation, would have learned better: to stick around and remain a vital loving presence in our sons' lives when they weren't on the ball field, or to enable them to feel our love without it being contingent on athletic prowess.

Just as surprising as the immediacy of guys' emotions was how apparently raw and unstudied they seemed to be. Maybe this was why they seemed so inarticulate: Somehow sports touch them in a way that is so deep that they find it nearly impossible to speak of it. Sports make us aware of the love we crave. Here's Ted, 26, a Pittsburgh native now a technical consultant in a division of an investment bank:

> My father [an accountant] was never there when I was growing
> up. Always on calls, always working, even on weekends. I wanted
> so much to get his attention, earn his respect. I knew he loved
> sports—God, the only time I saw him relax was when he would
> be watching the Steelers on TV. I went out for football, I think,

because it was cool, and everyone was into it, sure. But I think I went out for football because it would get *his* attention.

"Did it?" I ask.

No, not really. I mean, well, yeah, I guess. He said he was proud of me and all. But then I separated my shoulder in my second game, and that was pretty much the end of my football career. He never mentioned it, never talked about it, never really paid much attention to me after that.

"Did you ever talk about it?" I ask.

It's funny, you know. The year before he died, before we knew about the cancer and everything, he said something to me about it. In his own way, sort of indirect, you know? He told me one Christmas when I was visiting, that his dad had never paid any attention to him, and that he always felt that he had been a disappointment to his dad. He tried out for the baseball team as a kid in the fifties, but didn't make it. "I was so proud of you when you played football," he said to me. "I hope you know that."

I told him that actually I didn't. I didn't even think he was paying attention. "Oh, I didn't want to make too big a deal out of it. Your mother wasn't happy about it, and then your brother wasn't going to ever be good at anything. I didn't want to seem like I was singling you out."

Funny, but suddenly it wasn't like I finally got what I wanted from him, you know? It was more like I finally realized that I had been trying for so long for something that actually was there all the time.

Guys carry those early moments with them, both in their relationships with male authority figures like their coaches, teachers, and others, and in their relationships with each other. Sports are a place of intense emotion; it's the glue that holds male friendships together. Some friendships that have lasted for decades are based on sports talk. It both facilitates sharing feelings and enables us *not* to talk about our feelings—what's *really* going on in our lives. As long as we talk about how we feel about our team, our players—as long as *they* break our hearts—then we can both talk about heartbreak and not talk about it at the same time.

Sports vs. Girls

There's another reason guys love sports. It's not just a return to boyhood, it's a return to a specific moment of boyhood—the moment before girls. Remember the movie *Stand By Me?* This boy-bonding movie is about a group of pre-adolescents enjoying the last summer before they're saddled with high school and other adult responsibilities. High school, the boys feel without ever saying, will change everything, thrusting them into a world where the purity of their friendships will be tainted by competition for girls' attention, accolades, and rewards.

Through this lens, loving sports is also about loving your friends and hating what you see as the forces that threaten to break up that merry band of brothers. Sociologists Mike Messner and Don Sabo, two of the most insightful writers about the place of sports in men's lives, call men's experience with other men in sports a moment of "dominance bonding." It's not just innocent connectedness, there's an edge to it, a sense of superiority. It's where the safe haven of sports can turn dangerous for others.

It's the threat to dominance bonding that elicits the defensiveness when women invade formerly all-male spaces—whether professions such as medicine or law, or the science lab, or the military, or the sports locker room. At these moments, men feel threatened by women's equality, because equality includes access to those private spaces.

Fields of Dreams

Those spaces needn't be real, of course. One of the fastest-growing sports in America is fantasy leagues, in which "owners" organize a league and each owner selects his team in a draft (where they are limited by salary caps and other constraints). These teams are disaggregated teams—that is they are composed of players who are actually on any team in the sport, so that charting your team consists of tabulating the results of each of the individual players on your team. It doesn't matter how your home team does—it matters how any particular player that you "own" does.

Fantasy leagues exist in virtually every sport, and 15 million American men are playing them. U.S. businesses lose about $200 million in productivity each football season because employees are managing their fantasy football teams instead of working. One journalist writes that fantasy sports "allow you to indulge your inner Theo Epstein [General Manager of the Boston Red Sox] from the comfort of the couch; and for the hyper-competitive, adrenaline-craving, statistics-spouting sports geek, there is no modern ritual more sublime than the fantasy draft."

"It's better than sex," said Evan, 27, explaining how he and his friends wait all year for the fantasy football draft. In a recent popular film, *Knocked Up*, one character's wife suspects her husband is having an affair, and so she enlists the help of her sister and her sister's boyfriend and together they troop off to catch him in the act. She finds him in a suburban house, dressed in a Baltimore Orioles uniform, participating in a fantasy baseball draft. When she asks just what in the world he is doing, he gushes, "It's a fantasy baseball draft. I got Matsui!" (She considers this as much of a betrayal as if he had been sleeping with her best friend.)

The all-male competitive camaraderie is sort of the point. In their recent book, sports writers Erik Barmack and Max Handelman explain, as their title puts it, *Why Fantasy Football Matters (And Our Lives Do Not)*. To Handelman, it's innocent regression. "The whole trash-talking and chest pounding and borderline immaturity that guys revel in that they can't otherwise do in adult society," is what it's about. "Guys' egos ride a lot on this stuff, which is kind of crazy because it's numbers and it's fantasy."

But, he hastens to add, it's precisely that adolescent inanity that poses its charm. "The vast majority of fantasy football fans, myself included, revel in the absurdity of it all. It's like adult Dungeons and Dragons—

it's ridiculous. We know we're a bunch of clowns." And then, "When a woman pops up in the group, it brings an air of legitimacy to it. And we're thinking, we can't have that." Women remind us that we are supposed to be grown men. Other guys allow us to be immature boys. No wonder guys get so easily pissed off at women's intrusion.

The Stronger Women Get, the More Men Love Football

The passion men have brought to playing and watching sports has been a relative constant. What has changed dramatically in recent years is the participation of women and girls. In the past three decades women's sports have undergone a revolution—women have gone from being cheerleaders and occasional spectators to being active participants, and even commentators.

Just look at the numbers. In 1971, fewer than 300,000 high-school girls played interscholastic sports in America, compared with 3.7 million boys. By 2005, the number of boys had risen to 4.1 million, but the number of girls had skyrocketed tenfold, to 2.9 million. In 1972, the year Title IX was enacted, requiring gender parity in collegiate sports, women's sports teams averaged about two sports per campus; by 2004, it had increased by more than 400 percent to 8.3 teams per campus.

In one sense this dramatic increase in such a short time is a testament to the joy of sports—the camaraderie, the competition, the sense of physical efficacy. But it's also a testament to the sway of Guyland. For decades girls had heard that sports was where it was at, the same way that their mothers heard that the workplace was where real life happened. And so, naturally, if those fields were the place to be, they wanted to be there too. And once the obstacles were removed, they swarmed onto them. It sort of proves the axiom that begins *Field of Dreams*, perhaps the quintessential guy flick of all time: "If you build it, [they] will come."

Women have definitely arrived in the sporting arena. But let me be clear: This does not mean that women and girls have achieved anything close to equality in sports. According to sociologist Mike Messner, female athletes still face inadequate resources and substandard coaching and are often funneled into more "gender appropriate" sports like softball instead of baseball. Few universities are in compliance with Title IX, "as funding for recruitment, scholarships and ongoing support of women's athletics teams lags far behind that of men's teams." Indeed, a decade of conservative efforts to stop Title IX in its tracks has resulted in as many lawsuits by men's teams citing discrimination as women's teams.

In Guyland, the story isn't about the empirical fact of girls' entry into the sporting arena. It's about the impact of their entry on boys' ideas about how to prove masculinity. And that impact has been dramatic.

When women first began to seek entry, the response by men was simply to try to exclude them. Biologically, they said, women just cannot compete. They can't do it physically or temperamentally; they have neither the bodies nor the competitive fire that men have. "A woman can do the same job I can do—maybe even be my boss," said one athlete to sociologist Messner. "But I'll be damned if she can go out on the field and take a hit from Ronnie Lott." True enough. But then, neither could I—nor could virtually any of you, for that matter. Does that mean we should be disqualified from playing—or enjoying—sports?

Even today, the concern over the cutting of men's sports to achieve some warped vision of equality is but a surface-level mask over the efforts to push women back out of the athletic arena. Often it's simply a scare tactic to try to turn back the clock to pre-Title-IX-mandated equality. It's as if women's sports and men's sports exist in a zero-sum universe, in which if women get more, men have to get less.

But the response of most men hasn't been to bar the doors and keep women out. Rather, it's been to circle the sex-segregated wagons, and try and ignore them. A 1989 study of coverage of women's sports found that the three network affiliates devoted only 5 percent of their air-time coverage to women's sports. Fifteen years later, as women's participation had mushroomed and professional leagues had taken off in soccer and basketball, coverage had increased a whopping 1.3 percent—to 6.3 percent of total air time. And the two sports highlights shows are even worse: ESPN's *SportsCenter* devotes about 2 percent of its air time to women's sports, virtually exclusively tennis and golf.

Sporting men seem to deal with what they perceive as an invasion by retreating to those sports and those arenas in which women can't compete equally or aren't interested in doing so. The rapid rise in popularity of sports like rugby, ice hockey, or lacrosse testify to this. On websites like EXPN.com and extreme.com, there's plenty of coverage of surfing, skateboarding, mountain boarding, off-road ATV driving, and other extreme sports. Women, when they appear at all, do so in bikinis.

In the past couple of decades, the scene of masculine resistance to women's entry has also shifted from the playing field to the locker room. All those female journalists, were they to have access to the locker room, might see men—gasp!—naked! How many blogs and sports-radio commentators—as well as threatened male athletes—have weighed in on that score, conveniently forgetting that women professionals do what any competent professional does—their job.

And then, of course, there is football, the one field of dreams on which women usually don't—and can't—tread. Football has gained in popularity in part because it remains so steadfastly single-sex. As Mariah Burton Nelson, a former Stanford basketball star turned women's sports activist titled her book, *The Stronger Women Get, the More Men Love Football*. Yes, there are female players and teams and leagues, but they pale in comparison to the men's side.

If the playing field was occupied territory, and the locker room invaded, men had to figure out another place where they could be men with other men. The solution was sports *talk*. And that, sports fans, might be the real story.

Dialing for Dominance

Among young men, watching sports and talking about sports has replaced playing sports as the line of demarcation between women and men. Girls may be running around the next soccer field, and women can be working out and toning up as much as the next guy, but the one thing women don't do is talk, endlessly, about sports. They may even be sports fans, and watch sports on TV or in the stands, but they don't pore over the box scores as if it were the Talmud. The woman you work with, or the one sitting across from you in a chemistry lecture, may be as athletic as you are, but she wouldn't be able to tell you Roger Clemens's ERA in 2005, or how many triple doubles Jason Kidd racked up in the 2004–5 season. (FYI, the answers are 1.87 and 8, respectively.) Nor would she care. For most women, sports are something you *do*, not necessarily something you *are*.

Of course, there is one big difference between the world of sports and the other public spheres that women have entered so decisively in the past three decades. Unlike every other arena, sports remains sex-segregated. While there may be coed volleyball or softball leagues in many places, and little kids might play on integrated U8 AYSO soccer teams or T-ball, the overwhelming majority of sports play is done on same-sex teams. This means that the accomplishments of female athletes are rarely compared to, and thus rarely threaten the accomplishments of, male athletes. Even so, men seem to need a place where women don't typically go: the radio dial, the TV, the sports pages, the sports bar. If girls can compete *on* the field, then sports-talk—and talk radio, ESPN Zone, and the host of sites and blogs and commentary—is the new boys' club, the place where the homosocial purity of the locker room is reproduced.

In 1987, a failing country music radio station in New York City was purchased and transformed into an all-sports all-the-time format, WFAN (The Fan). Currently, there are nearly 400 all-sports stations in the U.S. Only sports radio, Christian-themed programming, and "alternative" radio have shown any appreciable growth over the past few years—indeed, they're the only niches that haven't declined precipitously. And eight out of ten listeners are male.

The most popular sports radio show, *The Jim Rome Show* boasts about two million listeners daily. The announcement heralding his show suggests a slightly older demographic than 18- to 26-year-olds, but allows for significant cross-generational bonding as well: "Your hair is getting thinner, your paunch is getting bigger, but you still think the young babes want you! That's because you listen to Sports 1140 AM. It's not just sports talk, it's culture."

It's as homosocial a space as you are likely to find on your radio dial—or, indeed, virtually anywhere in the country, real or digital. Between 85 and 90 percent of the audience is male.

Communications scholar David Nylund has been interviewing guys who listen to sports talk radio, and especially to Jim Rome. Here is what one 27-year-old told him:

> It's a male bonding thing, a locker room for guys in the radio. You can't do it at work, everything's PC now! So the Rome Show is a last refuge for men to bond and be men. . . . I listen in the car and can let the maleness come out. I know it's offensive sometimes to gays and women . . . you know . . . when men bond . . . but men need that! Romey's show gives me the opportunity to talk to other guy friends about something we share in common. And my dad listens to Romey also. So my dad and I bond also.

Male bonding in a purified all-male world. Sports talk, write sociologists Don Sabo and Sue Curry Jansen, "is one of the only remaining discursive spaces where men of all social classes and ethnic groups directly discuss such values as discipline, skill, courage, competition, loyalty, fairness, teamwork, hierarchy, and achievement."

Sports radio depends on listener participation; listeners call in with comments, criticisms, and observations. It's the pure democracy of the New England town meeting. If you know your stuff, you get to participate in the conversation. If you are the informed citizen, you win the admiration and respect of your community.

Well, sure, it's filled with as many masculine virtues as an all-night bull session with Alexander the Great. But its function, I believe, is somewhat less than heroic. Sports radio provides what so many other venues, now lost to the steamroller of political correctness, used to provide. Sports talk is decidedly *not* politically correct. It's offensive—especially to women and gays. That's because much of sports talk turns out not to be about sports but about those other groups. Joking about gays and women, putting them down, this is the ground on which male sports bonding often takes place. It's hardly innocent; in fact, it has a kind of defensively angry tone to it. "This is our space, dammit, and it's the last place where we can say what we really feel about them!"

Sports Talk as Racial Healing

In sports radio, guys have permission to be as sexist and homophobic as they want to be, without guardians of the Nanny State policing them.

But the one thing that is out of bounds is racism. Say what you want about women and gays—but since sports radio is also the ground for racial healing among men, racism is not tolerated. This is what fabulously popular and defensively politically incorrect talk show host Don Imus found out to his eternal discredit. It wasn't the sexism in his comment that the Rutgers women's basketball team (which made an unpredicted run to the national finals in the 2007 NCAA basketball tournament) was "a bunch of nappy-headed hos" that got him in trouble. Everyone calls women bitches and hos on talk radio. It was the "nappy-headed" part—that old-school racism—that immediately mobilized everyone from the Reverend Al Sharpton to New Jersey's governor.

As guys talk about sports, there may be many other conversations taking place. But none is more important than the conversation about race. Sports talk brings men of different backgrounds together, bridging a racial or class divide that would otherwise be hard to breach. In the sports bar, or on sports-talk radio, white and black men share a similar love for a team, or a player, and find out that they have a lot in common. Their gender is suddenly more important than being black or white.

Sports talk "can temporarily break down barriers of race, ethnicity, and class," as literary scholar Grant Farred put it. "White suburbanites, inner-city Latino and African-American men can all support the New York Knicks or the Los Angeles Dodgers." And the rage expressed at women (especially "feminists") and gays is the foundation of that cross-racial bonding.

For black men, this cross-racial bonding through sports talk may serve as a way to assert their intelligence, their ticket for entry into a white-dominated world. Jason, a black 20-year-old junior at Lafayette College recounted his first year on campus.

Whenever I would run into kids during the first weeks of school—you know, like freshman orientation or something—the white kids would be all friendly and come up to me and say, "Hey, what sport do you play?" like to break the ice and to be friendly and all. But the joke was that I don't play sports. I am actually here because I had the grades to get in. But these nice suburban white kids—well, they couldn't imagine a black kid on campus who wasn't an athlete. So when they'd ask me what sport I played, I'd say, "Chess."

Black guys are accustomed to white scrutiny of their physical prowess on the athletic field; talking about sports is a way for them to also assert that they can exercise the muscle between their ears.

If sports talk enables black men to enter a largely white-dominated arena, it also enables white guys to enter what they often perceive as a black-dominated arena. Like those legions of white suburban guys who listen to gangsta rap, talking about sports with black guys is a form of self-congratulatory racial reassurance, many guys' way of demonstrating to themselves and others that they are not racists. Talking about sports with black guys is often the only time they actually talk with black guys at all, and sports is the only safe subject they can talk about. It's a moment of racial healing, a way to feel that they are part of the solution, not part of the problem.

At times, this can be a genuine effort to bridge the racial divide—at least as individuals. At other times, it can be a substitute for the serious conversation about race—and racial inequality—that is so necessary to truly bridge that social divide. When it replaces that social and political conversation with a moment of bonding, sports talk may reproduce the very problem its adherents seek to transcend.

Sports talk is the *lingua franca* of Guyland. It is a currency that one can spend in any male arena in the nation. Sports talk enables conversation across race and class, even if it sometimes offers a false sense of racial healing. It enables men to bond in a pure homosocial world, a world free of the taint of women's presence. It offers the solace of masculine purity, and the cement of those bonds. Sports—and talking about them—is a way for guys to feel close to each other and still feel like real men, feel closer to their fathers and, perhaps, further separated from their mothers. Sports provide a way for men to have their emotions without feeling like wimps. Sometimes, sports serve as the only way for men to talk, to connect, or the only way they can express their emotions at all.

But if the athletic field has been Guyland's most sacred space, it is challenged today by the "intrusion" of women. So the boundaries of Guyland are pushed ever outward, toward some pure homosocial Eden where men can get to be men. Once, that pristine world existed at the edge of civilization—riding the range, huddled in the trenches, manning the space capsules. Today, it may be that the frontier is entirely virtual—radio and TV waves, cyberspace and the landscape of video games.

7 | BOYS AND THEIR TOYS: GUYLAND'S MEDIA

The brothers of Alpha Beta Gamma at Colorado State University are an affable bunch of guys—clean-cut, all-American jocks, attired in the general issue uniform of Guyland: faded baseball cap, T-shirt, cargo shorts, and flip flops. On the day I visit, four of them are sitting around the TV. One is wearing headphones, and, a joystick in hand, is rocking and reeling to an online game of *Grand Theft Auto: San Andreas (GTA)*. Beer bottles sit open on the coffee table. In an adjoining room, five more guys are huddled around a computer monitor, relaxing over a game of online poker. As if to show they are serious about their gambling, their baseball caps are turned backward. The stakes, they inform me, are relatively low, about $100 to over $1,000 a pot. (This does not strike me as low.) One guy's laptop is streaming a porn video, almost as an afterthought. Occasionally one of the guys glances at the screen. It is 11:00 A.M. on a school day. Not a book in sight.

Take a leisurely stroll into any college dorm room or fraternity, any apartment or house shared by a bunch of guys in any city or town in America. Whether they are white-collar young professionals or blue-collar workers, chances are they're all doing the same thing—staring at their TV or computer screens, or operating their PlayStations and Xboxes and other consoles. The only differences will likely be by class or race, and will revolve around how fancy their equipment is: The TVs are plasma flat screens or older models, their computers are cable-linked or dial-up, and they have the latest game consoles and fabulous speakers or not. Walk into any video arcade, Internet café, or "adult" video store. Cruise the poker tables in any casino, or look through the door of your neighborhood sports bar. Who's there? Guys.

Guys Watching Screens

Today's young people—from little kids to adults in their late twenties and early thirties—represent the most technologically sophisticated and media savvy generation in our history. The average American home—where most of these guys grew up—has three TVs, two VCRs, three radios, two tape players, two CD players, more than one video game console, and more than one computer. And when we leave home, we take this media with us in our laptops, iPods, MP3s, Gameboys, and portable DVD players. American kids ages 8 to 18 spend about 7 hours a day interacting with some form of electronic media; the average 13- to 18-year-old spends two hours a day just playing video games.

The most avid consumers of this new media, from video game consoles and online technologies to television and movies, CDs, DVDs, and MP3s, are young men, 16 to 26. It's the demographic group most prized by advertisers who dole out major ad revenue to popular "guy" radio shows such as Jim Rome, Howard Stern, and Rush Limbaugh; guy magazines such as *FHM* and *Maxim*; and TV stations including ESPN and "Spike" ("The First Network for Men").

As we saw in the last chapter, much of the television and radio content watched in Guyland is sports related, and as we'll see in the next chapter, many of the digital downloads are pornographic. But guys are also playing video games, gambling online, and buying up the majority of rap and heavy-metal CDs on the market. Guyland is big business in the entertainment industry.

Video games are its fastest-growing segment, outselling movies, books, CDs, and DVDs by a landslide. In the United States, video games earn about $6.35 billion on sales of over 225 million computer and console games every year. That's nearly 2 games purchased *per household* every year since 2000. Three-fifths of Americans age 6 and older play video games regularly—and three-fifths of those players are male.

Another favorite activity of guys, online poker, has now become one of America's favorite "sports," and has taken off on college campuses, where hundreds of thousands of guys are playing every day—and for hundreds of millions of dollars. According to PokerPulse.com, which tracks online poker games, some 88,000 players were betting almost $16 million in online poker every day when the first World Poker Tournament was held in 1997. Today, those figures have increased by a factor of ten—1.8 million players bet $200 million online every single day.

Guys are Instant Messaging (IM), watching TV and videos from their cell phones, digitizing music, photographs, and everything else they touch. They don't buy records; they download songs. They don't make phone calls; they text. They don't read books; they . . . well, let's just say they don't read very many books. Instead, they lock themselves in their rooms and stay up until all hours of the morning surfing the web, chatting online, downloading music, and playing video games. Sure, not all guys are hooked up to technology 24/7. But almost all guys have at least a passing familiarity with most of the media I've mentioned.

True, boys have always had their toys: I remember the guys in high school poring over *Road & Track* and discussing the thrills of four on the floor. And the college guys who played pinball for what seemed like days, or the guys who spent their time researching the flattest and simplest turntable for their immaculate high-end stereo systems. But the size and scale are different now. Those guys I knew were a bit outside the mainstream, less concerned, I thought, with the drinking, sports, and girls that preoccupied everyone else. The car guys were working-class Fonzie wannabes; the stereo junkies were campus geeks. Now those media-obsessed and media-savvy guys *are* the mainstream. The new weirdos are often more likely to be the kids whose parents didn't let them watch TV, or who don't gamble online, talk about sports, watch porn, or play video games for hours.

If you ask guys about the appeal of all this media, most will give you the same answer: They do it to relax, to hang out, to have fun. It's entertainment. Like sports, they do it as a way to spend time together without actually having to talk about anything significant that might be going on in their lives. In fact, in many cases they do it to avoid what's going on in their lives. All these distractions together comprise a kind of fantasy realm to which guys retreat constantly—sometimes sheepishly, sometimes angrily—because it's a way to escape, even for a few hours a day, their tedious, boring, and emasculating lives. They're avoiding the daily responsibilities of adulthood that in their minds first begins with being a conscientious student and then morphs into being a loving and attentive husband, an involved father, a responsible breadwinner. They are escaping what they think of as the burdens of adult masculinity. And in a world where guys are afraid to grow up at all, the Guyland Arcade helps them delay adulthood for a few moments more. "Here we are now," shouted Kurt Cobain, of the band Nirvana, with more of an anthemic challenge than a simple embrace of consumer culture, "entertain us."

So what exactly are they consuming? Why? And what are the consequences?

Before answering these questions, let's go back for a moment to the guys at Alpha house, hanging out at 11:00 in the morning in the middle of the week. Being a professor, I asked about reading for classes. The guys looked at me blankly, almost patronizingly. "Not a problem," said Blake, not looking up from the computer screen. "But when do you guys study? And don't you have to go to classes?" I asked. At this point several guys sort of rolled their eyes and looked up from their various screens. "And what about writing your papers? How do you get them done?"

The guys looked at each other, knowingly, but with a questioning look, as if deciding whether or not to tell me. Todd shrugged. They smiled and said in unison, "Brainiac."

"Brainiac?" I asked.

"Uh, a.k.a. Andrew. A pledge. He's the man."

I caught up with Andrew later that afternoon, where you might have expected to find him: the library. At first glance, Andrew didn't look like he stepped off the set of *Revenge of the Nerds*. In fact, he looked like the other guys in the fraternity: shorts, flip flops, CSU football T-shirt, glasses, and an easy smile. The giveaway was the Dodgers hat.

"Yeah, I'm from LA—well, the Valley actually. So I'm an out-of-stater, and for us admission is a whole lot harder than if you're from here, you know? Like I had really good grades and SATs, but I just wanted to get away from the whole LA scene, and I wanted to ski. So I came here. And when I wanted to pledge a frat, the guys said, 'Great! You can be our DH.'"

"DH?" I asked, "like 'designated hitter?'"

"Designated Homeworker," he laughed. Andrew's acceptance was conditional on his accepting the assignment as the house's DH. "It's okay. I mean, I don't exactly love it. But I do get out of a lot of the bullshit of pledging, like having to drink till I puke on the other guys. I just tell them that I have to go write their papers and they pretty much leave me alone. It works out, I guess."

Having a DH makes it possible for the rest of the brothers to do what they came to college to do: play video games, hang out, gamble online, drink copious quantities of beer, and hook up with girls as often as possible. If, on the one hand, contemporary students are increasingly professionalized—narrowly constructing their educations to prepare them for their eventual career—their actual experience of collegiate life remains remarkably juvenile.

Across the country, the guys I talked to spent most of their time playing at what are essentially escapist games. In video games, guys can play at being ideal versions of themselves in fantasy worlds. In aggressive music and violent movies, guys can see manifested the anger they feel inside. At online poker tables, guys feel empowered and skillful, as they do in few other arenas.

Though entertainment has always been escapist, the level of dedication—of time, of money, of energy—that guys today exhibit is astounding. Escape from daily life often becomes their top priority. So is it any wonder that these guys, on their way to manhood, so closely resemble boys?

What's All the Fuss?

Most guys react somewhat defensively when they hear the latest dire warnings about media use—that the anonymity of Internet chat rooms is deleterious to social development, or that violent rap and heavy metal music encourage violence in the real world, or that video games are so highly addictive they often result in players gradually disengaging from real life. Since they know that *they* are unlikely to play *World of Warcraft* for so long that they lose track of what day it is, and since they know that *they* aren't likely to use violent films as a prelude to mass murder, they are easily and casually accepting of media saturation. And, by and large, the rest of us go along with it. We rely on facile explanations like "consumer sovereignty" to justify the violent content, or we think, "No harm, no foul" and accept that there are no deleterious incremental effects of all that media consumption. Or we focus only on the form—the game playing, the porn watching, the radio shows—and resignedly shrug our shoulders and sigh that "boys will be boys." But such shrugs are often ways to shirk our own responsibility. We need to look at what guys are watching, listening to, and downloading because the media they are engaging with is not just entertainment. It is entertainment with a vengeance.

The dominant emotion in all these forms of entertainment is anger. From violent computer games to extreme sports, from racist and misogynistic radio show content to furious rap and heavy metal music, from the X-rated to the Xbox, the amount of rage and sensory violence to which guys have become accustomed is overwhelming. It doesn't even occur to them that all this media consumption might be extreme.

Jeff, a 20-year-old junior at the University of Illinois who dedicates a large part of his time to playing *GTA*, is an example. "Oh, no, not another grownup telling us that this stuff is all bad for us!" He looks at me skeptically. "I mean we all know the PC drill, blah blah blah. But c'mon, man. It's only a goddamned game after all. It's just entertainment."

"Yeah, so what, I play video games," says Dave, the 24-year-old behind the counter at my local video store. "I don't care that they're not PC; I like that. It's the one place I can go—well, that's not exactly true, since

I listen to Rush and Howard Stern and all those talk show guys—but it's one of the places I can go where I feel like I can just relax, be myself, and not worry about offending anyone. I can offend everyone!"

Why are these guys so angry and defensive? In part because they feel a little guilty that they are spending so much time doing something they know is so purposeless. And all their macho blustering about being proudly not PC is belied by the fact that most of them wouldn't dream of expressing such blatantly racist and sexist opinions in the company of women, for example, or in the presence of a person of color, or in front of their parents or teachers. They know these attitudes are wrong and indefensible: that, in part, is what makes them so attractive. Adolescents have been "proving" their independence with rebellion against their parents' values for generations.

But it goes deeper than that. Guys' defensiveness also has to do with the rage that's both covert and overt in much of what passes as entertainment in Guyland. Because as it turns out, the fantasy world of media is both an escape *from* reality and an escape *to* reality—the "reality" that many of these guys secretly would like to inhabit. Video games, in particular, provide a way for guys to feel empowered. In their daily lives guys often feel that they don't quite measure up to the standards of the Guy Code—always be in control, never show weakness, neediness, vulnerability—and so they create ideal versions of themselves in fantasy. The thinking is simple: If somebody messes with your avatar, you blow him away. It's a fantasy world of Manichean good and evil, a world in which violence is restorative, and actions have no consequences whatsoever.

Is a Steady Diet of Violence Dangerous?

The moment some violent event involving young men captures the headlines, we immediately blame—or defend—the media and its hold on young people's consciousness as if it were somehow the cause of all evil. Yet the public debate is often simplistic and ill-informed. On one side are the shrill jeremiads against "the media"—some vague, amorphous, yet simultaneously monolithic and omnipotent force corrupting the minds of young people, seducing them away from more wholesome pursuits with postures of badass gangstas, or hypermuscular technology-laden gladiatorial avatars blowing away enemies. People have been blaming the media for decades, and for a wide variety of problems—from voter apathy to random school shootings. They argue that media violence serves as a set of user manuals for rape, random acts of violence, crime, and generally represents the decline of civility in modern life.

On the other side of the argument are those who suggest that media simply reflect the society we live in, and that, in many cases, engaging with media has valuable effects. Some argue that watching violent movies or playing a violent video game enables one to experience a kind of catharsis, to safely express anger and aggression *without* actually acting it out. Others, like Steven Johnson in his bestselling book *Everything Bad Is Good for You*, argue that video games, for example, may be more cognitively challenging and beneficial than reading a book; they make elaborate cognitive demands, requiring players to "manage a dizzying array of information and options," process massive amounts of information to make complex decisions, and interweave complex narratives while increasing eye-hand coordination. *The Economist* recently chimed in with the opinion that plenty of games "far from encouraging degeneracy, are morally complex, subtle and, very possibly, [intellectually] improving."

While modern games, movies, TV shows, and other media may indeed offer more complex plot lines and make greater cognitive demands, these laudatory comments are really celebrating form not content. Even those who believe that media technology has cognitive value would certainly not attribute any value to using those cognitive skills in the service of murder and mayhem. In many video games geared to guys, violence is not punished; indeed, it is regularly rewarded. Women are prizes to be collected, conquered, and then discarded or murdered. In some games, the steady stream of explosive, lethal, and strategic doses of what Anthony Burgess called "ultra-violence," in his harrowing, futuristic tale, *A Clockwork Orange*, are the only way for the avatar to move to the game's next level.

The claims of the preservers of wholesome family entertainments are equally myopic. The virtual world of new media is hardly the mono-tonic avalanche overwhelming America's children that these contemporary Chicken Littles would suggest. Even if every single video game taught family values, and if every online porno site was transformed into a feminist seminar, many critics would still be unhappy because they think the technology itself is mind-numbing.

Current debates about the negative effects of video games, music lyrics, and other forms of Guyland entertainment are the latest installment of a debate that has been going on in our society for decades. Does the media *cause* certain behaviors, or merely reflect what is already going on in society? Would censorship reduce the actual (as opposed to virtual) problem, or simply create a new problem that would be, politically speaking, far worse?

Unfortunately, social science research hasn't been much help thus far in informing the debate. That's not from lack of trying, but rather because the findings have often been so complex and inconclusive that few partisans feel they need to pay any attention. To be sure, the research has shed significant light on different aspects of the subject, but light does not translate well when those debating the issues only want fuel for their heatedly polarized positions.

As a social scientist, I'm not convinced that a steady diet of violent video games leads inevitably and inescapably to increased violence by young teenage males. These critics almost always propose a sort of "monkey see, monkey do" model of behavior that reduces human complexity to a series of operant conditioning experiments: If we see it, we'll want to do it, and if we want to do it, we will do it. Most of us are clever enough to create wide gaps between what we see and what we want, and especially between what we want and what we do. There is "little evidence of a substantial link between exposure to violent interactive games and serious real-life violence or crime," observes Cheryl Olson, a professor of psychiatry at the Harvard Medical School Center for Mental Health and Media. Mark Griffiths, a psychologist and professor of gambling studies at Nottingham Trent University in Britain, and perhaps the leading researcher on online games also finds "little evidence that moderate frequency of play has serious adverse effects."

Nor, even, is the research that proposes that repeated viewing of violent media leaves us numb particularly convincing. Craig Anderson, the Iowa State psychologist, finds that kids become agitated and aggressive after playing video games. That's something virtually any parent could tell him. But to conclude that such agitation will persist for more than a few minutes is an illogical leap—again, as most parents could tell him. Nor can one infer that after watching violent films a kid will then be prompted to pick up a real gun and open fire. Nor can one claim that playing a game or watching a porn video provides enough catharsis to actually reduce anger or sexual aggression. There is absolutely no empirical evidence for any of these claims.

It's certainly true that repeated exposure to terrible, disgusting, or traumatic images leads to a certain amount of "psychic numbing," but this kind of self-protective indifference does not necessarily carry over into real life. After viewing 40,000 car crashes and 10,000 murders in movies and television, a guy will certainly not feel "numb" if he witnesses a car crash or murder in real life.

This link between watching and doing, or even between watching and justifying, may not be definitively proven by researchers, but that doesn't mean that there aren't moral issues in question. What does it mean that so many young men find images of ultraviolent urban mayhem so exciting that they stay glued to their video consoles for hours at a time? What does it mean that the portrayal of women not only in pornography but also in video games and music lyrics (and on TV, and on the radio, and on the Internet, and in every single type of media that is geared toward young men) is not only sexist and denigrating but also often outright and unapologetically hateful, violent, and misogynist? What does it mean that people of color continue to be portrayed by stereotypes that have been recognized as racist, offensive, and unacceptable for more than thirty years? These are questions about how guys view *masculinity*, not simple questions about the "effects" of some media on people.

So if it isn't a "license to kill," what are guys getting out of all their media consumption? They're getting a parallel education to the formal curriculum—complete with its own Three R's: Relaxation from the weight of adult demands and of the rules of social decorum (also now known as political correctness); Revenge, against those who have usurped what you thought was yours; and, Restoration to your rightful entitled position in the world.

Let's look at how these Three R's play out in some of the most popular media in Guyland.

We Got Game(s)

Video games began innocently enough with a computer generated ping-pong game in 1972. Who would have predicted that video games would become what they are today? Video games outsell movies, books, CDs, and DVDs by a landslide.

While the age range of gamers is wide—the median age is 28—they tend to appeal most to guys in their teens and twenties. The average teenage boy plays video games for about 13 hours a week; girls play about 5 hours a week. More than one-third of Americans rank computer and video games "the most fun family entertainment."

The games vary a lot: by type, by format, and, of course, by gender. Some games are played by one or two (or a few more) players on a console box, hooked up to the TV. Others are played online, on a computer. And some, called Massively Multiplayer Online Role-Playing Games (or MMORPGs), are played live, with thousands of people all over the world playing simultaneously.

Of video games, sports games, like Madden NFL or the various baseball and basketball games, command a large share of the market. Adventure and action games, like *GTA* and *Halo*, are by far the most popular genre. And strategy games, like *The Sims*, involve players in real-life decision making and strategic thinking, not simply adventures in the land of blood and guts.

While the majority of players of every game format and genre are male, the percentages vary enormously. At a recent World Cyber Games competition (WCG) in Singapore, 700 boys and men—and one woman!—crossed cyber-swords in online game competition. According to Mark Griffiths, console games (75 percent male, 50 percent over 19 years old) are only slightly more gender-equal than online games (85 percent male, 60 percent over 19 years old). Sports and adventure games come close to 95 percent male players; while strategy games, like *The Sims*, are the only genre where female players have made any inroads. In *The Sims*, the "action," such as it is, has to do with domestic situations. People get jobs, get married, have kids, and even clean the house. "All the men in my class HATED that game," comments William Lugo, a sociology professor at Eastern Connecticut State University, who studies video games and teaches a college course on them. "It was a little too realistic for them."

A new online game, *Second Life*, provides people with an alternative life. Currently, more than 8.5 million people have signed on to a site where they buy and sell real estate and other goods and services (using real money), develop relationships, get jobs, and create families. About $1.6 million real dollars are spent every 24 hours in the game, and the site recently celebrated its first millionaire. Over half of all players are under 30. Many players say they have more authentic experiences in their second lives than they do in their real ones. When fantasy becomes reality, one's real life can only pale by comparison.

Nina Huntemann certainly understands the gender of gaming. A punky feminist professor of communications at Suffolk University outside Boston, she's an avid lifelong gamer and a keen observer. Her research informs a documentary, *Game Over: Gender, Race and Violence in Video Games*, that she created for the Media Education Foundation.

"I constantly got the message that gaming was for guys," she told me. The computer labs in college were "completely dominated by guys and the fact that I liked games, and liked them for the same reasons that they did, made more than a few somewhat uncomfortable." The gaming world, many gamers believe, is part of Guyland, and for women to enter this virtual men's locker room is unacceptable. Recently, a female gamer complained to the video games columnist for the *New York Times* that "the frat boys have taken over video games" pandering to "the lowest common denominator."

Much of Guyland's media is restorative, designed to provide that sense of power and control that men do not feel in real life. There is an old psychoanalytic maxim that what we lose in reality we re-create in fantasy. And what men believe they have lost is their unchallenged privilege to run the show. Guys play video games, gamble, or pose and posture to the musical stylings of inner-city black youth because these poses give them the feeling of being in control. They spend so much of their lives being bossed around by other people—teachers, parents, bosses—it's really a relief to be the meanest, most violent, and vengeful SOB around. And they spend so much of their lives in a world that is, if not dominated by women, at least is characterized by women's presumed equality, that it's nice to turn back the clock and return to a time when men ruled—and no one questioned it.

Both in their form and in their content, games give you the feeling of power and control. They take the control out of the hands of the director and put it in the hands of the consumer. That's why Dan Houser, 31, one of the cofounders and creative vice-presidents of Rockstar Games, predicts that "games are going to take over from movies as the mainstream form of entertainment." Books, he explains, "tell you something. Movies show you something. But games let you *do* something."

By and large, of course, video gaming is harmless fun. My son, Zachary, just turned 9 and is already in love with video games on his PSP. Every one of his male friends—and not one of his female friends—is already playing what seem to be innocuous computer games, sports games like MLB and World Cup Soccer, and *Star Wars*. And when he's not playing games, he checks out YouTube videos of teenagers lip-synching Weird Al Yankovic parodies or backyard *Star Wars* light-saber battles.

"What I like about video games is that you get to play as someone else, you get to pretend to be someone else," he explains to me. "It's like playing dress up. And you get to decide what the person does. Like in skateboarding, you get to decide which side he goes on, or if he does an Ollie or a grind. So I like that I get to make the decisions."

And it doesn't seem to cut into his love for playing sports—he plays on soccer and hockey teams, and plays other sports with me—or his school work, or reading, playing the drums, or guitar, or singing, or any of the other things he loves to do. It's a big part of his life, but it hasn't displaced any other parts. Yet, because gaming is so gender-asymmetrical, his mother and I worry that these videos will create a false fissure between the play worlds of boys and girls that becomes a chasm by middle school. The signs are already there.

"There are a couple of boys in my [third grade] class who I think are already playing too much," Zachary says. "Like, every single lunchtime they say that they just beat the seventh level on *Lego Star Wars*. It's ridiculous. It's like the only thing they can talk about."

The problem is less about form—how much they play or how often. These sorts of discussions distract us from the important conversations we need to have about content. We need to engage with the steady diet of violence, fighting, and misogyny. If that's their steady diet, they're consuming cultural junk food.

But it's junk food that packs a punch. Reality is disappointing; video fantasy is exciting. "Video games have the quality of being so explicit, so blatant, in their representations of men, women, of power, of control, that they lay out some of the key ideologies of the culture in absolutely unmistakable, vivid ways," comments Michael Morgan, a professor of communications at the University of Massachusetts, in the documentary *Game Over.*

The characters are almost always massively exaggerated gender stereotypes: The male characters in their torn T-shirts and army fatigues have biceps that would make GI Joe look puny; indeed their upper torsos are so massive, their waists so small, and their thighs so powerfully bulging that there is no way that most of these characters could actually stand up. They're cartoons, in the same way that the characters embodied in professional wrestling are cartoon versions of hypermasculine stereotypes.

While they may look like they just left the shower room of a Christopher Street gym, all the avatars in game-land are straight. And so are the women: powerful, strong enough to be threatening, but always straight, always with blond disheveled "bedroom" hair—a sort of recently sexually ravaged look—with breasts so large and a waist so small they make Barbie look well proportioned. And they're eternally grateful to their hypermasculine muscle-bound rescuers. In one game, *Duke Nukem*, the "Everyman American Hero," finds a landscape in which all the men have been killed and only Duke can rescue a million "babes" who have been captured by aliens. The women are, of course, swooningly grateful. Even Lara Croft, the female action-game icon, is a hypersexualized babe—who happens to know how to handle a grenade launcher.

Let's return for a moment to *Grand Theft Auto: San Andreas*, among the most popular and widely discussed video games on the market. The set-up for the game, what the producers call the "cinematic," is a thin justification for the violence and mayhem that your character, or avatar, then creates. After the introduction, it becomes back story, never again referred to. In the fictionalized cities of Los Santos and San Fiero—Los Angeles and San Francisco—your goals are to sell drugs, build your crime empire, kill cops. You can kill anyone you want. You can increase your health by picking up a prostitute and having sex with her in your car. And you can recoup the money you paid by following her out of your car and killing her.

GTA has been so popular that its creators, Rockstar Entertainment, have created a new, East Coast urban setting, based on the 1979 cult classic, *The Warriors*. Like *GTA*, *The Warriors* is a "dark urban fantasy set in a dystopian city dominated by gangs." The cinematic offers a multiracial street gang that has been falsely accused of murder. They then have to fight their way from the burned-out projects in the Bronx to Coney Island. Unlike many games, in this one they don't use assault weapons, rocket grenades, or other heavy artillery; in *The Warriors*, it's baseball bats, chains and knives, and lots of hand-to-hand combat.

Of course, most guys who play *The Warriors* will never find themselves in a rumble in real life—and this, too, is part of the appeal. Games offer safe risk-taking, power without pain. You can be a master of the universe, a gangsta blowing away the police and scoring the babes, without ever leaving the comfort of your dorm room or apartment, let alone venture into the real hood. The thrills are visceral and exciting, yet safe and contained. For young white guys playing *GTA* in their suburban dens, rapping and posing in their family-room mirrors, some of the thrill comes from being a badass dude with no real consequences.

Gaming for Real

That boundary-blurring between game and reality also seems to be part of the thrill of online gambling, especially the dramatic proliferation of online poker.

The single largest group of online poker players is young men, 14 to 22 years old, according to the National Annenberg Risk Survey (NARSY) in 2003 and 2004. In 2004, 11.4 percent of high-school and college males reported betting on cards at least once a week, nearly double the number from the year before. These increases were similar between high-school gamblers (5.7 percent in 2003 to 10.8 percent in 2004) and college guys (7.3 percent in 2003 to 12.5 percent in 2004). That means that one in eight college guys is betting on poker games online at least once a week. In fact, it's increasingly younger guys. In 2003, 25.9 percent of youth who bet on cards weekly were under 18; by 2004, it was 43.2 percent who were under 18.

A front-page story in the *New York Times* recently profiled Michael Sandberg, a 22-year-old senior politics major at Princeton, who's won more than $120,000 this year alone at PartyPoker.com, and paying for four years at one of the nation's most expensive and prestigious universities. Playing up to ten hours a day, Sandberg considers his poker playing more of a career move than collegiate recreation. "I don't think I can make $120,000 doing anything but poker," he told the reporter. "I was half-studying for my politics exam today, but I got bored and started playing poker on my computer instead."

Poker parties are now standard fare on campuses all across the country. This past December, a sorority at Columbia held an 80-player tournament; they expect triple that next year. At North Carolina, 175 players anted up $10 minimums to play in one tournament. At the University of Pennsylvania, private games are advertised every night on a campus email list.

Routinely, guys at MIT and Cal Tech work out complicated algorithms to stack the odds in their favor, and many of them end up winning a lot of money. But online poker is a sophisticated pyramid scheme—some at the top win big, while hundreds of thousands of less-clever guys wager more modest amounts and end up losing the money they were supposed to be spending on books, clothes, laundry, or food.

Recently, I changed planes in Las Vegas, and had a two-hour layover, which would have enabled me to gamble in a variety of ways without ever leaving the airport. Instead, I watched as plane after plane disgorged its passengers. About half the arrivals resembled the Las Vegas I had seen during my last visit, about twenty years earlier: old ladies with silver hair and a twinkle in their eyes as they headed off to slot machine heaven; middle-aged and overweight couples, there to renew their marriages and hopefully pay off their crushing mortgages; young starry-eyed couples off for the shows and the drive-through weddings.

But at least half the arriving passengers were guys in their twenties, with nary a hatless head among them (baseball caps outnumbered cowboy hats by about 4 to 1). They were already somewhat rowdy, checking each other's poker strategies, ready for action. Like Dave, a 26-year-old who said of his job "it doesn't matter, just put that I work in an office." According to Dave, he and his six friends saved for a year for this trip, and they were each carrying several thousand dollars. They would splurge on a suite (into which they would all cram), and were hoping to "put all that nickel-and-dime-poker-every-week knowledge to good use" in Vegas.

Would they take in any of the shows, or try and meet girls? He winced, and looked at me as if I were asking if he intended to get a bikini wax. "Uh, we're here for the money," he said. End of story.

Guy TV and Guy Radio: Politically Incorrect and Loving It

All day long, in every waking sphere of life—at work, in school, at the dinner table—guys feel like they have to be so polite, socially acceptable, respectful, and politically correct. In the fantasy world of Guyland media they can re-create what they feel they've lost in reality—entitlement, control, unchallenged rule, and the untrammeled right to be gross, offensive, and politically incorrect. Many of the radio and television programs specifically geared toward the Guyland demographic are unapologetic about (and even proud of) their offensiveness. *Spike*

TV appears to take the attitude that television has been so effectively colonized by women that guys need a room—or a network—all their own where they can be themselves.

Some Guy TV is simply regressive. More than one-fourth of all viewers of *SpongeBob Squarepants* are over 18 years old, according to Nickelodeon. "I'm 22, and my favorite show on TV is *SpongeBob*, and I watch Jimmy Neutron all the time," says one guy.

In the car, at work, or during those few minutes a day when the TV is off at home, young men are tuning into "Guy Radio"—the steady stream of right-wing political pundits whose main stock in trade is outrage. From the liberal Howard Stern to the ultraconservative Rush Limbaugh and Michael Savage, the radio hosts and their legions of fans spend most of their time fuming at lost privileges, seething that white men are now society's victims, arguing that "they" are enacting injustices on "us." "They" refers to pretty much everyone not like middle-class white men—minorities, gays, women, and, of course, a "feminizing" government bureaucracy. The participatory town meeting quality of Guy Radio, with its steady stream of callers, ups the emotional ante. Sure, there's plenty of defensive anger to go around. But the tone expresses a sense of aggrieved entitlement.

Matt, 22, and a senior at Vanderbilt who has just been accepted to law school tells me:

> I was raised to believe in the whole enchilada, you know, like truth, justice, and the American way. Fairness and equality. And I busted my ass to get in here, and to get good enough grades to go to a good law school. And did I get into Duke or Virginia? No. And are there guys in my classes who had lower grades than me and lower LSATs and did they get in just because they were minorities? Uh, yeah. And girls?! Unbelieveable. More of them than guys applied and yet they get in because they're girls? They're richer than shit, and their daddies paid for everything. I'm fed up with it. It's not fair. My family didn't own slaves. We're from Pennsylvania, for Chrissakes. I'm not racist; I don't care what color you are. But I shouldn't be penalized because of my race, my color, right? I mean, that's just not fair.

Matt was among the more articulate when it came to discussing substantive issues like affirmative action or race and gender preferences in admissions. Most of the guys mouthed platitudes they took directly from the radio shows, without so much as actually thinking if they applied to their situations or not, lines like "it's not the government's money, it's the people's money" in response to tax policy.

Of course, not all guys subscribe to this "white-man-as-victim" mentality. Many are more thoughtful than that, were raised in households where such talk was unconditionally unacceptable, and are intelligent enough to see through the rhetoric. Yet so many of them do buy into it that it demands our attention. And, to be fair, guys didn't come up with these attitudes all by themselves. This kind of outrage is learned—and the "teachers" are both the adults in guys' lives and, perhaps especially, media personalities such as Rush Limbaugh and other members of the furious media punditocracy. Guys are seduced by such easy answers to the problems that face them as they come of age in an economy in which they will probably never be able to live up to their parents' standards. The rhetoric of Guy Radio assures guys that the problems in their lives are not their fault. Yet rather than point to the actual causes of these problems, rather than take a well-informed and thoughtful approach to looking at the world around them, these media personalities point instead to the easiest and most available scapegoats—those just below "us" on the social ladder.

Despite modern advances, the idea of white male privilege still hasn't disappeared—it's simply found a new home in and anger-and-resentment-fueled "good old days" rhetoric. "Man, you got screwed. In the good old days you would have a great job by now. You would have had a nice house, a nice car, a wife who takes care of you. You got robbed. In fact, now you're even worse off, because if you're white and you're a man you don't stand a chance. Everybody hates you. Everybody blames you for their oppression. Women, gay men, blacks, Asians, Latinos, Native Americans, everybody. And you didn't even *do* anything!" And while none of this is actually true (even the good old days were only good for a very few), that's not the point. The point is that angry right-wing radio personalities give permission for a very low level of discourse and a very high level of rage. This permission not only allows but encourages guys to be as angry as they want to be, boosting guys' sense of entitlement and importance.

Macho Stylin' in Black and White: Music in Guyland

When guys are not being angry white guys, they often adopt the stylings of angry black guys, in speech, dress, and culture, particularly rap music.

The rap on rap music has long been its vile misogyny, its celebration of gangsta thuggery, predatory sexuality, and violence. In its defense, rap's promoters and fans argue that the genre's symbolic assertions of manhood are necessary for an inner-city black youth for whom racism and poverty have been experienced as so emasculating. Rap is a "loud scratchy, in-your-face aesthetic" that "sprang off the uptown streets of New York City" and has come to represent to the world the current generation of black male teenage life. So what if rap basically confirms every vile stereotype of African Americans—violent, out-of-control, sexual predators—that racists have long held. It's an "authentic" expression.

Besides, rap's defenders argue, rap's misogyny and homophobia are not all that different from the violence and macho swagger of heavy metal, hard rock, or punk music. They do have a point. Indeed, in response to the success of rap and hip-hop, hard rockers have ratcheted up their own misogynistic proclamations of manhood. But debating whether heavy metal or hip-hop is more misogynist is an empty debate, one that skirts the key similarity between them: Both genres celebrate a particular image of masculinity—an image that seems to appeal to middle-class white guys. What does it mean that so many white guys appropriate inner-city musical genres—as well as the fashion, language, and physical gestures and idioms? Mark Anthony Neal argues that "hip hop represents a space where [white guys] work through the idea of how their masculinity can be lived—what they literally take from the hyper-masculine 'black buck.'"

True enough, but I also think that an essential element of this masculinity is that it is seen as *authentic*. White suburban masculinity has become so safe and sanitized, the lives of these guys so tracked—school, college, job, marriage, family, death—that they search for something that feels "real." "We spend our entire days trying to fit into a perfect little bubble," said one young man to author Bakari Kitwana. "The perfect $500,000 house. The perfect overscheduled kids. . . . We love life, but we hate our lives. And so I think we identify more with hip-hop's passion, anger and frustration than we do this dream world." And, in a psychological flurry worthy of Freud, they project that credibility and authenticity onto inner-city black youth, and then consume it in the form of hip-hop music, Sean John clothes, and appropriation of ghetto jargon.

"We love life, but we hate our lives." An astonishingly revealing phrase. What is it that white guys hate so much about their own lives? And what does their consumption of African-American cultural styles mean—culturally and politically? What they hate is the inauthenticity, the requirements that they be good, polite, and decent toward women, that they suffer through experiences they feel are emasculating and humiliating. Defiant rebellion is what they project onto black culture—because they subscribe both to the surface reading of badness being cool, and because they accept the racist idea that black people are "naturally" like this—i.e., that such a "cool pose" is actually a gendered response of black men to racial inequality. They embrace the badness, but avoid engaging with its historical origins. Repackaged as music, black anger is sanitized for white consumption.

And consume it they do. According to market researchers and music impresarios, between 70 percent and 80 percent of hip-hop consumers are white. While young white guys also buy the majority of hard rock and heavy metal CDs, those same young white guys are in rather scarce supply at hip-hop concerts. Consumption of the inner city stops at the borders of the ghetto. As media critic and journalist Kevin Powell puts it, white fascination with hip-hop is "just a cultural safari for white people." It's safe because you "can take it off. White hip-hop kids can turn their caps around, put a belt in their pants and go to the mall without being followed," noted one observer. The "Afro-Americanization of White Youth," as Cornel West calls it in his bestselling book, *Race Mat-*

ters, turns out to coexist easily with white guys' opposition to affirmative action. Cultural identification does not necessarily lead to political alliance, which might explain the meteoric rise of Eminem to the pop pantheon.

Eminem's got credibility—he may be white, but he's the real deal, an authentic rapper not just a fabricated product of white music producers like Vanilla Ice was. Eminem's credibility is based on class, not race. His impoverished, downwardly mobile working-class Detroit background matched that of many other whites who had drifted to the far right; but Eminem took himself into the urban ghetto rather than into the woods with the Michigan Militias. In his autobiographical film, *8 Mile*, his ultimate success comes as he defeats a middle-class black rapper, thus asserting class solidarity over racial divisiveness.

Eminem speaks to young white guys as few others of their generation, capturing their anger and malaise-driven angst while maintaining his credibility among inner city blacks, who are the arbiters of the musical genre. Like other rappers, he draws from a deep well of class-based, gendered rage, as well as adolescent declarations of manhood that are part protest and part phallic fluff. But unlike other rappers, Eminem is white, and thus enables guys' identification in a way that doesn't feel like they're ventriloquists, staking a claim to authenticity by speaking in another group's tongue.

White Guys as Winners—Finally!

What it all adds up to is that guys—young guys, guys in their teens and twenties—are sick and tired of feeling sick and tired. One might expect this sort of thing from middle-aged men who feel as if they've been sold a bill of goods and feel ripped off by a system that cares not a whit about them. Older men who have watched their meager savings trickle up to monstrous corporate salaries, who land with a thud after being downsized or laid off, who watch their bosses float happily in their golden parachutes. But you wouldn't expect it from young guys, guys full of the promise of their entire adult life ahead of them. What have they lost?

Their sense of entitlement. Their sense that the world is their oyster, their home, their castle. It no longer feels like "this land was made for you and me," as Woody Guthrie sang, but for somebody else. They're tired of "being made to feel like losers," as many of them put it. They're tired of feeling that the game is over before they've even started to play. They're tired of putting the damned toilet seat down every time, of saying "he or she" on their term papers, of calling people of color "people of color." They're tired of feeing like there is no mobility—or, if there is, someone else is climbing over them on the ladder of success. They want to escape to a world where men rule and where reality doesn't get in the way. "Where else can you get the chance to storm the beach of Normandy or duel with light sabers or even fight the system and go out for a pizza when you're done?" asks David, an avid gamer for over twenty years.

In the gaming world, they get the world as they wish it would be, the world as they had imagined it would be if they played their cards right and subscribed to the Guy Code. They get the world they feel entitled to.

In their media world more generally, they turn the tables. More, they turn the tables over. They do it angrily—but they also do it in disguise. In some of their media consumption—rap music or some video games— they do it in blackface, symbolically appropriating the idiomatic expressions of the racialized "other" to gain access to and express their own emotions. Video games in which your avatar is an inner-city hood on a drug-propelled crime spree, or gangsta rap in which newly minted millionaires grab their genitals and flash their bling-bling while surrounded by gyrating big-bootied babes in g-strings—these are racialized fantasies in which white suburban youth do more than play at being "bad."

At the turn of the last century, as historians have explained, young white male performers would don blackface to express their anxieties and emotions, especially as lonely immigrants in a bewildering new world. They longed for the comforts of home and family—"de ol' folks at home" and "Mammy," a "universal lamentation for homeland and birthplace," as one historian put it—but the demands of masculinity required stoic emotional sturdiness. Blackface gave them access to their feelings, a way to express their anger, impotence, confusion, and longing.

GTA and gangsta rap are racist not simply because they traffic in every single racial and sexual stereotype that have now been banned by campus hate speech codes or workplace harassment rules. The safe and secure white middle-class guys project their needs onto these others, and then take those feelings back. Appropriation "allows Whites to contain their fears and animosities toward Blacks through rituals not of ridicule, as in previous eras, but of adoration," writes University of Hartford communications professor Bill Yousman.

In fact, much of white guys' appropriation of black styles says more about whiteness than it does about racist projections of blackness. For white guys, blacks are all violence, athletic prowess, aggression, and sexual predation—that's what they adore about it. It's all so utterly unapologetically politically incorrect, a massive middle finger to the forces that constrain free speech and make us feel guilty about the racist and sexist stereotypes that we "know" everyone still holds but no one has permission to say. It's *The Man Show* 24/7, with buxom blondes bouncing on trampolines and men with permission—again! finally!—to ogle.

Despite the ubiquitous presence of babes in guys' media world, the presence of real women is often seen as an invasion. Few things provoke more anger than women's invasion of this last all-male world. Whether it's a mother asking her adolescent son to do his homework or wash the dinner dishes, a young woman who wanders into the game zone and wants to play, or a girlfriend or young wife asking that her partner actually spend time with her, men resent the intrusion of real women into their fantasy worlds.

Guyland's expansive and expanding entertainment arcade is to the beginning of the twenty-first century what the western novel or the adventure yarn was to the beginning of the twentieth century: an untrammeled world of homosocial purity, a pristine natural landscape where men can test themselves against the forces of nature and other men, uncorrupted and untainted by the feminizing influence of women. It's a world of surface thrills and excitement, masking a growing disquiet with guys' roles in life, and a gnawing sense that what they were told would be theirs is no longer their birthright.

The electronic environment of Guyland structures the fantasy lives of young men. Instead of embarking on this new stage of life with energy and enthusiasm, as they face the future, these relatively affluent and certainly privileged young guys seem defensive and angry, listless and indifferent. Instead of actually taking control of their lives—exploring career paths, lifestyles, and relationships that might leave them with an authentic feeling of power—they opt to live in a world that grants the illusion of control, as if to say, "It doesn't matter if I'm in control, as long as I get to feel as if I am." Guyland is seductive, easy, and suggests you never have to grow up. Peter Pan now has a joystick. Why would he ever leave Neverland?

But Guyland is also crippling young men, making it more difficult for them to negotiate real relationships with real women, or to commit to careers and family lives. And nowhere is this more evident than when it comes to fantasies about sex.

8 | BABES IN BOYLAND: PORNOGRAPHY

Guys are preoccupied with girls. But sometimes, they just can't show it. Or, rather, they can show they are girl crazy, but not that they actually *care* about girls. It's a fine line. If a guy isn't preoccupied with girls, then other guys might begin to wonder about him (and his sexuality). Being girl crazy reminds the other guys, with whom he is spending virtually all of his waking hours, that he's not interested in *them*, the other guys, not like that. The homosociality of Guyland, the fact that so much of guys' lives take place with and is judged by other guys, requires the relentless assertion of heterosexuality. At the same time, a guy can't appear too eager, too needy of girls' attention, or he'll come across as desperate. He must remain cool, calm, in control, both for the sake of appearances among the other guys and to increase his chances of success with a girl. It's the guys who appear the most disinterested who end up being the coolest, the ones that the girls find most attractive.

The time-honored way for a guy to prove that he is a real man is to score with a woman. It indicates both his desirability and his virility, and proves that he's succeeding in the often complicated task of attaining manhood. The problem, however, is that for guys, girls often feel like the primary obstacle to proving manhood. They are not nearly as compliant as guys say they would like them to be. By declining guys' sexual advances and not allowing guys to use them as currency, they are often as much of a threat to masculinity as they are a booster. This is why pornography is so appealing to guys: The pornographized woman's middle name is compliance. Even when she doesn't comply right away, she always comes around eventually—and passionately.

Porn in the USA

Staring at naked women is one of Guyland's greatest pleasures. And guys are staring—in real life, online, in magazines, on TV, in movies, and on DVDs—all the time. Pornography has been a massive industry in the United States for decades but the recent numbers are startling. Today, with gross sales of all pornographic media ranging between $10 and $14 billion annually, the porn industry is bigger than the revenues of ABC, NBC, and CBS—combined. Sales and rentals of pornographic videos and DVDs alone gross about $4 billion a year. More than 260 new pornographic videos are produced every week. Adult bookstores outnumber McDonalds restaurants in the United States by a margin of at least three to one. On the Internet, pornography has increased 1,800 percent, from 14 million web pages in 1998 to 260 million in 2003 and 1.5 *billion* downloads per month in 2005.

Equally important is not the size of the pornographic market but its pervasiveness. It's creeping into mainstream media as well as growing in the shadowlands to which it has historically been consigned. A large percentage of Americans use pornography "as daily entertainment fare." Of the 1,000 most visited sites on the Internet, 100 are adult-sex oriented. Our society has become, as journalist Pamela Paul titles her book, *Pornified*. As she puts it, pornography today "is so seamlessly integrated into popular culture that embarrassment or surreptitiousness is no longer part of the equation." Even pole-dancing, once the domain of professionals, is catching on among suburban wives "in book club country," according to the *New York Times*.

Young men have posted pictures of young women on their walls for decades—from Betty Grable on the lockers of World War II flyboys to

Marilyn Monroe, Raquel Welch, Farrah Fawcett, and Pamela Anderson. But what is different today is that these images of husky blondes (with "bedroom hair" and surgically augmented breasts) aren't simply the dorm room posters of college freshmen. They bombard the senses everywhere you look. What this means is that guys (and girls, too, for that matter) are growing up looking at sexualized images of women long before they're even thinking about sex. Is it any wonder that as they come of age they feel entitled to women's bodies?

Go to a basketball game and every time-out is filled with gyrating, skimpily clad "dancers" who limn the boundary between pole dancers and athletes. Open any mainstream magazine and you'll find ads with women's bodies selling everything from makeup and jewelry to cell phones. *Sports Illustrated*'s bestselling issue is the Swimsuit Issue. Watch any music video and you'll see dozens of barely dressed playthings bumping and grinding their way across the dance floor. Even the "Victoria's Secret Fashion Show," a two-hour-long commercial in which nearly naked models parade their own wares as well as the company's airs on network television.

And that's for mainstream consumption. Guys, magazines like *Maxim* or *FHM* feature bikini-clad buxom babes, drenched in sweat or water, on every front cover. Inside, along with articles about fitness, cars, technology, muscles, and sexual performance, are nearly naked starlets, models, and other assorted hotties, all suggestively posed. "All Babes All the Time!" is, apparently, the only way to successfully launch a new magazine geared exclusively to this demographic. According to the editors of *Maxim*, their 2.5 million subscribers are overwhelmingly male (76 percent), unmarried (71 percent) and young (median age is 26).

Maxim is but one of a spate of new "lad" magazines that began in Britain. According to journalist Tim Adams in the *Sunday Observer*, these magazines are in part an anti-feminist backlash aimed at helping men "regain their self-esteem" having been "diminished by the women's movement." By being brazen enough to make every magazine cover a wet T-shirt contest, these magazines have solved the problem of Madison Avenue advertisers who had tried unsuccessfully for years to market cosmetics—shaving paraphernalia, colognes, skin care products—to straight white men. *Men's Health*, the most successful of the new magazines launched in the 1980s and 1990s, followed suit. Once devoted to organic foods and herbal medicines for various men's illnesses, it reincarnated itself into a magazine that caters to men's sexual anxiety. Next to articles that offer pointers on how to develop abs of steel and buns of iron, flows a steady stream of articles about how to drive her wild in bed, how to be bigger, thicker, harder, and have more sexual endurance. Like so many other marketers, *Men's Health* panders to sexual anxiety by suggesting one can never be potent enough or enough of a sexual athlete. By presenting the illusion that the world is absolutely teeming with gorgeous women who are far more "into" sex than any generation in history, the media in general completely undermines these young men's vulnerable male identities. If there is so much available sex, these guys ask themselves, why is it so hard to get laid?

To mollify this insecurity, guys turn to porn.

Pornography as Reassurance

The sexual mandate of the Guy Code—have sex with as many women as possible, as frequently as possible, no matter what—is so unattainable that virtually every young man feels at least a little bit inadequate. But knowing that other guys are judging you on those impossible standards also puts guys in a position of feeling insatiable. Add to this the impossible idea that the world is filled with women who are available to everyone but you and you have a toxic brew of entitlement and despair. And that is the fuel for both voyeurism and predation.

Those softest of soft-core guy magazines serve to reassure young men that their desire to look at girls is not only their birthright as guys but a biological imperative. Guys seem to need that reassurance in part because they feel so besieged by gender equality, so trampled by the forces of political correctness, that they can't even ogle a woman on the street anymore without fearing that the police will arrest them for harassment.

That reassurance is also one of the chief functions of pornography for this age group. It's no wonder that the bestselling issue of *Playboy* each year is the "back to school" issue in which a dozen or so "coeds" from some collegiate athletic conference playfully disrobe. "Women of the ACC!" "Women of the Southeast Conference!" "Women of the Ivy League!" Men are eager—even desperate—to believe that those college girls, the ones who are their equals in chemistry class, on the debating team, or even on the soccer field, are really, underneath it all, "just girls" who are happy to bare their breasts and let men look.

"I know it sounds sort of stupid," says Greg, "I mean I lived in a coed dorm, and besides you can see everything 24/7 online and all, but I buy that damned *SI* Swimsuit Issue every year." A 25-year-old law student, Greg pauses for a moment to think about it.

> I think it's because the women are so *posed*, you know, like they're posing for the camera, for me; they're not doing some other guy and I'm supposed to get off on that. They're trying to look sexy— for me! And same thing about that *Playboy* back to campus issue. God I love that one. It's like whatever college you go to, there are such hot babes there who love to pose naked and turn guys on. They're the best antidote to all that feminist stuff about staring at women. They're begging you to stare at them. No, that's not quite it. They're daring you *not* to stare at them!

Pornography is a moment of reassuring voyeurism for these almost-men. Most of them have certainly had less experience with women than they'd like, and they are still trying to figure out how they measure up. Women in pornography are portrayed as the fantasized ideal—always ready and willing, always orgasmic, completely satisfied with you and always wanting more. It's no surprise guys want to look.

The world of pornography is an egalitarian erotic paradise where both women and men are constantly on the prowl, looking for opportunities for sexual gratification. The typical porn scene finds a woman and man immediately sexually aroused, penetration happens instantaneously, and both are orgasmic within a matter of seconds. That is, the pornotopic fantasy is a fantasy where women's sexuality is not their own, but is in fact a projection of men's sexuality. In the erotic paradise of pornography, both women and men act, sexually, like men—always ready for sex, always wanting sex, and always having sex that involves penetration and intercourse to an immediate orgasm. It's *his* orgasm that is the thrilling climax of the scene; hers is taken for granted and, in some ways, irrelevant. It's the complete reversal of real-life sex, where his interest is a given and hers must be elicited, where *his* orgasm is usually taken for granted (and, in fact, he often has to work like crazy to delay it) and her orgasm is the prize to be achieved.

Of course this equality of desire is a fiction, as any adult can tell you. But younger guys are more gullible. In fact, most guys are so desperate to believe it that they suspend disbelief in a way that is itself hard to believe. Consistently, young men who have grown up in an era of staged photo ops, Photoshop, and planted news stories actually believe that these women are so amazingly turned on that they are experiencing orgasm. "Naturally, I like good-looking women, but even more important is that *they* like what they're doing," one guy tells a journalist. "There are incidents where it's clear that someone has a real orgasm, and I like that." Another says he completely believes the women are consenting— he believes that a woman might "choose" a career in pornography just as she would choose to be a surgeon or a teacher. "She may be role playing an unwilling participant, but at bottom she is there by choice." And that choice implies "enormous amounts of trust, lust, and sexual confidence" so that these guys might feel trusted, lusted after, and sexually confident themselves.

No wonder anti-pornography activist John Stoltenberg writes that pornography "tells lies about women, though it tells the truth about men." The most prevalent lie is that women's sexuality is as predatory, depersonalized, and phallocentric as men's sexuality. Women's sexuality in real life, by contrast, usually requires some emotional connection. "For sex to really work for me, I need to feel an emotional *something*," commented one woman to sociologist Lillian Rubin. "Without that, it's just another athletic activity, only not as satisfying, because when I swim or run, I feel good afterward."

In my opinion, pornography also tells lies about men—that sex is inevitably vile and degrading, an animal urge that propels men to fuse disgust and desire. Some lies may be ones men really want to hear, the major one being that every woman really, secretly, deep down, wants to have sex with *you*. In a sexual marketplace where they feel completely dominated by women—from women having the power to decide if you are going to get sex in the first place, to all those dispiriting reminders that "no means no"—pornography gives guys a world in which no one has to take no for an answer.

Of course, this turns out not to be true. And so the sexual fantasies of many young men become more revenge fantasies than erotic ones—revenge for the fact that most of them don't feel they get as much sex as they think they are supposed to get—or as they think everyone else is getting.

Getting Off as Getting Even

The ubiquity of pornography in Guyland is more than simply a matter of female availability and never-ending desire. It's also about guys' anger at women for withholding what they, the guys, believe is their due: sex. It's about an arrogant in-your-face entitlement that guys feel, and the fact that they feel it all the time. Daily life is filled with beautiful and sexual women everywhere they look—in the dorm, in classes, on the street, at work. And the Guy Code is playing an endless loop in their heads: "Gotta get laid, you're not a man unless you try for it, keep going, what's wrong with you?" One guy, interviewed by Pamela Paul, notes that daily life presents so many situations that leave guys feeling impotent and undesirable. He cites what he calls the "street dilemma"—walking down the street seeing all these girls you want to have sex with. "And it makes you angry in a way," he says. "Not violently angry, but just pissed off. It pains us every time we see another woman we can't have sex with. You want to see all these women naked and you know you never will. It's really frustrating."

Seen in this light, the success of the smash hit video series, *Girls Gone Wild* is not surprising. In *Girls Gone Wild*, a video camera follows girls on spring break and at campus parties and offers them a free tank top in return for baring their breasts; it earns about $40 million a year for producer Joe Francis. *Girls Gone Wild* is just what guys want to see: drunken girls, in bikinis, willing to bare their breasts for nothing but a cheesy tank top, to show how "liberated" they are. Despite the fact that this must be the most impoverished definition of "liberation" imaginable, *Girls Gone Wild* has become so successful that Francis is currently planning to open a chain of fast-food restaurants to rival Hooters.

Some extremely popular websites take the *Girls Gone Wild* theme a little farther—and quite a bit more explicitly. On sites such as slutbus.com, bangbus.com, and bangboat.com, a couple of young guys who appear to be in their early twenties go cruising in a minivan (or boat) with a video camera looking for young women. They offer the women a ride, and once she gets in the van, they offer her money, typically $100, to take off her clothes. Gradually, the guys up the ante until she agrees to have sex for money. The rest of the video shows her having sex with several different guys in the van. When it's over, and the woman gets out, one of the men leans out with a wad of bills. But just as she reaches for the money, the driver revs the engine and the van peels off, leaving her running after it, angry and frustrated that she's been both "had" and "taken." The guys in the van have a good laugh at how "stupid those bitches are." On the slutbus website there are trailers for ten of these videos at a time; on bangbus, there are more than 200 trailers. All use roughly the same plot structure.

After I found out about these websites, I asked a few guys about them. About half had heard of them and visited them. They thought they were "funny," "silly," or "stupid" but also "kind of cool" because, as one guy said, "those girls think they are so hot and all stuck up, and for a couple of hundred, they'll do it doggy-style." What was most interesting, however, is how well the ruse worked on its intended audience. Although the website describes the fact that "all models" in the video are over 18, none of the guys I spoke with thought these were staged events; instead they saw them as documentaries, as reasonable depictions of reality. And that's the problem. Because what this tells us is that the guys who watch these videos actually believe that women will have sex with strangers for money even if they're not desperate. That walking home from the store, or out jogging, or seeking help when her car has run out of gas, a woman will expose herself, perform oral sex, and have intercourse within minutes—and all for money. We also learn that the guys think that after using these women for sex, it's funny to humiliate them by not paying them. All women are basically whores and will have sex if the price is right. But since they are whores anyway, why pay them? Better to just peel out and leave them angry too.

At the very least, websites like slutbus.com help guys to solve the "street dilemma." Pornotopia is the place where they can get even, where women get what they "deserve," and the guys never have to be tested, or face rejection. And so the pornographic universe becomes a place of homosocial solace, a refuge from the harsh reality of a more gender equitable world than has ever existed. It's about anger at the loss of privilege—and an effort to restore men's unchallenged authority. And, it turns out, that anger is worse among younger men.

How to Think About Pornography in Guyland

Twenty years ago, as the feminist debate about pornography reached its zenith and feminist-inspired efforts to challenge it were legally debated (and enacted) in several major cities, I assembled a collection of writings by men who tried to get underneath these roiling debates and dig into their own experiences and those of other men, to find out what men looked to pornography to find. *Men Confront Pornography* was the first such collection in which men actually talked about pornography—not simply by asserting what pornography does to some passive spectator, but how pornography worked within the fabric of their own lives.

Now, after reading the social science research on the effects of pornography, interviewing adult men—both consumers of and producers of pornography—and talking with young men about their use of pornography, what has gradually become clear is that young men's experiences of pornography differ markedly from the way that adult men use pornography. To be sure, there are similarities—both young and adult men experience the same male entitlement to look at women's bodies, and both are fully able to suspend disbelief and enter the pornotopic spectacle.

But while pornography may be gendered speech, men of different ages hear that speech differently.

Nearly every compensatory behavior, and every obsessive assertion, actually belies itself. "Underneath all the assertions of liberty and 'healthy fun,' lie the desperation and anxiety, the shame and fear, the loneliness and sadness, that fuel the endless consumption of magazines and strip shows, x-rated films, visits to prostitutes," writes the poet David Mura. And beneath the pornographic spectacle is sadness—a deep sadness that men carry with them about their own sexuality, a sadness born in intimations of inadequacy, of a collapse of their unchallenged prerogatives in the boardroom as much as in the bedroom.

This sadness turns out to be a dominant emotion among adult male consumers. Journalist David Loftus and sociologist Michael Putnam each talked to middle-aged men, mostly in their thirties and forties, about their use of pornography. Consistently, those men's experiences were edged with resignation; they were sheepish, and their consumption had an air of desultory utility. "It gets me away from the ordinariness of life, makes me a hero of some sort," says one. "So there is this big gap, a chasm between the way I'd like things to be and the way they are, and there's a certain amount of sadness that comes in realizing that," says another. Pornography "helps for a brief period of time, you no longer feel the sorrow about that, because for that second it's all right, that chasm's not there."

Middle-aged users turned out to be apologetic. Some just talked about how it was harmless fun, or a vacation from relationships—from the requirements of courtship and caring that invariably precede heterosexual sex. "You don't have to buy them dinner, talk about what they like to talk about," says Seth, a computer programmer in New York. "And even when you do, there's no guarantee that you're gonna get laid. I mean with pornography, no one ever says no."

As performance artist Tom Cayler explained in a theatrical piece,

I come home from work and I am tired. I wanna take a shower, see the kids, get something to eat and lie down, watch a little TV. Maybe if there's not a ballgame on, I'll read a book, okay?

So, there I am, I'm reading this adventure novel and I get to the portion of the book where the hero has got this gorgeous dame writhing above him, biting her lips with pleasure. I mean, how do you even do that? That doesn't feel so good to me.

But I am getting turned on by this. I am getting turned on by this imaginary, illicit, sexual liaison. And I say to myself, "Hey, there's the wife. She is lying right next to you. She is gorgeous, available, warm, loving, naked." But am I turned on by her? No, I am turned on by these little black dots marching across the page.

Because, see, if I wanted to have sex with her, I would have to put down my book, I would have to roll over, I would have to ask her to put down her book, I would have to say . . . "How ya doin'? Are the kids in bed, is the cat out, is the phone machine on, are the doors locked, maybe we should brush our teeth, is the birth control device handy?" Then I would have to turn on the sensitivity. I would have to ask her what's been goin' on with her, what she's been dealin' with, I mean with the kids and the house, and the budget, and her mom, and everything like that. I'd have to tell her what was happenin' with me. My problems, my worries. I'd have to hold her, I'd have to stroke her. I would have to tell her how important she is to me. I would have to commit myself to an act which these days I may or may not be able to consummate. You think that is easy? The little black dots, they are easy.

The world of escape offered by pornography is "easy." It makes few relationship demands; it asks little of men morally, intellectually, politically, and offers so much in return: the illusion of power and control. Pornography allows "gratification without vulnerability, without risk to the self," writes journalist Tim Beneke in his book *Men on Rape*. But while adult men experience the absence of power and control with sadness and resignation, almost-men experience it with anger and contempt.

What Does Pornography Really "Do"?

Even though guys spend a lot of time watching pornography, there is little convincing research showing a definitive link between this activity and extreme antisocial behavior. Separate studies by Edward Donnerstein, a communications professor at University of California, Santa Barbara, Neil Malamuth, a psychologist at UCLA, and University of Alabama psychologist Dolf Zillman found that watching violent pornography produced some behavioral and attitudinal changes among young male viewers who were more likely to subscribe to various rape myths (such as women say no when they mean yes, and that women eventually like it when they are forced to have sex) and more likely to acquit rapists in mock trials. Yet two months later those attitudinal changes had nearly evaporated. And the changes held only for the most violent of images; images of consensual sex produced no changes at all. In fact, the changes caused by the violent pornography were identical to those produced by images that were only violent, with no sexual content, leading the researchers to conclude it is the violence, not the sex, that exerts a greater influence.

Most research on pornography has been undertaken by college professors with the subjects of that research being college-age male students. Male students are a convenient group to look at—they're there, they're relatively sexually uninhibited compared to the rest of the population, they're likely to be users of pornography and thus familiar with it, and the modest financial "incentive" to participate in the research is usually an actual incentive. But researchers on pornography have tended to generalize their findings to "men" in general, as if there were no differences among different age groups. In fact, men's sexuality changes as they age; their fantasies change, their likes and dislikes change. What turns men on at 18 might be light years away from what turns men on at 48. What men like to do, and have done to them, changes with age as well. Wouldn't the same hold true of how they experience images of sexuality?

By contrast, virtually every man that both journalist David Loftus and sociologist Michael Putnam talked to was over 30. The subjects joked about how they'd been using porn for years, how they found it "functional," if uninspired, and how they were aware, for the most part, that the people in them seemed unreal for a reason. But instead of the unreality—the massive breasts, the enormous penises—being a turn-on, these adult men seemed somewhat jaded, wishing for something that looked more "real," more like them.

This suggests some of the differences and there are many. Guys and adult men watch different sorts of porn, for different reasons, and under different circumstances. Guys tend to like the extreme stuff, the double penetration and humiliating scenes; they watch it together, in groups of guys, and they make fun of the women in the scene. Adult men watch by themselves, or sometimes with a partner, and they tend to like the ones where the women look like they are filled with desire and experience pleasure. This is a significant counterpoint to those who feel called to mind the public's morality: It turns out that pornography use over time does not up the ante and lead men toward increasingly violent and extreme images. Quite the opposite. Violence and aggression in pornography is more likely to be skewed toward the younger consumer.

Older men often experience their masculinity wistfully, with nostalgic glances backward over their shoulders at the carefree boys they once were. As Robert Bly found out a decade ago, when he escorted thousands of men on retreats to retrieve their lost playfulness and innocence, the sober responsibilities of adult masculinity often require that men give up their dreams of adventure; daily lives with adult partners and family obligations often mute the ecstatic sexualities of youth.

But guys in their early twenties don't see it that way at all. They experience their masculinity not in terms of what they had to give up in order to become men, but rather they experience it as anticipation—what they *will* experience. And, more to the point, what they are *entitled* to experience. And as they begin to bump up against the reality that they're unlikely to become masters of the universe, omnipotent sex gods, and billionaire celebrities hounded by hordes of groupies, they begin to feel a bit resentful. It is "the men who do not feel secure in their manliness, who do not feel a solid part of the larger culture, who are more likely to take pornography's lies seriously and to abuse the women in their lives," writes Loftus. After all, younger men are not established in their careers, don't feel solidly anchored in their families or their communities, face an uncertain financial future, and daily confront a baffling combination of sexually active yet seemingly unavailable women. Anxiety, insecurity, and emotional impotence make up the potent cocktail that fuels guys' pornographic imaginations.

"Oh, man, I love it when those women get on the bangbus," says Greg, a 22-year-old senior at UMass.

My friends and I share a membership so we can all watch it together. It's like they get all these girls who are like 19 or 20, and they're just walking around town, going to the mall, and some of them are going to classes at college for God's sake, and then these guys offer 'em some money and they like are naked and sucking and fucking these guys they don't even know, and loving it, for like a couple of hundred bucks. Un-fucking-believable. We're all like "oh, bang that bitch!" and "fuck that little ho." And they're like college girls! It's like so cool. Why aren't they like that here in Amherst?

The guys I interviewed consistently spoke of women more with contempt than desire. Women were "hos," "bitches," and "sluts"—words that are rarely, if ever, used by adult men (who almost invariably used "girl") in innumerable research studies. In Guyland, young men see a relentless war between the sexes, and, as far as they can tell, the only way to keep from losing is to fool the women: to treat them as if you believe they are goddesses, while secretly demeaning them to your friends. You don't have sex with women because you desire them; sex is the weapon by which you get even with them, or, even, humiliate them.

"I'll confess, although I know it's not very, uh, PC or anything, but I love all those *Girls Gone Wild* videos and the porn that shows girls on spring break and all," says Matt, 18, a first-year student at the University of Georgia.

I love where these stuck-up college bitches are like drunk and finally just give head to like 20 guys and get fucked by the whole football team and all. It's like they're always walking around campus in their little shorts and you can see their shaved pussies sometimes, but they think they are like, way too hot for me. But then these films, man, they're like these same bitches, and they finally get what's coming to them.

He laughs. "I mean they get what's coming *on* them!" He laughs again. Granted, guys like Matt have every intention of getting married, falling in love, and raising children. But for now, watching these girls' sexual humiliation is a way to level the playing field just a little bit.

Racial and Ethnic Differences Among Guys

If age matters in pornography, so too, do race and ethnicity. When I raised the question with black or Latino or Asian-American guys, I heard different sorts of statements entirely. Virtually none of the Asian-American men I spoke with expressed much interest in pornography, for example, nor did many of the Chicano men on the West Coast or in the Southwest. Latino men in the Northeast, particularly Puerto Rican and Dominican men, and African-American men across the country showed some interest, but it paled in comparison to the consumption by white men. Here's Jason, a 22-year-old Asian-American student at Lehigh:

Yeah, I've seen a bit of porn in the dorms and all. It's completely stupid. It all looks so fake. I just don't think that girls are out there all the time looking for cocks to suck. It's gross.

Across the country, William, a 24-year-old Asian-American engineering graduate student at UCLA, has a somewhat different spin:

I'm offended by it. Seriously. I've seen some porn that my fraternity brothers had at Berkeley. All those Asian women who acted like whores. They were like all dressed up in some exotic fantasies about what Asian women are like. And they're always with white guys. It's like the Asian male is invisible. So it's this sort of racist fantasy where Asian women use all these like "exotic Asian things" with the like "me love you long time" fake-Asian accents [he uses air quotes] but always for white guys' fantasies about what Asians are like. I think it's really offensive.

Survey research bears out these impressions. In the most comprehensive study of American sexual behavior ever undertaken, University of Chicago sociologist Edward Laumann and his colleagues found that rates of masturbation among black men were about half the rates of white men. If we assume that at least one function of pornography is to facilitate and accompany masturbation, then these lower rates among black men may indicate lower rates of consumption of pornography. "I know y'all think we're like porn connoisseurs," says Derek, a 23-year-old black graduate of Emory whom I met in Atlanta and who now works in the music business.

But that's probably because y'all have been looking at gangsta rap videos, man, and thinking all black guys are pimpin' niggas with like posses of bitches around them. But those videos are made for white kids, man. We know who buys these CDs, we know who watches the videos. We make the videos for them—it's what they think about life in the hood. They think that's street. I call it "MTV-street."

Black men are certainly represented in pornography. There are specific genres of pornography utilizing old racist themes of the enormously endowed black stud and the sexually voracious black woman, themes that are as old as slavery itself. But the consumers of such racialized images are, as we might expect, likely to be white guys, whose imaginations facilitate a certain projection onto these racial "others" that legitimate racial inequalities. Race is sexualized; sex is racialized. Says Chase, a 26-year-old African-American graduate student:

Yeah, I sometimes look at it. But it doesn't really get me. It's not about me. Something else is going on, like white guys doing black

girls to get something racial, or like black guys doing white girls—
for those same white guys to get something racial. It's weird, but
it doesn't feel like it's about *me*, even if it's black guys in it. I can't
exactly describe what's wrong, but I know it's not about me. Not
for me.

For Chase, mainstream pornography offers fantasies of racialized
revenge that use black people, but aren't about black people. White men
with black women, tasting that animal passion. Or black men with enormous penises having sex with white women, which affords both racialized revenge for black men—of the sort advocated by Eldridge Cleaver
in the 1960s who famously said that black men raping white women
was a revolutionary act of retaliation for black men's emasculation—and
white men's revenge against uppity women, using bigger and stronger
black men as proxies to subordinate them.

It's younger white men, then, both gay and straight, who are the most
avid consumers of pornographic images. And it's the straight white guys
for whom the anger and contempt are at its height. This is especially
ironic, as we saw earlier, because often the white guys adopt the imagined language of the street—that is, imagined African-American masculine idiomatic expressions—to express that contempt and anger at the
"bitches" and "hos" that surround them and tempt them and then turn
them down. This appropriation of racial images to enable the expression
of white people's feelings is familiar to us, from the discussion of gangsta rap and video game avatars. It's more than racialized, of course. It's
also racist—for which group has the power, the sense of entitlement, to
appropriate the language of the other?

The Costs of Porn

For young men, especially, pornography serves in part as a course in
sex education, however distorted that image of sex might be. For many
boys and young men, images of sex in pornography are the first images
of actual sex that they have ever seen. Yet rather than instructing men
to commit rape, pornography whispers, cajoles, teases, urges, and begs

men to masturbate. Pornography is nothing if it is not utilitarian: If you can't get off to it, it is not "good" porn.

Since one can assume that masturbation is at least in part a product of sexual excitement and gratification, then the appropriate questions about pornography are of an ethical and political nature, not only social scientific ones. What does it mean that many guys get erections and masturbate to images of women being degraded or humiliated? What does it mean that a scene depicting a woman being gang raped, slapped, spanked, and then ejaculated on would be arousing?

The men who make the pornography have a good idea what their viewers want. Over and over again, they describe a male consumer who is angry, sexually frustrated, and eager to exact some sort of revenge on women. In interviews with pornography producers, journalist Robert Jensen found this sort of motivation as a constant theme. "I'd like to really show what I believe the men want to see: violence against women," said one producer to Jensen, explaining why the "money shot" (the man ejaculating on the women, usually on or near her face) is the critical moment in the pornographic spectacle. "The most violent we can get is the cum shot in the face. Men get off behind that, because they get even with the women they can't have."

But what does pornography actually *do* for these young men? They are unlikely to enact any of the images they see. I've talked to dozens of guys about their use of pornography and while many admitted that they had learned a new position or two only a handful said they ever tried out something more. But even if what they see is not what they want in real life, why is it the stuff of fantasy? And what relationship does fantasizing about women being raped and humiliated have with their actual day-to-day relationships with women?

Curiously, the answer to that question may well be "Nothing." Watching porn in Guyland has as much to do with the relationships among the guys themselves as it has to do with actual relationships with real-life women. Guys use porn to bond with other guys.

One of Guyland's most interesting spectacles is a bunch of straight guys sitting around a dorm lounge, the living room of a fraternity house, or an apartment, sharing a pizza, and watching pornography together.

The "function" of pornography ostensibly is to arouse the viewer sexually but when you are sitting on a sofa in someone else's living room, it would be more than a little bit "gay" to reveal any interest at all in the progress of other guys' erections and their interest in masturbation. So the viewers sit, increasingly sexually frustrated as the pornography "works" on them. They don't masturbate, they don't discuss wanting to masturbate—indeed to devolve into a circle jerk is the last thing that these guys would have on their minds, since it would only reveal the obviously homoerotic scene of a bunch of straight guys sitting around watching sex together.

So what do the guys do? They get angry. Each time I happened on a group of guys engaged in group pornography consumption, they spent a good deal of time jiving with each other about what they'd like to do to the girl on the screen, yelling at her, calling her a whore and a bitch and cheering on the several men who will proceed to penetrate her simultaneously.

Some research I undertook with my graduate students a few years ago sheds some light on this curious spectacle. In one project, Martin Barron and I examined the content of pornography in three different media: magazines, videos, and online chat rooms. We found that the amounts of violence increased among the three, from magazines to videos to online chats. But it wasn't because the technology allowed for more explicit violence. It was because the social context of the media changed. Magazines, and to a large extent videos, are intended for individual consumption. But online chat rooms are, by their nature, spaces of social interaction among men. These chat rooms are the closest thing to a pornographic locker room, in which bonding is often accomplished by competing with the other guys. In the online chat rooms, a description of a violent sexual encounter might be followed by another user's "Oh yeah, well, last night I did this to the woman I was with . . ." which would be followed by another response designed to top even that. The competition can become heated—and violent—rather quickly. What we had stumbled on was the "homosocial" element in heterosexual porn viewing, the way in which anything, including intimacy with a member of the opposite sex, can be turned into a competitive moment with other guys.

It's a classic illustration of the frustration-aggression principle of social psychology, the axiom that thwarted impulses become transformed into aggression. Or, put the other way around, aggression is simply the expression of frustrated impulses—in this case, the frustrated desire for sexual release is translated into aggression against the weaker and more vulnerable object, the one who can't fight back, the woman on the screen. The men desire; the pornography informs and elicits that desire. But they cannot satisfy that desire. So whose fault is that? It's not the guys' fault: They were just sitting there, minding their own business, with no intention of feeling horny. But then this beautiful girl seduced them, elicited the desire from them, and they can't have her, and can't do anything about it. Pornography evens the score by offering a fantasy of revenge.

So, what are guys getting out of getting off? They're getting back. They're not getting mad; they're vicariously getting even. Getting back at a world that deprives them of power and control, getting even with those haughty women who deny them sex even while they invite desire, getting back at the bitches and hos who, in the cosmology of Guyland, have all the power.

While these violent images are indeed disturbing, what might be more disturbing is that by viewing pornography, and by relying on pornography to inform them, guys are sustaining an "us against them" attitude toward women that is not going to serve them in the long term. They're missing out on developing the skills—sexual and otherwise—that might help them to sustain relationships with women in the real world. Because actual sex with an actual woman is about a lot more than what's depicted on the screen. Actual women are far smarter than that, want more from sex, aren't immediately orgasmic, don't appreciate being used, have feelings, make demands, and believe themselves to be entitled to at least a modicum of dignity, respect, and care.

There are unforeseen costs to the virtual universality of the pornographic spectacle in Guyland, to say nothing of modern society in general. Even if it doesn't directly cause violence or rape, it can sexualize violence against women, make it look acceptable. Pornography rarely enhances our sex lives; it is more likely to impoverish it, reducing emotionally complex erotic encounters to a few-minutes' formula of physical acrobatics so that our experience of being sexual can become, as the seventeenth-century British philosopher Thomas Hobbes said of life in a state of nature, "solitary, poor, nasty, brutish and short." Even if it's sex education, it's all form and no content, all body and no soul.

It may even be the case that the ubiquity of pornography in Guyland "is responsible for deadening male libido in relation to real women," as feminist writer Naomi Wolf argues. Increasingly, guys who are logging on to cyberporn or watching hardcore DVDs seem less likely to be able to marshal the emotional resources to sustain a serious sexual relationship with another person. "Dude," says one 26-year-old to journalist David Amsden, "all my friends are so obsessed with Internet porn that they can't sleep with their girlfriends unless they act like porn stars." You thought those little black dots were easy? Try megapixels. Now *they're* easy!

9 | HOOKING UP: SEX IN GUYLAND

I know it's different at other schools," Troy patiently tried to explain to me. "I mean, at other schools, people date. You know, a guy asks a girl out, and they go out to a movie or something. You know, like dating? But here at Cornell, nobody dates. We go out in groups to local bars. We go to parties. And then after we're good and drunk, we hook up. Everyone just hooks up."

"Does that mean you have sex?" I ask

"Hmm," he says, with a half-smile on his face. "Maybe, maybe not. That's sort of the beauty of it, you know? Nobody can really be sure."

My conversation with Troy echoes an overwhelming majority of conversations I have had with young people all across the country. Whether among college students or recent grads living in major metropolitan areas, "hooking up" defines the current form of social and sexual relationships among young adults. The only point Troy is wrong about is his assumption that traditional dating is going on anywhere else. Dating, at least in college, seems to be gone for good.

Instead, the sexual marketplace is organized around groups of same-sex friends who go out together to meet appropriate sexual partners in a casual setting like a bar or a party. Two people run into each other, seemingly at random, and after a few drinks they decide to go back to one or the other's room or apartment, where some sexual interaction occurs. There is no expectation of a further relationship. Hookups can morph into something else: either friends with benefits or a dating relationship. But that requires some additional, and complex, negotiation.

Many adults find this promiscuity hard to grasp. What is this hooking up culture all about? What does it mean exactly? What's the *point* of all that sex? Is it even fun? For the past two years, I've been involved in a study to find out. The Online College Social Life Survey was developed initially by Paula England, a sociology professor at Stanford, and has now been administered to about 7,000 college students at nine campuses—large and small, public and private, elite and nonelite—including Stanford, Arizona, Indiana, Radford, UC Santa Barbara, SUNY Stony Brook, Ithaca College, and Evergreen State. We asked participants about their sexual behaviors, their experiences of various sexual activities, orgasm, drinking behavior, and their romantic relationships. We asked both women and men, gay and straight—but mostly straight. All were between 18 and 24. I've also consulted with other researchers at other schools, and compared our data with theirs. And I've looked at data from several large, nationally representative studies of sexual behavior among young people.

Some of what's going on won't come as that much of a shock; after all, young adulthood since the sixties has been a time of relative sexual freedom and well-documented experimentation. What may be surprising, though, is how many young people accept that hooking up—recreational sex with no strings attached—is the best and most prevalent arrangement available to them. Once, sexual promiscuity co-existed with traditional forms of dating, and young people could maneuver between the two on their way toward serious and committed romantic relationships. Now, hooking up is pretty much all there is; relationships begin and end with sex. Hooking up has become the alpha and omega of young adult romance.

And though hooking up might seem utterly mutual—after all, just who are all those guys hooking up *with*?—what appears on the surface to be mutual turns out to be anything but. Despite enormous changes in the sexual attitudes of young people, the gender politics of campus sex don't seem to have changed very much at all. Sex in Guyland is just that—guys' sex. Women are welcome to act upon their sexual desires, but guys run the scene. Women who decide not to join the party can look forward to going to sleep early and alone tonight—and every night. And women who do join the party run the risk of encountering the same old double standard that no amount of feminist progress seems able to eradicate fully. Though women may accommodate themselves to men's desires—indeed, some feel they have to accommodate themselves to them—the men's rules rule. What this means is that many young women are biding their time, waiting for the guys to grow up and start acting like men.

Yet the hooking-up culture so dominates campus life that many older guys report having a difficult time making a transition to serious adult relationships. They all say that eventually they expect to get married and have families, but they have no road map for getting from drunken sloppy "Did we or didn't we?" sex to mature adult relationships. It turns out that choosing quantity over quality teaches them nothing about long-term commitment. Nor is it meant to. The pursuit of conquests is more about guys proving something to other guys than it is about the women involved.

As a result, most guys drift toward adulthood ill prepared for emotional intimacy better suited to fantasies of being "wedding crashers" (hooking up with women who are attending a friend's wedding) than becoming grooms themselves. They know little more about themselves and their sexuality at 28 than they did at 18, and the more subtle aspects of romance and partnership likewise remain a mystery. They barely know how to date. While the hookup culture might seem like some sort of orgiastic revelry, in truth these guys are missing out. It's not just that they're delaying adulthood—it's that they're entering it misinformed and ill prepared.

A Brief History of Campus Sexual Patterns

In the 1930s, Michigan sociologist Willard Waller described campus romance as a complex dance that he called "rating-dating-mating." Waller saw a competitive romantic marketplace in which students rated themselves in reference to both the other sex and the evaluations of their same-sex friends ("rating"). They then sought to date appropriately—slightly up, but not too much. In their eyes, dating "up" too much would make the relationship too insecure; dating "down" would decrease your own rating.

In order to have what he called a "Class A" rating, men, Waller wrote, "must belong to one of the better fraternities, be prominent in activities, have a copious supply of spending money, be well-dressed, be 'smooth' in manners and appearance, have a 'good line,' dance well and have access to an automobile." Women, by contrast, may need "good clothes, a smooth line, ability to dance well," but paramount, by far was her already determined "popularity as a date," since her "prestige depends on dating more than anything else."

What is immediately striking about Waller's comment, written nearly three-quarters of a century ago, is how accurate it continues to be—for men. *His* prestige still depends, in large part, on his social networks and his material assets. *Her* datability, though, no longer depends simply on social attributes. To be sure, women have to be pretty and sociable—that hasn't changed. But, according to a recent survey at Duke, they *also* have to be sexy, and accomplished, and ambitious, and athletic—and not to show that they are expending any energy at all doing any of it. "Effortless perfection" was the phrase the university gave the phenomenon.

In Waller's time, all this rating and dating was ultimately in the service of mating—romantic (and sexual) relationships between committed intimate partners that would lead, eventually, to marriage. But today, the sequence of rating, dating, and mating has been all but abandoned among young adults. To be sure, they still rate themselves and each other. Men have to be cool, women effortlessly perfect. But the idea of dating seems quaint but irrelevant. Today, campus culture is no longer about dating to find an appropriate mate. Now, it's more about mating to find an appropriate date!

"A date for me is, like, when a guy calls you up and says, 'would you like to go someplace,' you know, like to dinner, or to a movie," says

Debbie, a 21-year-old senior at the University of Virginia. "That never happens here!" She laughs. "Now it's like you see a guy at a party and he says, 'What are you doing now? Can I walk you home?' It's like, you know, the beginning of the date is like the end of the date. He walks you home, and then you hook up."

In some ways this is not news. College campuses have always been sexual hothouses, places of sexual experimentation, freedom, and predation. Many of the reasons are obvious: Young people are out from under direct parental control and feel freer to experiment with different activities. The fact that many are away from home means they are also freed from the critical scrutiny of their high-school and neighborhood friends, free to try on new identities with different cliques. And, of course, their hormones are in full gear.

To many parents, the sexual shenanigans of the contemporary college campus sound like some drunken bacchanalian orgy. But this isn't because parental restrictions have disappeared or because sexual liberalism pervades campus life. All this sexual activity on college campuses also has a lot to do with simple demography: the onset of fertility in adolescence, first sexual experiences, and the delayed age of marriage.

Stated most simply, *a college student today will never again be in a place where there are so many sexually active unmarried people.* Nor will college students ever again be around so many sexually active people *like themselves*—with roughly similar class and race characteristics (since most college sexual activity takes place with people of one's own race and class background). Prior to college, not as many people are sexually active. And after college, not as many people are sexually available—either in terms of their physical proximity or in terms of their relationship status. College is the quintessential gathering place for middle-class white Americans aged 18 to 22. They don't even need to plan much—like they do in high school when they live with their parents, or after they graduate from college, when they actually have to go somewhere to meet others. In college dorms they bump into each other randomly, frequently, seemingly spontaneously, with little planning, like excited atoms, eager to discharge.

Hooking Up

In recent years, scholarly researchers and intrepid journalists have bravely waded in to demarcate the term "hooking up," map its boundaries, and explain its strange terrain. But the definitions are vague and contradictory. One research group refers to it as ". . . a sexual encounter which may nor may not include sexual intercourse, usually occurring on only one occasion between two people who are strangers or brief acquaintances." Another study maintains that hooking up ". . . occurs when two people who are casual acquaintances or who have just met that evening at a bar or party agree to engage in some forms of sexual behavior for which there will likely be no future commitment."

Our collaborative research project, The Online College Social Life Survey, found that hooking up covers a multitude of behaviors, including kissing and nongenital touching (34 percent), oral sex, but not intercourse (15 percent), manual stimulation of the genitals (19 percent), and intercourse (35–40 percent). It can mean "going all the way." Or it can mean "everything but." By their senior year, we found that students had averaged nearly seven hookups during their collegiate careers. About one-fourth (24 percent) say they have never hooked up, while slightly more than that (28 percent) have hooked up ten times or more.

As a verb, "to hook up" means to engage in any type of sexual activity with someone you are not in a relationship with. As a noun, a "hookup" can either refer to the sexual encounter or to the person with whom you hook up. Hooking up is used to describe casual sexual encounters on a continuum from "one-night stands" (a hookup that takes place once and once only with someone who may or may not be a stranger) to "sex buddies" (acquaintances who meet regularly for sex but rarely if ever associate otherwise), to "friends with benefits" (friends who do not care to become romantic partners, but may include sex among the activities they enjoy together).

Part of what makes the hookup culture so difficult to define and describe is the simple fact that young men and women experience it in very different ways. They may be playing the same game, but they're often on opposing teams, playing by a different set of rules, and they define "winning," and even "scoring," in totally different ways. Sameness doesn't necessarily mean equality.

Indeed, the current patterns of sociability and sexuality among heterosexuals have actually begun to resemble the patterns that emerged in the mainstream gay male community in the late 1970s and early 1980s, the pre-AIDS era. Sex was de-coupled from romance and love, and made part of friendships that may—or may not—have anything to do with romantic relationships. "Fuck buddies" are the precursors to "friends with benefits." Sex was seen as recreational self-expression, not freighted with the matched baggage of love and relationship. When it comes to scoring, then, gay and straight men have a lot more in common with each other than either group does with women. To put it another way, it is gender, not sexual orientation, that is the key to understanding these campus sexual patterns. If we want to understand the complexities of the hookup culture we must do so with gender in mind.

Deliberate Vagueness

The phrase "hooking up" itself is deliberately vague, which is why any attempt to define it concretely will inevitably fall short. In fact, it is its very vagueness and ambiguity that characterize it. "It's, like, anything from like making out to intercourse," says a 19-year-old female sophomore at Radford University. "[A]nything from, in my opinion, kissing to having sex," says another. "Having sex," says another. But then she pauses.

> But see, hooking up and having sex can be two different things. It's really hard. When people say "we hooked up," you don't really know what they mean by that. Because I don't really consider having sex hooking up. I think that's a different thing. Like having sex is separate from hooking up. I think it should be anyway. Because everyone can just be, like, "yeah, we hooked up," and you never know what they did. They could be having sex every night and you're assuming that they probably just made out or something like that.

Maybe, as one woman suggested in an interview, hooking up is the "yada yada yada" of sex.

Did you ever see that episode of *Seinfeld* where they're, like, "yada, yada, yada." And you're, like, "what does that mean?" She's, like, "I went home with him and yada, yada, yada." And that's kind of, like, what a hookup is. Because you don't really know exactly what it means, unless you're talking to a really good friend and they're telling you all the details.

Judging from our survey, there's a whole lot of yada yada yada going on. Yet that vagueness serves men and women in very different ways. When a guy says he "hooked up" with someone, he may or may not have had sex with her, but he is certainly hoping that his friends think he has. A woman, on the other hand, is more likely to hope they think she hasn't.

In a sense, hooking up retains certain features of older dating patterns: male domination, female compliance, and double standards. Though hooking up may seem to be mutually desired by both guys and girls, our research indicates that guys initiate sexual behavior most of the time (less than a third of respondents said this was mutual). Hookups are twice as likely to take place in his room as in hers. And, most important, hooking up enhances his reputation whereas it damages hers. Guys who hook up a lot are seen by their peers as studs; women who hook up a lot are seen as sluts who "give it up." According to Duke's study of campus sexual behavior, "Men and women agreed the double standard persists: men gain status through sexual activity while women lose status."

"There is definitely a double standard," says Cheryl, a sophomore at Creighton. "I mean, if I do what my friend Jeff does [hook up with a different girl virtually every weekend], my friends wouldn't talk to me! I mean, that's just gross when a girl does it. But a guy, it's, like, he's like Mr. Man."

"If a guy hooks up with a girl, he sort of broke down her wall of protection," explains Terry, a Stanford junior. "She's the one that let her guard down . . . her job going into the night . . . was to like protect herself, protect her moral character and her moral fiber, and it's like you came in and went after her and she was, like, convinced to let her guard down . . ."

This is a somewhat surprising view of things, given just how much we think everything has changed. It not only echoes the 1950s, but even farther back to the Victorian age. Despite the dramatic changes in sexual behavior spurred by the sexual revolution, sexual experience still means something different for women and men. "It's different from what it used to be when women were supposed to hold out until they got married. There's pressure now on both men and women to lose their virginity," is how one guy put it. "But for a man it's a sign of manhood, and for a woman there's still some loss of value."

The vagueness of the term itself—hooking up—turns out to be a way to protect the reputation of the woman while enhancing that of the man. In addition to that conceptual vagueness after the fact, hookups are also characterized by a certain vagueness before and even during the fact as well. Most hookups share three elements: the appearance of spontaneity, the nearly inevitable use of alcohol, and the absence of any expectation of a relationship.

Planned Spontaneity

In order for hookups to work, they have to appear to be spontaneous. And they do—at least to the guys. One guy told me it's "a sort of one-time, spur-of-the-moment thing. Hookups generally are very unplanned."

"Oh, sure," said Jackson, a 22-year-old senior at Arizona State, "you go to parties on the prowl, looking to hook up. But you never know if it's going to happen. And you certainly don't know who you're gonna hook up with. That takes several drinks."

Yet such spontaneity is nonetheless carefully planned. Guys have elaborate rituals for what has become known as "the girl hunt." There are "pregame" rituals, such as drinking before you go out to bars, since consuming alcohol, a requirement, is also expensive on a limited budget, so it's more cost-effective to begin the buzz before you set out.

There are defined roles for the guys looking to hook up, like the "wing man," the reliable accomplice and confidant. "The wing man is the guy who takes one for the team," says Jake, a sophomore at Notre Dame. "If there are, like, two girls and you're trying to hook up with one of them, your wing man chats up the other one—even if she's, like, awful—so you can have a shot at the one you want. Definitely a trooper."

When guys claim that the hookup is spontaneous, they are referring not to whether the hookup will take place, but with whom they will hook up. Women have a different view of spontaneity. Since they know that hooking up is what the guys want, the girls can't be "spontaneous" about it. They have to think—whether or not, with whom, under what conditions—and plan accordingly, remembering a change of clothes, birth control, and the like. They have to decide how much they can drink, how much they can flirt, and how to avoid any potentially embarrassing or even threatening situations. The guys lounge in comfort of the illusion of alcohol-induced spontaneity; the women are several steps ahead of them.

"Girls, like, before they go out at night, they know whether or not they're going to hook up with somebody," says Jamie, a 21-year-old senior at Arizona State. "It's not spontaneous at all."

Yet the illusion of spontaneity remains important for both guys and girls. It's a way of distancing yourself from your own sexual agency, a way of pretending that sex just happens, all by itself. It helps young people to maintain a certain invulnerability around the whole thing. It's not cool to want something too much. It's better to appear less interested—that way no one will know the extent of your disappointment if your plans don't come to fruition.

The Inevitability of Alcohol

Drinking works in much the same way. Virtually all hooking up is lubricated with copious amounts of alcohol—more alcohol than sex, to tell the truth. "A notable feature of hookups is that they almost always occur when both participants are drinking or drunk," says one study. In our study, men averaged nearly five drinks on their most recent hookup, women nearly 3 drinks. Says one woman:

> Like, drinking alcohol is like a *major* thing with hooking up with people. A lot of the times people won't have one-night stands unless they're drunk. Actually, I can't tell you I know one person who has had a one-night stand without drinking or being drunk, and being, like, "oh, my head hurts. I can't believe I did that."

To say that alcohol clouds one's judgment would be an understatement. Drinking is *supposed* to cloud your judgment. Drinking gives the drinker "beer goggles," which typically expand one's notion of other people's sexual attractiveness. "After like four drinks a person looks a little bit better," explains Samantha, a 21-year-old senior at the University of Virginia. "After six or seven that person looks a lot better than they did. And, well, after ten, that person is the hottest person you've ever seen!" Or, as Jeff puts it, "Everybody looks more attractive when you're drunk."

But intentionally clouding judgment is only part of the story. The other part is to cloud *other people's* judgment. If you were drunk, you don't have to take responsibility for what happens. For guys, this means that if they get shot down they can chalk it up to drunkenness. The same holds true for their sexual performance if they do get lucky enough to go home with someone. In fact, drunkenness provides a convenient excuse for all sorts of potential sexual disasters, from rejection to premature ejaculation to general ineptitude born of inexperience. For a lot of guys, the liquid courage provided by alcohol is the only thing that makes them able to withstand the potential for rejection that any sexual advance entails in the first place.

While both sexes might get to enjoy the lack of responsibility alcohol implies, this turns out to be especially important for the women, who still have their reputations to protect. Being wasted is generally accepted as an excuse. "What did I do last night?" you can legitimately ask your girlfriends. And then everyone laughs. It's still better to be a drunk than a slut. "A hangover," Laura Sessions Stepp writes in her book, *Unhooked*, "is a small price to pay for exoneration."

The Absence of Expectations

One of the key defining features of hooking up is that it's strictly a "no strings attached" endeavor. Young people in college—and this seems to hold true for both women and men—seem generally wary of committed or monogamous relationships. The focus is always on what it costs, rather than what it might provide. And if you consider that half of young adults come from divorced households, their cynicism is neither surprising nor unfounded. "I don't know if I even know any happily married couples," one young woman says. "Most of my friends' parents are divorced, and the ones who aren't are miserable. Where's the appeal in *that*?"

Hooking up is seen as being a lot easier than having a relationship. Students constantly say that having a relationship, actually dating, takes a lot of time, and "like, who has time to date?" asks Greg, a junior at the College of Wooster in Ohio. "I mean, we're all really busy, and we have school, and classes, and jobs, and friends, and all. But, you know," he says with a bit of a wink, "a guy has needs, you know what I mean? Why date if you can just hook up?"

When one older teenager explained her most recent hookup to a *New York Times* reporter, he asked if she thought the relationship might lead to something more. "We might date," she explained. "I don't know. It's just that guys can get so annoying when you start dating them."

"Serial monogamy is exhausting," one young woman tells journalist Stepp. "You put all your emotions into a relationship and then you have to do it all over again." Says another:

Dating is a drain on energy and intellect, and we are overworked, overprogrammed, and overcommitted just trying to get into grad school, let alone getting married. It's rare to find someone who would . . . want to put their relationships over their academics/future. I don't even know that relationships are seen as an integrated part of this whole "future" idea. Sometimes, I think they are on their own track that runs parallel and that we feel can be pushed aside or drawn closer at our whim.

Which is a pretty revealing statement since it wasn't so long ago that Doris Lessing remarked that there had never been a man who would jeopardize his career for a love affair—and never been a woman who wouldn't.

Guys seem to agree, but for a different set of reasons. Brian says:

> Being in a real relationship just complicates everything. You feel obligated to be all, like, couply. And that gets really boring after a while. When you're friends with benefits, you go over, hook up, then play video games or something. It rocks.

Guys may hook up because they get exactly what they want and don't have to get caught by messy things like emotions. "A lot of guys get into relationships just so they get steady [expletive]," another teen tells journalist Benoit Denizet-Lewis. "But now that it's easy to get sex outside of relationships, guys don't need relationships." "That's all I really want is to hook up," says Justin, a junior at Duke. "I don't want to be all like boyfriend and girlfriend—that would, uh, significantly reduce my chances of hooking up, you know?"

Yet the absence of expectations that supposedly characterizes the hookup seem not to be as true for women. And this is not a simple case of "women want love, men want sex." Rather, it's a case of women being able and willing to acknowledge that there is a lot of ground between anonymous drunken sex and long-term commitment. They might not want to get married, but a phone call the next day might still be nice.

Young women today are more comfortable with their sexuality than any generation in history. There are certainly women who prefer hooking up to relationships. Women also hook up to avoid emotional entanglements that would distract them from their studies, professional ambitions, friendship networks, and other commitments. Or they hook up because they don't think they're ready for a commitment and they just want to hang out and have fun. Yet many also do it because it's the only game in town. If they want to have sexual relationships with men—and by all appearances they certainly do—then this is the field on which they must play. Some women may want more, some may not, but since more is not available either way, they take what they can get. As one young woman explained it to sociologist Kathleen Bogle,

> Most of the girls I know are looking for something, you know, someone, even if it's not serious, someone that is there to hang out with and talk to. [Girls want] a feeling of being close to someone and I don't know if it's even that guys don't want that, it's just that they don't care if they have that, it's like "whatever." It could be any other girl any night and you know that's fine with them.

And for the women who do want relationships, hooking up seems to be the only way to find the sort of relationships they say they want. They hope that it will lead somewhere else. Says Annie, 23, who recently graduated from George Washington University, in response to "Why do women hook up?"

> Because they want to find love. They want, even though people don't care about consequences, they want to find love. At least girls do. At least I do. I wanted to find love. I wanted to be happy and in love and just have that manly man hold me. They just want to find that. And even if the consequences are bad, it's a lot better going through the consequences and being loved than it is being alone and never loved.

Race and Hooking Up

Hooking up may be a guy thing, but it is also a *white* guy thing. Of course there are exceptions, but minority students are not hooking up at the same rates as white students. This is partly because minority students on largely white campuses often feel that everything they do is seen not in terms of themselves as individuals but representative of their minority group. "There are so few blacks on campus," says Rashon Ray, a sociologist at Indiana and part of our research team. "If one guy starts acting like a dog, well, word will get around so fast that he'll never get another date." As a result, on some large campuses, black athletes will hook up with white women, but will date black women.

"I know we don't do what the white kids do," said one black male student at Middlebury College in Vermont. "That's right, you don't," said his female companion. "And I don't either. If I even thought about it, my girls would hold me back." Said another black student at Ohio State, "if I started hooking up, I mean, not like with some random white girl, but like with my sisters, Oh, God, my friends would be saying I'm, like, 'acting white.'"

As a result, minority students are likely to conform to more conventional dating scripts, especially within their own communities. Our survey found that blacks and Latinos are somewhat less likely to engage in hooking up, and Asian students are *far* less likely to do so.

Hooking Up and Relationships: "The Talk"

In general, women tend to be more ambivalent about hookup culture; some report feeling sexy and desirable, others feel it's cheap and rarely leads anywhere. But when it comes to forming an actual relationship, the tilt is almost entirely toward the women. They are the ones who must negotiate whether the hooking up will proceed to a deeper level of intimacy. On many campuses, women are the ones who typically initiate the "Define the Relationship" conversation—the "DTR," or, more simply, "The Talk." "Are we a couple or not?" she asks.

Some women don't even bother to ask. "I didn't want to bring it up and just be, like, 'so where do we stand?' because I know guys don't like that question," says one woman to sociologist Kathleen Bogle. Another tells her it's the women who want the relationship and the guys who make the final decision. "It always comes down to that," says Ann, a junior at Wright State University.

> You know, women see hooking up different from men. I mean it's fun and all, but like after once or twice, like, where is it going? I mean, are you or aren't you, you know, like a couple? Me and my girlfriends always talk about how to bring it up, how to start the

talk. I know he doesn't want to hear it. But otherwise, what's all that hooking up *for*?

Justin, a junior at George Washington, offers the apposite retort:

Oh, man, don't get me started on "the talk"! It's like as soon as you hook up with someone, and you, like, have a good time, or whatever, and suddenly she's all, like, "well are we a couple, or not?" Of course you're not! You just hooked up, man!

"So," I ask him, "what do you do when she wants to have that talk?"

Avoid it. Like if she says, all serious, like, "Justin, we have to talk," like you know what's coming, right? That's when I get busy doing something else. Or I don't call her back. Or I try and avoid seeing her in private and only like bump into her on campus or something. But I definitely do not want to have that talk. It ruins everything.

But why are guys so relationship-phobic? Virtually every guy I spoke with said that he wanted to get married someday, and that he hoped he would be happy. Just not now and probably not until his early thirties. Their relationship phobias are less related to fears of romantic entanglements from which they would have trouble extricating themselves, and more to do with the purposes of hooking up in the first place. Hooking up, for guys, is less a relationship path than it is for women. In fact, it serves an entirely different purpose.

Sex as Male Bonding

In some ways hooking up represents the sexual component of young men's more general aversion to adulthood. They don't want girlfriends or serious relationships, in part, because they don't feel themselves ready (they're probably not) and also, in part, because they see relationships as "too much work." Instead they want the benefits of adult relationships, which for them seem to be exclusively sexual, with none of the responsibility that goes along with adult sexuality—the emotional connection, caring, mutuality, and sometimes even the common human decency that mature sexual relationships demand. Simply put, hooking up *is* the form of relationship guys want with girls.

Yet it's a bit more complicated than simple pleasure-seeking on the part of guys, because as it turns out pleasure isn't the first item on the hookup agenda. In fact, pleasure barely appears on the list at all. If sex were the goal, a guy would have a much better chance of having more (and better) sex if he had a steady girlfriend. Instead, guys hook up to prove something to other guys. The actual experience of sex pales in comparison to the experience of talking about sex.

> When I've just got laid, the first thing I think about—really, I shouldn't be telling you this, but really it's the very first thing, before I've even like "finished"—is that I can't wait to tell my crew who I just did. Like, I say to myself, "Omigod, they're not going to believe that I just did Kristy!"

So says Ted, a 21-year-old junior at Wisconsin:

> Like I just know what will happen. They'll all be high-fiving me and shit. And Kristy? Uh, well, she'll probably ask me not to tell anyone, you know, to protect her reputation and all. But, like, yeah, right. I'm still gonna tell my boys.

Hooking up may have less to do with guys' relationships with women and more to do with guys' relationships with other guys. "It's like the girls you hook up with, they're, like, a way of showing off to other guys," says Jeff, a proud member of a fraternity at the University of Northern Iowa. "I mean, you tell your friends you hooked up with Melissa, and they're like, 'whoa, dude, you are one stud.' So, I'm into Melissa because my guy friends think she is so hot, and now they think more of me because of it. It's totally a guy thing."

He looks a bit sheepish. "Don't get me wrong," he adds, with little affect. "I mean, yeah, Melissa is very nice and blah blah blah. I like her, yeah. But," he sort of lights up again, "the guys think I totally rule."

Jeff's comments echo those I heard from guys all across the country. Hooking up is not for whatever pleasures one might derive from drunken sex on a given weekend. Hooking up is a way that guys communicate with other guys—it's about homosociality. It's a way that guys compete with each other, establish a pecking order of cool studliness, and attempt to move up in their rankings.

"Oh, definitely," says Adam, a 26-year-old Dartmouth graduate now working in financial services in Boston. "I mean, why do you think it's called 'scoring?' It's like you're scoring with the women, yeah, but you're like scoring *on* the other guys. Getting over on a girl is the best way of getting your guys' approval."

His friend, Dave, 28, sitting next to him at the bar, is also a Dartmouth grad. He nods. "It's not just like keeping count," he says. "Not a simple tally, you know? It's like 'how many have you had?' yeah, but it's also 'who did you get?' That's how my guys . . . well, that's how we evaluated you for membership in the worldwide fraternity of guys." They both laugh.

Of course, the awesome insecurity that underlies such juvenile blustering remains unacknowledged, which is interesting since that insecurity is the driving force behind so much of sex in Guyland. The vast majority of college-aged guys are relatively inexperienced sexually. Most of them have had some sex, but not as much as they'd like, and nowhere near as much as they think everyone else has had. Perhaps they've received oral sex, less likely they've performed it, and if they have had intercourse at all it is generally only a handful of times with one partner, two if they're lucky. There are virtually no trustworthy adults willing or able to talk honestly about sex with young people. Talking to their parents is far too awkward. Sex education in schools is often restricted to a quasi-religious preaching of abstinence. Any information that they do manage to cobble together—how it works, what to do, what women like, what they expect—comes almost entirely from their peers, and from pornography. In fact, pornography winds up being the best source of sexual information available to them, and as we've seen pornography is filled with lies.

Yet most guys think that they are alone in their inexperience. They think that other guys are having a lot of sex, all the time, with a huge number of women. And they suspect, but would have no way of knowing, that other guys are a lot better at it than they are. Seen in this light, the hookup culture, at least for guys, is more than a desperate bid simply to keep up. It's a way to keep up, and keep quiet about it—while being rather noisy at the same time.

Hooking Up vs. Good Sex

Mature sexual relationships are complex; good sex takes time to develop. It usually helps to be sober enough to know what is happening. Hooking up may provide quantitative evidence of manly sexual prowess, but it cannot answer the qualitative insecurities that invariably attend sexual relationships. Hooking up may make one feel more like a man when talking with other guys, but it doesn't help—indeed, it may actually hinder—healthy and mutually satisfying sexual relationships with women. And it certainly cannot answer the anxieties that haunt guys when they are alone. Hooking up offers sex without entanglements, but it is attended by so many possibilities for ego devastation, misunderstanding, and crises that it can still become quite entangled. And since there is so much surface interaction in hookup culture, but so little actual connection, most of this stays buried.

With all this hooking up, friends with benefits, and booty calls, guys should feel they have it made. But there is a creeping anxiety that continually haunts guys' sexual activities, particularly these almost-men. They worry that perhaps they're not doing it enough, or well enough, or they're not big enough, or hard enough. Though the *evidence* suggests that men are in the driver's seat when it comes to sex, they *feel* that women have all the power, especially the power to say no.

And these days, those women have a new "power"—the power to compare. Many of the guys I spoke with became suddenly uneasy when the topic of women's sexual expectations came up. They shifted uncomfortably in their seats, looked down at the floor, or stared into their soft drink as if it were an oracle.

Jeff, a sophomore at UC San Diego said,

Uh, this is the tough part, you know. I mean, well, like, *we're* supposed to have hooked up a lot, but now so are they, and they, like, talk about it in ways that we guys never would. So, like, you feel like you have to be this fabulous lover and they have to come at least three times, and like, your, you know, your, uh, dick isn't the biggest she's ever seen, and, like, you always feel like you're being measured and coming up a bit . . . [he laughs uncomfortably], short.

"I think guys in your generation were more worried about whether or not you were going to get laid at all," says Drew, a senior at Kansas State. "I'm pretty sure I can hook up when I want, and I have several FWBs and even the occasional booty call. But I worry about whether I'm any good at it. I hear all this stuff from other guys about what they do, and how crazy they get the girl, and I think, whoa, I don't do that."

Guys feel a lot of pressure to hook up, a lot of pressure to score—and to let their friends know about it. And they feel a lot of pressure to be great in bed. In Bogle's study, some students estimated that some of their friends were hooking up twenty-five times every semester. And, they believed that while *they* thought hooking up meant kissing and other stuff, they thought their friends were actually having intercourse. "It's always the *other* student who, they believed, actually had intercourse every time they hooked up," she writes.

I asked guys all across the country what they think is the percentage of guys on their campus who had sex on any given weekend. The average answer I heard was about 80 percent. That is, they believed that four out of every five guys on campus had sex last weekend. Actually, 80 percent is the percentage of senior men who have *ever* had vaginal intercourse in our college survey. The actual percentage on any given weekend is closer to 5 to 10 percent. This gives one an idea of how pervasive the hooking-up culture is, how distorted the vision of young men by that culture is, and the sorts of pressures a guy might feel as Thursday afternoon hints at the looming weekend. How can he feel like a man if he's close to the only one not getting laid? And if so many women are available, sexually promiscuous, and hooking up as randomly as the men are, what's wrong with him if he's the only one who's unsuccessful?

As it turns out, guys' insecurity is not altogether unfounded. Most hookups are not great sex. In our survey, in their most recent hookups, regardless of what actually took place, only 19 percent of the women reported having an orgasm, as compared to 44 percent of the men. When women received cunnilingus, only about a quarter experience an orgasm, though the men who reported they had performed cunnilingus on their partner reported that she had an orgasm almost 60 percent of the time.

This orgasm gap extends to intercourse as well. Women report an orgasm 34 percent of the time; the men report that the women had an orgasm 58 percent of the time. (The women, not surprisingly, are far better able to tell if the men had orgasms, and reporting rates are virtually identical.)

Many women, it turns out, fake orgasm—and most do so "to make that person feel good, to make them feel like they've done their job." But some women said that they faked it "just really to end it," because they're, "like, bored with it."

"He was, like, trying so hard to make me come," says Trish, a senior at Washington University in St. Louis. "And there was, like no way it was going to happen. I felt so bad for him. I mean, I had gone down on him and he came already, and he was, like, trying to be a good sport about it, but really . . . So I just faked it, and he felt good and I felt relieved."

Hooking Up and Gender Politics

Hooking up seems disadvantageous to women in so many ways, and not only because the sex isn't so great. In fact the disincentives appear so numerous that one eventually might wonder why women bother. The hookup culture appears to present a kind of lose-lose situation. If they don't participate, they risk social isolation—not to mention that they also forego sex itself, as well as any emotional connection they may be able to squeeze out of the occasion. If they do participate, they face the potentially greater risk of "loss of value," and there's a good chance that they won't even have any fun.

On the other hand, one ought not overstate the case. Anti-feminist jeremiads fret constantly about women's lost modesty, chastity, or even their capitulation to male standards of sexual conduct. Conservative columnists complain about ever-loosening sexual mores, and use the gender inequality of hookup culture to advise women to keep their legs crossed. Women, they counsel, must remember the message that their grandmothers might once have told them, "men want only one thing." And so women, if they yearn for commitment and marriage, have to re-learn how to just say no.

Since the 1990s, abstinence campaigns have been encouraging young people to take a "virginity pledge" and to refrain from hetero-sexual intercourse until marriage (the campaigns assume that gay and lesbian students do not exist). Abstinence-based sex education is pretty much the *only* sex education on offer in the majority of American high schools. And many parents see abstinence as the best advice they can offer their children about how to reduce their risk for sexually transmit-ted disease, unwanted pregnancy, or sexual assault.

At first glance, such campaigns appear to be somewhat successful. One study found that the total percentage of high-school students who say they've had heterosexual sex had dropped from more than 50 per-cent in 1991 to slightly more than 45 percent in 2001. But teen preg-nancy rates have risen, and whatever decline in abortion rates may have occurred is due largely to the restrictions on its availability, not a cur-tailment of sexual behavior. Nor do abstinence campaigns offset the other messages teenagers hear. Sociologist Peter Bearman analyzed data from over 90,000 students, and found that taking a virginity pledge does lead an average heterosexual teenager to delay his or her first sexual experience, but only by about eighteen months. And the pledges were only effective for students up to age 17. By the time they are 20 years old, over 90 percent of both boys and girls are sexually active. Another campus-based survey found that of the 16 percent who had taken virgin-ity pledges, 61 percent of them had broken their pledge before graduating. Pledgers were also less likely to use condoms, although they were just as likely to practice oral sex as nonpledgers.

What's more, because abstinence-based programs are often used instead of actual sex education, few people really know exactly what "counts" in keeping your pledge. In one recent survey of 1,100 college freshmen, 61 percent believed you are still abstinent if you have participated in mutual masturbation; 37 percent if you have had oral sex; and 24 percent if you have had anal sex. On the other hand, 24 percent believed that kissing with tongues broke their abstinence pledge. In the survey by Angela Lipsitz and her colleagues, the majority of those who said they "kept" their vows had experienced oral sex.

At first glance, abstinence might be seen as the antithesis of the Guy Code, since promising not to have sex would negate the drive to score that is central to the Code. But abstinence actually sits easily within the Guy Code. Abstinence pledges put all the responsibility on the girls to police sexual activity—and to bear all the consequences and responsibilities if something goes wrong. Abstinence pledges also make it a lot easier for guys to maintain the good girl/bad girl, Madonna/whore dichotomy that has kept the sexual double standard in place for decades. "Does having sex with, like, a ho, actually violate your abstinence pledge?" one first-year student asked me recently. "I mean, I definitely respect the nice girls, and I am abstinent with them."

Even those who advocate prudence rather than abstinence nonetheless seem to focus all their attention on the women. If a woman ever intends to marry, and most do, hooking up is exactly the wrong way to go, say several recent commentators on the issue. In a 2001 survey by the Independent Women's Forum, a conservative anti-feminist think tank, authors Elizabeth Marquardt and Norval Glenn tell us that while more than four out of five college women surveyed say they want to get married, there are too many elements in college culture that "undermine the likelihood of achieving that goal." Marquardt and Glenn propose reviving a "culture of courtship" to encourage those old-fashioned dates—and that old-fashioned sexual frustration.

Laura Sessions Stepp in her book *Unhooked* claims that hooking up is "a replacement for dating," in which "intimacy is disposable"; "a way of playing at romance while controlling the unruly emotions that come with real romance." Stepp argues that "young people have virtually abandoned dating and replaced it with group get-togethers and sexual behaviors that are detached from love and commitment—and sometimes even from liking." She worries that this will make it more difficult to date, mate, fall in love, and marry. And indeed it might, for both sexes. Yet at the end of her book she offers advice only to mothers and daughters—mostly about how women should be far choosier about their dating and sexual partners, lest they permanently impair their ability to develop those relationships—ever.

Such advice ignores the pleasure-seeking behaviors and intentions of both women *and* men, and assumes that women are naturally chaste and virginal, were it not for those rapacious men. Such an image is obviously insulting to men, since it imagines them as no better than predators. And it is also probably insulting to women, who have shown themselves fully capable of seeking and enjoying sex in ways that their mothers—and certainly those grandmothers!—could never have imagined. Both women and men are pleasure-seeking creatures, especially on campus, and it lets guys entirely off the hook if the focus of all the advice is only the women.

The truth is, hooking up is not the end of the world—it's a time-out, like college. And more important, it's a political time-out; that is, it is experienced differently, and unequally, by women and men. Focusing all one's moralizing attention on young women only perpetuates that inequality, rather than challenges it.

Hooking Up: The New Norm

What these earnest warnings miss, of course, is not the opposition between hooking up and courtship, but that hooking up *is* today's culture of courtship. It is certainly not true that all the women are hooking up in order to develop relationships, nor are all guys hooking up in the hopes of avoiding precisely the relationships that the women are seeking. Most actually want relationships. But, most say, not quite yet.

Today's college students will get married—eventually. It'll be about eight years later than their mothers and fathers did. And they'll do that by choice, because before marriage they want to establish careers, enjoy relationships, and develop autonomy. The contemporary culture of courtship is not their parents' culture of courtship, but it is no less a "culture" and no less legitimate because of that.

The students I interviewed in depth following our quantitative survey were convincing on this score. Hooking up, in their minds, is not an alternative to relationships—it's the new pathway to forming relationships. Even if only a small percentage of hookups result in relationships, most relationships do begin with a hookup. For some, hooking up is most definitely in the service of a relationship—just not this particular one.

"Of course I'll eventually get married," says Anne, a Princeton junior who happens to be sitting with Dave when I speak with him. "Just not yet. Right now, I have to focus on my career, getting through medical school, establishing myself. Hooking up's about as much as I can handle. It's the means to an end, not the end itself." And with that, she gives Dave a peck on the cheek, picks up what appears to be twenty pounds of science textbooks, and is off to the lab.

Dave looks at me, shrugs his shoulders, and grins. "All the girls at Princeton are like that," he sighs. "You know that expression from, like, your generation," he eyes me warily, " 'you can look but you better not touch?' " I nod and scowl slightly at being cast as over-the-hill. "Well, around here it's more 'you can touch but you'd better not look'—as in look for a girlfriend."

Kathleen Bogle, a sociologist, argues that hooking up has become the normative path to relationships on campus. "There's something about the way people define college life as a time to party and a time to kick back," she told a journalist. "They're postponing marriage, so they have time to play the field."

Postgraduate Sex in Guyland

Playing the field takes a somewhat different shape after graduation. Though young people still go to bars or parties in groups, and some still drink a lot, fewer are slinking off to empty rooms to hook up. On the whole, post-college-aged people are returning to more traditional dating patterns. Bogle followed recent graduates of two colleges, and found that women and men exchange phone numbers or email addresses, and some time in the next few days they will contact each other and arrange to go to dinner or something more conventionally social. It turns out that hooking up in college has added a new act in an old drama, but it is hardly a new play.

Of course, the fact that most young people move beyond hooking up still doesn't neutralize its more negative aspects. Though the hookup culture may be the new norm, that still doesn't make it ideal. Even if guys are having sex in order to assuage an understandable insecurity, they are nonetheless using women. And even if women are themselves conscious sexual agents, there remains an undeniable aspect of capitulation in much of their behavior.

"Hookups are very scripted," one woman tells Laura Sessions Stepp. "You're supposed to know what to do and how to do it and how to feel during and afterward. You learn to turn everything off except your body and make yourself emotionally invulnerable."

What kind of sex is this, where a young woman prepares by shutting down and becoming invulnerable? Where a young man thinks more about his friends than about the woman he's having sex with, or even than his own pleasure? Where everyone is so drunk they can barely remember what happened?

Much of what passes for sex in Guyland is not the kind of sex that adults—those with considerably more experience in this arena—would think of as healthy. It sometimes feels as if it doesn't build a relationship but rather is intended to be a temporary stand-in for one. Nor does it seem to be particularly good sex. And the real skills that young people will need as they take on adult sexual relationships rarely feature in the hookup culture. They're not learning how to ask for what they want, or how to listen to their partners, how to keep monogamous sex interesting, how to negotiate pleasure, how to improve their techniques. And while much of adult sexuality is also a learn-as-you-go endeavor, that doesn't mean there isn't plenty of room for advice and counsel.

Yet most adults aren't talking. The more religious among us may have firmly held beliefs that dictate abstinence and tolerate no middle ground, while the more liberal among us may give our adolescent children books that explain the physiological aspects of what they need to know but say nothing of the emotional component inherent in sexuality. But rarely do mature adults actively engage their sons and daughters in the kinds of candid conversations that might actually prove useful to them. Rarely do we talk about a sexuality that can be both passionate and ethical; rarely do we even explain that there is such a thing as ethical sexuality that doesn't promote or even include abstinence as a goal. Instead, the whole subject is so shrouded in embarrassment and discomfort that we generally avoid it, hoping that our kids will figure it out for themselves without too much trouble in the meantime. Lucky for us they often do.

But not always.

10 | PREDATORY SEX AND PARTY RAPE

The words ring in my ears today as if they were just spoken. "When it comes to sex, never take no for an answer." Or this: "Look, girls have to say no, even if they want to do it. It's part of being a girl. So if they say no, they're really saying yes. They still really want you to . . ."

Growing up in the suburbs in the 1960s, I heard those phrases as often as I heard my friends reciting the lyrics of the latest Beatles single or the line score of the Yankees games. Hippie or preppie, stoner or jock, nerd or hood, it's how guys talked about what guys talked about.

What I learned in the locker rooms of my youth was, "Tell her anything if you think it'll get you laid." I can still hear my friend Billy, who wrestled at 135 pounds, giving advice to his younger and lighter mat partner:

If she wants to hear that you love her, tell her you love her. If she wants to hear that you'll marry her, tell her you'll marry her. The most important thing is to keep going. Don't stop. If she says no, keep going. If she pushes your hand away, keep going. You only stop if she hits you.

I took this advice seriously; it constituted a how-to manual, a sort of mixed-company etiquette primer—"Mr. Manners", you might say. I called it, as did we all, "dating." And I followed it assiduously, although, alas, not especially successfully.

In the years since, of course, the rules have changed. Completely. My generation's "dating etiquette" is now called sexual assault. You can't keep going if she says no. You can't keep going if she says stop. You can't keep going if she pushes your hand away, or if she hits you. Today, guys know that the rules are completely different.

Or do they?

When I mentioned this story to my class recently at Stony Brook, one of the guys looked up at me and shook his head sadly. "It's not 'don't stop until she hits you.' It's 'don't stop until she *hurts* you.'" Time and again, on college campuses, guys told me something similar: Girls "have to say no" to protect their reputations, they "mean yes, even if they say no," and "if she's drunk and semiconscious, she's willing."

"It's really confusing," says Jake, who graduated from Yale two years ago.

I mean, like, really *really* confusing. On the one hand, like every week you have some dorm seminar or lecture on sexual assault, and like a constant buzz about what's "appropriate" and all, and on the other hand you go to a party on the weekend and it's like everything they said to avoid, everything that is, like, completely illegal and off-limits.

"Like what?" I ask.

Like trying to get girls drunk so they'll have sex with you. Like, I dunno, like lying to them, or like telling them how interested you are in them and how much you like them and all, when it's completely not true, and all you really want to do is have sex with them and then get the hell out of there.

"Omigod, the lies we tell," says Bill, his roommate and fellow grad, a big grin on his face.

Like sometimes I can't believe what I've done to get laid. Like, I've said "I'll only put it in a little"—can you fucking-believe that? Like, "I won't come in your mouth." Like . . .

At this point, though, Bill begins to look a little sheepish.

Like, well, look, I know this isn't PC and all, but a couple of times I've pushed girls' heads down on me, and like one time this girl was so drunk she was near passed out, and I kind of dragged her into my room and had sex with her. When she sort of came to a little bit, she was really upset and started crying and asked why I had done that. I think I said something like, "because you were so pretty" or some bullshit, but really it was because, well, because I was drunk and wanted to get laid. And she was, like, there.

Bill's comment is actually a little more than "not PC"; in most jurisdictions, he could be arrested for sexual assault. To many guys this ambiguity seems like a gray area, a zone where it is not absolutely clear where consent ends and assault begins. Often women agree that the lines get fuzzy and boundaries blur.

But Bill's confession also suggests at least one instance when this gray area is a fraud. Bill was not interested in the girl. He was interested in getting laid. And she was, as he puts it, ". . . like, there." The problem for guys like Bill is that even though they may think that the absence of clear refusal implies consent regardless of circumstances, young women are finally learning that what has been done is "assault."

Is it any wonder that rates of sexual assault are so high?

The Guy Code insists that men get as much sex as they can. And with hooking up the new norm on campus, they may assume that girls want the same thing. Getting drunk, and getting her drunk, is seen as foreplay—whatever happens after that has already been declared consensual.

Of course, not all guys are like Bill. And there are certainly cases where the gray area really is a gray area. As we have seen, alcohol is often used to *create* a gray area, a realm of plausible deniability where no one supposedly has to take responsibility for what he (or she) wanted to do. Alex, a senior at Michigan State, learned this the hard way. One night at a party in an off-campus apartment he and a girl got drunk—really drunk. He liked her, and he thought she liked him. They were dancing, getting close, kissing. She went into one of the bedrooms and lay down on the bed. The guy whose room it was asked her to get up, and she did. She went back into the living room and they danced more, drank more. Then she went back in the bedroom and lay down again. Alex thought it was because she wanted to have sex with him, so he "helped" her get undressed, then he got undressed. And when, moments before intercourse happened, she said, "What are you doing? Stop!" he stopped. She started crying. He apologized, explaining that he thought she wanted to have sex. She became hysterical, and accused him of attempted rape. Several days later she filed attempted rape charges with the local police. And though the charges were eventually dropped, it was not before his parents, her parents, and their lawyers all became involved.

Alex is not a rapist. He's a nice guy, a decent guy, who likes women and would like to have a girlfriend, or at least a "friend with benefits." He hasn't had a lot of sex, doesn't "score" every weekend with a different woman. To his thinking, he didn't do anything wrong, and he certainly didn't do anything that every other guy he knows would have done under the circumstances. In fact, he did less—when she asked him to stop, he actually stopped.

In a more traditional dating culture, boundaries are in place to protect both men and women from falling into this kind of gray area. Premarital sex certainly occurs, but it does so in the context of a relationship. In today's hookup culture, where sex is a casual affair that needn't be preceded by any kind of relationship whatsoever, where sexual encounters often occur after huge amounts of alcohol have been consumed by both parties, and where even consensual sex is marked by vagueness, lack of judgment, and misunderstanding, it is no wonder that cases like Alex's occur with alarming frequency.

Driven to Distraction: The Numbers Game

The public conversation about sexual assault on campus has primarily been a battle over numbers. In the 1980s, psychologist Mary Koss conducted some surveys that found what appeared at the time to be astonishingly high rates of unwanted, forced, or coerced sex among college students. The results were not easy to convert into tidy soundbites, and sparked hyperbolic and near-frenzied responses from both feminists and anti-feminists over the extent of campus sexual assault.

In the early 1990s, feminist writers like Naomi Wolf and Robin Warshaw drew on Koss's research to proclaim a virtual epidemic of campus sexual assault. They claimed that one in four women had had an experience that met the legal definition of rape, even if "rape" was not the term she used to describe that experience. Most women saw what had happened as a mistake, a date gone bad, a guy who got carried away. They blamed themselves for leading him on, for giving mixed signals, for not really knowing what they wanted, for being too drunk to say no clearly.

Quickly did the anti-feminists jump in to gainsay the results of these studies. Writers like Cathy Young and Camille Paglia pooh-poohed what they regarded as inflated numbers, and laid the blame for campus sexual assault entirely at the feet of the women. Some argued that inflated date rape statistics are symptomatic of campus feminism run amok; man-haters encouraging coddled liberal women at elite universities to impose their prudishly Pollyanna view of sexuality on the rest of the nation. Katie Roiphe's 1993 book, *The Morning After: Sex, Fear, and Feminism*, argued that young women must take responsibility for whatever happens to them for better or for worse.

Roiphe, Young, and Paglia all argue that boys will be boys, and that to constrain male sexuality is to do a disservice to young men. As Paglia explains, today's female students have the temerity to believe "they can do anything, go anywhere, say anything, wear anything." Well, she says, "No, they can't."

A woman going to a fraternity party is walking into Testosterone Flats, full of prickly cacti and blazing guns. . . . A girl who lets herself get dead drunk at a fraternity party is a fool. A girl who goes upstairs alone with a brother at a fraternity party is an idiot. Feminists call this 'blaming the victim.' I call it common sense. . . .

Every woman must take personal responsibility for her sexuality. . . . She must be prudent and cautious about where she goes and with whom. When she makes a mistake, she must accept the consequences and, through self-criticism, resolve never to make that mistake again.

But even if women could live their lives according to Camille Paglia's credo, the fact remains that women on college campuses are "at greater risk for rape and other forms of sexual assault than women in the general population or in a comparable age group." Regardless of how one tries to parse the numbers, the seamy underside of the campus sexual culture is sexual assault.

The numbers do have a story to tell. Whether they are as inflated as Wolf and other feminist activists report, or as low as even the more conservative estimates of Young, Paglia, and others promoting a more *caveat emptor* approach, they're still high. Perhaps the most reliable study, from the National Institute of Justice in 1997, found that between one-fifth and one-quarter of women are the victims of attempted or completed rape while in college. More than half were by a guy that the woman was dating. If they were "only" 10 percent instead of 20 percent that would be extraordinarily high. Even if they were 5 percent, that would *still* be extraordinarily high.

And at the same time, most everyone acknowledges that sexual assaults on campus are drastically underreported. In Bonnie Fisher's N.I.J. study, only 5 percent of the completed or attempted rapes were reported to law enforcement officials (either local or campus police) although two-thirds told someone about it. Only one-tenth of the rapes that are actually reported to campus crisis hot lines are also reported to the police. Most are reported only to friends, or to no one at all.

Why do so few women report sexual assault? There is a common list: shame, self-blame, fear of reprisal, fear of being ostracized. But remember, nine out of ten offenders were known to the victim—usually a classmate, a friend, or an acquaintance—and it's clearly easier to report strangers than a person you know. According to the survey, 12.8 percent of completed rapes, 35 percent of attempted rapes, and 22.9 percent of threatened rapes take place on a date. And somewhere around half of both perpetrators and victims had been drinking. Alcohol has a way of weakening resolve for taking police action.

Also, while researchers find that college women remain more frightened by the prospect of stranger rape, and curtail their activities to minimize their risk of stranger rape, the most treacherous time for a college woman is when she is at a party, drinking, with people she thinks she knows. Among the various categories of acquaintance rape—rape while on a date, rape by a former or current intimate partner, or rape in a nonparty, nondate situation—the most common of all is "party rape," which is defined by the Justice Department as a rape that "occurs at an off-campus house or on- or off-campus fraternity and involves . . . plying a woman with alcohol or targeting an intoxicated woman."

So it's entirely possible that women, as well as men, are likely to misperceive what would legally qualify as a rape or attempted rape as a "date gone bad." In fact, according to Fisher's survey, less than half of the women who had experienced something that fits the legal definition of rape actually described what happened to them as rape.

Yet one has to engage in some strange epistemology to conclude that if *they* don't define it as rape, it wasn't rape. For most crimes, the subjective experience of the victim plays little role in the labeling of a crime. A robbery is a robbery, whether or not you were dressed so nicely that the mugger thought you wanted it. It's still a robbery even if, in your drunken foolishness, you walked through a bad part of town in the middle of the night with an expensive camera around your neck, or if you "consented" in your fright and said, "Here, take my money!" Crimes don't often depend on victim confirmation; there are legally set standards that define it. But somehow when it comes to sex crimes against women, whether or not the victims actually label it a crime seems of paramount importance.

It's probably true that the rates of sexual assault have climbed recently not because more women are being raped or assaulted but because more women now recognize that what happened to them is not "a date gone horribly wrong," but an assault. What's more, they know that if they complain about it they are far more likely to be believed than were only a decade ago. Pat Connell, a 25-year veteran of the Cal-Berkeley Police Department, gives a more impressionistic version. Sexual assault, when he first started, was "almost always a guy jumping out of the bushes." Now, he says, "what we get are date-rape cases. It's the biggest problem we have here."

It's not that current rates have soared especially high. It's that those rates in the past were so artificially low—based on women either not recognizing the assault as being out of bounds, or feeling afraid to make a public issue of it by going to the police. Especially if she was likely to be blamed all over again for being in the wrong place, wearing the wrong clothes, or drinking the wrong drinks. Who needs that on top of everything else?

Guys and Sexual Assault

What's wrong with the date-rape debate is that until recently men were not included in the discussion. This changed when UCLA psychologist Neil Malamuth surveyed male students' "attraction to sexual aggression." In his research, between 16 percent and 20 percent of the male respondents said they would commit rape if they could be certain of getting away with it. That's one in six. When Malamuth changed the word "rape" to "force a woman to have sex," between 36 percent and 44 percent said they would—as long as they could be certain they wouldn't get caught. In another study, 15 percent of college men said they actually had used force at least once to obtain intercourse—a rate which does seem to corroborate the statistics provided by women.

The question for us, then, is why? Why would nearly two of every five college males in this study commit sexual assault if they believed they could get away with it? For one thing, it has to do with some distorted ideas about women and sex. As we have seen, many men subscribe to what sexual assault counselors call "date rape myths"—

that women want sex just as much as men do but are socialized to say no even if they mean yes; that women like to be forced to have sex; that drunk women are "fair game." In some interesting research in Germany, psychologists found that "as long as rape myths are not openly challenged in social interactions, men who endorse rape myths may assume that their own beliefs are shared by many others." These distortions can lead men to think that a sexual assault is simply a sort of after-the-fact change of mind by a girl who really did want to, but then thought better of it.

As we have also seen, for many guys the drive to score is a male-male competitive drive, a sort of "keeping up with the Joneses" around sex. Guys' incessant predation turns out to be a form of compensation—a way for guys to keep up with impossibly high, but imagined, rates of sexual activity.

University of Kansas psychologist Charlene Muehlenhard has been studying adolescents' sexual encounters for more than a decade, and her findings underscore this idea. She found that more men (57.4 percent) than women (38.7 percent) reported that they had engaged in unwanted heterosexual intercourse due to being enticed—that is, someone made an advance that he or she had difficulty refusing. More men (33.5 percent) than women (11.9 percent) had unwanted heterosexual intercourse because they wanted to get sexual experience, wanted something to talk about, or wanted to build up their confidence. And more men (18.4 percent) than women (4.5 percent) said they engaged in heterosexual intercourse because they did not want to appear to be shy, afraid, or unmasculine or unfeminine. Peer pressure was a factor for 10.9 percent of the men but only 0.6 percent of the women.

Sometimes, as we've seen, the pressure to have sex is so great that it eclipses the pleasure. Says Mark, now 24, reminiscing about a particularly unpleasant experience in college:

> I remember there was this party, and all my buds are like telling me that there is this really hot girl who sorta likes me, and, like, I already had a girlfriend back home, but they were like all, "Who cares, dude? It's a party and she's hot!" and so I got a little drunk,

got her a little more drunk, and we had sex and like the whole time it was because I had to tell the guys I did her, you know? I didn't even really like her or anything. But they would have been on my case forever if I passed it up. I think I had sex not because I wanted to have sex, but because I wanted to have *had* sex—so I could talk about it. How fucked up is that?

Already this is a potentially toxic brew of misinformation (beliefs about other guys' sexual activity) and disinformation (date rape myths). But it takes a little extra to push perceptions into activity: license. Women may be vulnerable to male predation, but only if the men exploit that vulnerability.

Some argue that sexual exploitation is a masculine trait, that men are hardwired from millennia of evolution to try and get over on someone for personal gain; that having sex with as many women as possible, with or without their consent, is the most successful strategy for ensuring your own genetic immortality. Of course, there are some evolutionary imperatives, deeply ingrained from millennia of adaptation. But while evolution may explain the largest scale patterns of human interaction, there is no possible way that it explains what will happen this weekend at that fraternity party on campus at State or Tech. There is, after all, such a thing, equally imperative from an evolutionary standpoint, which is called human agency, or, to be brief, *choice*. Rape is a choice, not a biological program.

And so, from an evolutionary standpoint, what is significant is that *most men don't make this choice*. Most men do not commit sexual assault. Most men do not have a date "go bad" or have her "change her mind afterward." Even if the most hyperbolic statistics were true and one-fourth of all college women were assaulted, that would mean that three-fourths were not. And if even *all* of the men surveyed by Neil Malamuth who said they would force a girl to have sex if they knew they could get away with it actually did it, it would still be "only" half of them. What kind of pathetic evolutionary imperative would it be if half of all members of the group don't do it?

Men choose to act this way. And they choose to act this way because they believe it to be justified and they believe that other guys, whose approval is the whole point of this exercise, will reward them for it. They choose to act because of ideology—the beliefs they have about what they should or shouldn't do, what they can or can't do, and why. In other words, what enables men to choose to commit rape and call it something else are some of the core elements of Guyland—the cultures of entitlement, silence, and protection.

Getting Over as Getting Back

Guys believe that they are entitled to women's bodies, entitled to sex. Unfortunately for them, a significant number of women don't see it that way. And, as we've seen, when entitlement is thwarted guys seek revenge. Curiously, while psychologists and feminists and the entire legal system see male sexual aggression as the initiation of violence, guys describe it in a different way—not as initiation but as retaliation. What are they retaliating against? The power that women have over them.

To listen to guys speak, it's women who have the power in sex, not men. Says Dave, a 25-year-old computer consultant in Chicago:

> Oh, definitely girls. They have all the power. They have the big power—the power to say no. I want them, I want sex with them, and they're the ones who decide whether it'll happen or not. Some bitch decides whether or not I get laid. I don't decide, she does. It's not fair.

Dave began his description in a sort of temperate voice, without much rancor. But a few seconds later, he looked frustrated and mad, and the tone of his voice had risen to match. Again and again, as guys described their feelings to me, they would at some point stop *describing* their feelings and actually start *feeling* them. Anger lies just below the surface of a conversation about sexual politics; it is remarkably easy to tap, and to activate into full-scale rage.

Tim Beneke, a journalist, once traveled around the country interviewing men about their views on rape. These men had never committed rape and yet the violence of their language is arresting. Here's what one 23-year-old who worked in a company in San Francisco told him:

> Let's say I see a woman and she looks really pretty and really clean and sexy and she's giving off very feminine, sexy vibes. I think, wow I would love to make love to her, but I know she's not interested. It's a tease. A lot of times a woman knows that she's looking really good and she'll use that and flaunt it and it makes me feel like she's laughing at me and I feel degraded. . . . If I were actually desperate enough to rape somebody it would be from wanting that person, but also it would be a very spiteful thing, just being able to say 'I have power over you and I can do anything I want with you' because really I feel that they have power over me just by their presence. Just the fact that they can come up to me and just melt me makes me feel like a dummy, makes me want revenge.

Guy after guy seemed to understand how their reactions to women made them feel surprisingly aggressive. Here was Stan, another guy Beneke interviewed:

> Growing up, I definitely felt teased by women. I think for the most part women knew I was attracted to them so women would sit in a certain way or give three-quarter beaver shot or give you a little bit of tit and maybe not give much more, or lift their skirts a certain way. I definitely felt played with, used, manipulated, like women were testing their power over me. I hated it with a passion! With a *fucking* passion!

These sorts of replies—which seemed to invert the power dynamics between men and women that analysts, feminists, and social scientists had been observing—stunned Beneke. Why does it look like men are in power when they constantly talk about being powerless? He looked at the language men use to describe female attractiveness. Women are "ravishing," or "stunning," she's a "bombshell" or a "knockout"; she's "dressed to kill," a real "femme fatale." Men describe themselves as being "blown away" and "knocked out." As suggested in metaphor, women's beauty is perceived as violence to men: Men use violence to even the playing field, to restore equality.

Recently, *Men's Health* magazine surveyed 444 readers (97 percent of whom were male). Forty-nine percent said that there were women in their office whose manner of dress was "pointedly provocative." And one-third believed that men should report such women for sexual harassment.

In a letter to the editor of the *New York Times* denouncing sexual harassment guidelines, William Muehl, a retired professor at the Yale Divinity School claimed that:

> From the moment a young male reaches puberty, he is bombarded with sexual stimuli by the culture in general and his female peers in particular. The way women dress and conduct themselves makes it virtually impossible for men to overlook their physical charms. Nothing is more absurd than a television talk show in which a feminine panel denounces sexual harassment, while dressed in such a way as to exhibit acres of its own flesh.

Muehl concluded by approvingly quoting "one college chaplain" who claimed "the way young women dress in the spring constitutes a sexual assault upon every male within eyesight of them."

Yet even the angriest of men, the most disempowered, would stop short of sexual assault if not for the culture of silence among his peers. Transgressing boundaries, ignoring a woman when she says no, or doesn't say yes, or is too drunk to know what exactly is happening to her—this doesn't happen in a vacuum, one guy and one girl. There are often bystanders whose silence might easily be mistaken for approval.

Usually the bystander absolves himself of any complicity. "Hey, don't look at me," he shouts in protest, "I never raped anybody." And he's usually right. But neither did he intervene at a party when it seemed clear that someone was about to be raped. Nor did he refrain from spreading the rumor about some girl who got "trained" or gang banged, nor say to anyone that he thought such behavior was gross and wrong, let alone illegal.

Rather, here is what he is more likely to say:

Girls are continually fed drinks of alcohol. It's mainly to party but my roomies are also aware of the inhibition-lowering effects. I've seen an old roomie block doors when girls want to leave his room; and other times I've driven women home who can't remember much of an evening yet sex did occur. Rarely if ever has a night of drinking for my roommate ended without sex. I know it isn't necessarily and assuredly sexual assault, but with the amount of liquor in the house, I question the amount of consent a lot.

That's one guy's description of a party at his fraternity house. He questions it, but doesn't ever have a chat with his roommate, nor does he intervene if he thinks there is the possibility of assault. This is where the dynamics of Guyland are in plain view: Bros Before Hos.

The culture of silence both enables the worst of the guys in their predatory behaviors and at the same time prevents the best of the guys from speaking up about what they really think about all this sexual predation. Challenging your roommates, stepping in to stop sex from happening when a woman is clearly too drunk either to consent or to refuse sex, is a betrayal of brotherhood. In a sexual culture where men and women are seen as being on opposite teams, where men are mandated to "get over" on women and women are mandated to "protect themselves" from sexual assault, scoring one for the team is crucial. If you refuse to "score" yourself, you are at least expected not to block the shot for your buddies. In this setup, defending or protecting a woman is worse than switching teams, it's an act of treason.

Even when sexual assault is called by name and reported, and when legal action is pursued, the culture of protection often kicks in to minimize the damage or to deflect responsibility away from the perpetrators and onto the victims. For example, in 2001, a group of college football players and recruits were accused of gang rape at the University of Colorado. I learned about this case when I was asked to be an expert witness for two of these women, Lisa Simpson and Anne Gilmore. After reading close to 5,000 pages of materials, including court testimony, depositions by the women, the athletes, and university officials, I was stunned by how well the case illustrated the cultures of entitlement and silence that surround sexual assault and muffle the cries of the women in a culture of protection. The collusion of athletic department officials and the corrupt complicity of university administrators who were unable or unwilling to challenge their winning football team was even more astonishing. Eventually they all—the coach, the athletic director, the president, and the chancellor—resigned, but not before they revealed exactly how the culture of protection operates.

In early December 2001, a group of high-school football recruits arrived on the campus of the University of Colorado for a weekend of recruitment activities. The university's football team had gone from being the doormat of the Big 12 to being a major collegiate powerhouse, able to compete with perennial conference powers like Oklahoma and Nebraska. The university had also become a hotbed of sexual assault by high-profile athletes. Several cases had been reported and adjudicated through the 1990s—a badge of dishonor that so irked alumnus Rick Reilly that he wrote a series of exposés in *Sports Illustrated*, where he was a columnist.

On the night of December 7, several of these recruits and a few of the team members had sex with a few female students at an off-campus residence. The next day, three of these women brought criminal charges against the men for rape and sexual assault, and they subsequently sued the university for facilitating the gang rape and failing to prevent it (which is actionable by law if the university "knew, or should have known" that such an assault was likely and made no moves to prevent it).

When the recruits first arrived on campus, they were met by team members whose charge it was to show them a good time, and encourage them to come and play for Colorado. Sometimes, at other schools, recruits are also met by pretty coeds who are paid by the alumni association to "escort" the recruits. Everyone knows that these escorts will have sex with them.

One of the recruits told the police after the assaults of December 7 that the football players promised to get him sex. "They told me that . . . we gonna all get laid and you know. See how . . . see how we do it so you can all come here so we can party like this' every weekend." He continued, "They told us, you know, this is what you get when you come to Colorado."

His expectations raised, he became angry when he hadn't had sex after one day. One player recalled that he became "kind of upset" and said he "didn't have fun because he didn't hook up with any women." And another player testified that the recruit "came up to me and was, like—he goes, 'What's up on the girls? You didn't give me no girls.' " A party was hastily arranged by some players and one or two of their female friends (not Simpson or Gilmore) who were themselves groupies.

Lisa Simpson, Anne Gilmore, and a couple of other girls had been hanging out at home in their pajamas that evening, playing some drinking games, and finally, at about 1 a.m., they decided to go to sleep. They were in their rooms, in their beds, with the lights off, when suddenly a group of players and recruits knocked on their door. Simpson, groggy and half-asleep, turned over in her bed to find a huge guy standing over her. "I'm a recruit," he said. "Show me a good time. Suck my dick."

Let's be honest: of course, there are groupies on many college campuses, a few women who hang out in various locales frequented by players, and who are willing participants in sexual encounters with them. College athletes are celebrities, after all, and like rock bands or movie stars—or even elected officials—their celebrity status, not to mention their wealth and notoriety for partying, is a sexual turn-on.

But this was not a case about groupies. This was a case of a planned "party" whose sole purpose was to get some black recruits some sex with some white girls. (The distasteful racist undercurrent is quite evident.) The players planned it with a couple of their male friends, and one female friend suggested Simpson's apartment, and then brought the recruits to the women's place. The only problem was that no one had told the women that they were "invited" to the same party.

The case eventually was resolved: Several of the recruits were not admitted to the university, and the players pleaded guilty to reduced charges and were sentenced to community service. That community service, incidentally, consisted of working out in the weight room on the chance that visitors might want a tour of the facility—which even the athletic director called a "sham." That's how the culture of protection works.

Was the football program chastened, the entire athletic department humiliated, the university disgraced? Eventually. Eventually, the coach resigned, as did the athletic director, the chancellor, and even the president—all proclaiming their lack of accountability. And eventually, the university settled the case with Lisa Simpson and the others for over $1 million, not because the university admitted any wrongdoing, but because they said it wanted to put the matter to rest. Responsibility was so diffused that a gang rape seemed to be nobody's fault.

And before that, when the story broke, everyone did more than run for cover; they tried to throw a blanket over the entire event. A year after his participation in the assault on Lisa Simpson, the football program tried again to get one of the participating recruits admitted. He was a good player, after all. Perhaps the best illustration of this culture of protection came from Joyce Lawrence, one of the members of the commission that was charged with investigating the recruiting scandal. "The question I have for the ladies in this is why they are going to parties like this and drinking or taking drugs and putting themselves in a very threatening or serious position," she said. (Remember, Simpson was in her PJs, in her bed, with the lights out.) Attitudes like this are what sustain predatory sexual entitlement.

Greeks and Jocks

Nowhere is the brotherhood more intense, the bonding more intimate and powerful, or the culture of protection more evident than among athletes and fraternity members. Greeks and jocks live at the epicenter of Guyland. It's one reason why the risk of sexual assault is higher among these high-prestige all-male groups. The example above is not an isolated event, not as much of an anomaly as we might like to believe. One survey of twenty universities with Division I athletic programs found that male athletes comprised 3.7 percent of the student population, but also comprised 19 percent of sexual assaults reported to the Judicial Affairs Office.

It's not the simple fact of being in an all-male group. There are plenty of all-male groups in which such activities seem to happen rarely, if at all. Members of the golf and tennis teams are rarely accused of sexual assault, let alone gang rape, nor are members of the all-male computer programmers club or math team. Nor are all fraternities equally at risk to promote and support sexual assault. In a fascinating study, sociologists Ayres Boswell and Joan Spade found they could distinguish between "rape prone" and "rape free" fraternities in part by the ideologies that the guys held and their beliefs in rape myths. Just like among athletes, higher-prestige fraternities promoted a higher level of sexual entitlement.

Campus athletes are especially prone to these ideas of entitlement. Journalist Robert Lipsyte calls it a "jockocracy"—a quasi-aristocratic culture in which privilege and prestige and other rewards accrue inordinately to athletes, and in which, therefore, they come to feel entitled to special treatment. One former professional basketball player put it this way:

> What happens when you come from nothing, or relatively nothing, once you're presented with something—in this case the natural, or unnatural adulation that comes from adults patting you on the back or sliding through classes, all that other stuff—you begin . . . to think that the world is handing out things to you . . .

As Edward Goldolf, an expert on campus sexual assault, put it,

> If you're an athlete in college, you're given scholarships, a nice dorm, doctors, trainers, a lot of support and attention from fans and cheerleaders who ogle you. That sense of privilege influences you, and some guys may then think "I deserve something for this. I can take women, the rules don't apply to me." They feel they're above the law.

In one study, 30 percent of Cornell football players reported high levels of sexual entitlement—a statistic that prompted the university to institute mandatory annual sexual assault awareness workshops for players.

In 1987, the NCAA imposed the "death penalty" on Southern Methodist University after it was revealed that football boosters had paid sorority women up to $400 a weekend to have sex with high-school football recruits. "I thought the young woman was one of the team groupies who hang out with team members and do whatever [the team members] want," one of these recruits said of a woman who was gang raped during a recruiting visit.

When questioned about these sorts of practices, coaches reply not with a moral compassion for the young women, but with a fear that if they *don't* do it, all the schools that *do* will gain a competitive advantage by getting all the good football players. In a radio interview, for example, Terry Holland, former basketball coach and athletic director at the University of Virginia, echoed these sentiments when he commented on the hostess programs and other "use" of female students:

> I think if you said to every AD in the country, "We're going to eliminate this practice of allowing whatever the group is called on campus to show football players and basketball players and other recruits around," every AD would buy into it immediately. The problem is it's very difficult for any institution, or even any conference, to react unilaterally to these types of suggestions because the competition is so fierce . . .

When one of the Boston Celtics was accused of rape, Massachusetts Superior Court Judge Robert Barton eloquently described this culture of protection:

> The athletes are spoiled. They're pampered. . . . They've been spoiled everywhere they've gone. Everybody has covered for them. The coach has covered for them. The professors have covered for them. The police cover for them . . . to make sure that the star

quarterback or basketball player or baseball player is going to be able to play next week.

But there is plenty of evidence that implementing successful sexual assault prevention policies for athletes and eliminating the opportunities for such assaults (especially during recruiting visits) does not result in uncompetitive athletic programs. Athletic directors at a few premier universities with nationally competitive football programs—including the University of Southern California, Miami, Penn State, Ohio State, Michigan, UCLA, and Stanford—have instituted mandatory sexual assault prevention programs for their players. Most programs use outside experts; some are done by the university police department. Interestingly, though it's important that coaches be briefed both before and after, they generally do not attend the programs. If they are present, the athletes pay little attention to the presentation and focus entirely on the coaches' reactions. At Stanford, one of the more enlightened athletic programs in the nation, the players' *parents* are encouraged to attend these sessions with their sons and they are housed in the same hotel—and often on the same floor—as the recruits.

Many of these competitive programs have abandoned the female hostess programs that Colorado has only recently abandoned. As Mike Karowski, assistant athletic director at Notre Dame, told a reporter:

We've decided not to have a bunch of women hosting football players. There's no need. In fact there's no need to have one of these programs anywhere. We're not selling sex here, and when you present a group of attractive females to a high school football player, that's the impression you're giving them.

In order for such a program to work, though, the culture of protection must be challenged. And that can only happen when not only the campus administration but also the coaches make it a priority. "When the coach gives a clear and consistent message that such behavior will not be tolerated," one trainer told me, "and backs it up with immediate action, you set a climate that can prevent sexual assault. Maybe not completely. But better." As one head coach of a Division I basketball team explained it to me:

> Look, my team is only as good as next year's recruiting class. We need to recruit the best kids out there. Gotta get 'em. And if we have one screwup, one dumb guy who does something really stupid, there are a dozen parents who are going to say, "The heck with this guy and his program, I want something better for my boy." I want to prevent sexual assault because I don't want those kids going somewhere else.

One coach who gets it appears to have been Pete Carroll, coach at USC. When he coached the New England Patriots, Carroll also instituted mandatory annual sexual assault prevention training from the Mentors in Violence Prevention (MVP) Program—one of the most impressively comprehensive programs in the country.

Homosociality, Status, and Gang Rape

I'd always considered the "gang bang" a sort of urban legend. It's a staple of adolescent male lore, but I suspect it was so incomprehensible to me because it was simply impossible to fathom that a bunch of guys could stand in line, with erections, waiting their turn to have sex with a girl who actually wanted to have sex with all of them.

But gang rape is found often enough on college campuses to cause concern. Like binge drinking and hooking up, gang rapes tend to be far more rare in guys' lives after college—it seems to be a phenomenon that requires both the intense bonding of day-to-day residential homosociality (as in a single-sex dorm or fraternity house) and also the relative safety provided by the American college campus.

On campuses, the research suggests, gang rapes are most often perpetrated by men who participate in intensive all-male peer groups that foster rape-supportive behaviors and attitudes. "Gang rapes involving members of close-knit fraternities or athletic teams have been viewed as groupthink phenomena where members of high-status groups become inculcated with the groups' moral superiority, invulnerability, and consensus" write psychologists Mary Koss and John Gaines. But not only there, of course. Dorm floors and off-campus apartments work just as well.

The gang bang actually confers status for the men involved. Anthropologist Peggy Reeves Sanday had been teaching anthropology at the University of Pennsylvania for a decade when a gang rape was reported to have occurred on her own campus. She spent the next couple of years interviewing every involved party—the women, the accused men, other students, the administrators, police, and court officers—to try to understand the different "frames" that each group brought to the event. Sanday, applying the same lens that she used in studying rape in pre-industrial societies, argued that rape was a cultural vehicle that initiated men into masculine roles and circumscribed aggression of young males toward one another by redirecting it toward women. "Whenever men build and give allegiance to a mystical, enduring, all-male social group, the disparagement of women is, invariably, an important ingredient of the mystical bond, and sexual aggression the means by which the bond is renewed." It was clear to her that the woman was the vehicle for a male-male experience; gang rape is "the glue that binds the brothers to the fraternity body."

In his coming-of-age memoir, *Makes Me Wanna Holler*, former street thug and now *Washington Post* journalist Nathan McCall recounts his own participation in a gang rape. At age 14, he was invited to what his friends called "running a train." In a carefully planned scenario, a girl was invited to what she thought was a party. She was assaulted and threatened. McCall felt compelled to join, afraid of being called soft, even though he felt too guilty to actually do anything. He faked intercourse. Afterward, though, he joined in the celebration of their conquest: "It sealed our bond . . . we served notice that we were a group of up and coming young cats."

Later, he reflected on gang bangs: Yes, they involved sex, but they weren't about sex. "It was another way for a guy to show the other fellas how cold and hard he was" by "using a member of one of the most vulnerable groups of human beings on the face of the earth—black females."

Gang rape cements the relations among men. But more than that, gang rape permits a certain homoerotic contact between men. Sometimes, it actually gets a little graphic. When one participant reported his pleasure at feeling the semen of his friends inside the woman as he raped her, one senses a distinctly homoerotic component. Was the woman merely the receptacle, the vehicle by which these men could have sex with one another and still claim heterosexuality?

On campus, gang rapes are often one type of "party rape," in recognition of where and when they seem to happen. But make no mistake about it: Party rapes don't just happen. They're planned. The victim has already been selected. "She is often drunk or high on drugs—in many cases, she is nearly or totally incapacitated and unable to understand or voice consent or resistance, let alone physically fight or escape from a group of stronger people," writes Robin Warshaw. In a now-classic study, Menachem Amir found that 71 percent of the gang rapes were planned; 11 percent were partially planned. Only 16 percent were spontaneous.

Alcohol is also almost always part of the equation. Alcohol may "release pent-up aggression, dull one's perceptions, and make one more vulnerable to peer pressure," says rape expert Andrea Parrot. As we have seen, alcohol can also be a strategy to avoid responsibility. And it can be used as part of a deliberate rape strategy. As sports scholar Todd Crosset writes, "[d]rinking may be part of some men's premeditated strategy to coerce women into unwanted sex or to be violent; it may also be a convenient and socially accepted means by which men can distance themselves from their violence."

So, athletes or frat guys are more prone to gang rape not because they are athletes or frat guys, but because being frat guys or athletes confers on them an elite status that is easily translated into entitlement, and because the cement of their brotherhood is intense, and intensely sexualized, bonding.

Those same guys are often fond of quoting that stirring passage from Shakespeare's *Henry V*, in which the young king inspires his badly outnumbered and overmatched soldiers to fight at Agincourt, proclaiming "he who sheds his blood with me shall be my brother." Yes, the cement of men's bonding is, as Churchill said, composed of blood, sweat, and tears. And apparently, in some cases, semen. How debased has become King Hal's noble proclamation.

Antioch Rules

What about everyone else? Challenging the culture of entitlement, breaking through the culture of silence, and dismantling the culture of protection involves everyone on campus.

A few years ago, Antioch College, long a bastion of educational progressivism, had decided that consent to sexual activity required more than not saying no. It required that people say *yes*—to everything. Verbal consent, the new Code of Conduct stated, is required for any sexual contact that is not "mutually and simultaneously initiated." "Do not take silence as consent; it isn't," the policy stated.

When this rule was first enacted at Antioch, the reaction was overwhelmingly negative. The anti-feminist chorus howled in derision at feminist protectionism gone berserk. Charlton Heston added it to a list of campus political correctness completely out of control. Can you believe, he told an audience at Harvard in 1999, that "at Antioch College in Ohio, young men seeking intimacy with a coed must get verbal permission at each step of the process from kissing to petting to final copulation . . . all clearly spelled out in a printed college directive."

Women on college campuses generally applauded the change. Guys, however, did not seem happy at all. "If I have to ask those questions I won't get what I want," blurted out one young man to a reporter. But is explicit consent the wettest blanket ever thrown over adolescent sexual fumblings? Is hearing "yes" a turnoff? Is hearing yes to "Can I touch you there?" "Would you like me to?" "Will you lick me?" "Can I fuck you?" a guarantor of instant detumescence? Probably not.

Interestingly, when Canada introduced similar language into its *national* policy on sexual assault, no howls of protest seem to have gone up from the millions of Canadian men who were suddenly going to be deprived of that hard-earned sex. Indeed, it seems to work just fine.

And Antioch students seem to have taken their new sexual assault policy in stride. Instead of saying, "Do you want to have sex?" which, admittedly, might be a little forward for people just beginning their sexual adventure, they simply say, "Do you want to implement the policy?" Perhaps it's that sense of humor that will break the ice.

Those rules of sexual conduct—simply codifying what would be civil behavior in any decent society—only hint at the conversations we need to be having, both on campus and off. Most of the time, on campus today, the programs on "Rape Awareness" focus on women—helping them to reduce their risk of sexual abuse. Women learn that they have to pay attention to their surroundings, monitor their drinking, and make sure they are safe. Such an emphasis is, of course, necessary and important.

But also incomplete. What do such programs assume about men? They assume that *unless* women take these preventive steps to self-police, guys, those basically out-of-control predatory sexual animals, will prevail. Or, maybe a little better, that while most guys wouldn't even fantasize about sexual assault, let alone do it, neither will they lift a finger to interrupt it, challenge other guys, or in any way disturb that enabling code of silence that protects the bros, no matter what they may do to the hos.

I think we can do better, and ask a little more of men. Nowhere is this better expressed than on a "splash guard" that a colleague devised for Rape Awareness Week at his university. (A "splash guard" is placed in a urinal in a men's room to sanitize it, and prevent splatter.) He had thousands made up for every public urinal on campus with a simple and hopeful slogan: "You hold the power to stop rape in your hand."

11 | GIRLS IN GUYLAND: EYES ON THE GUYS

To ask a group of teenage girls and young women about their lives is to enter a world of entitlement and often even enthusiasm. As far as they're concerned, all those rights that their mothers and grandmothers had to fight for—the right to choose, to have control over their bodies, to enter any school, any profession, to be free of sexual harassment on the job or sexual assault on a date—are a done deal. Feminism's so over. Who needs a women's movement any more? They've already won!

They assume they'll have equal access to education and employment opportunities, and that they are just as capable as their male peers (if not more so) of achieving success. They're competing in sports with as much vitality and drive as men, and entering the job market—including the military, police and fire departments, and the political sphere—in unprecedented numbers. And no wonder—female characters like Zoey and Carly on Nick TV shows, and the acerbic Juno in the recent hit movie—are more clever by half than any of the somewhat clueless male friends and classmates.

Psychologist Dan Kindlon, author of *Alpha Girls: Understanding the*

New American Girl and How She Is Changing the World, argues that today's generation of girls, born in the early 1980s and beyond, have undergone a kind of collective psychological transformation that is the natural result of the gender equality of recent history. They are ambitious, driven, competitive, assertive, and confident as never before. "I mean, I know I can do anything, be anything, go for anything I want," says Kristy, a 17-year-old senior, a star student, and a star athlete who is headed for Princeton next year from Dalton, a prestigious private school in New York.

"I've heard it all my life. Go for it! Don't quit! You can do it. Sure, *some* people won't make it. *Some* people don't have what it takes. But me? No way. My future is wide open and I can do whatever I set my mind to do."

"How do you know?" I ask.

"I just know. It's mine."

It's true: Girls today are unlike any generation in our nation's history. Decades of change in the options for women have had their effect. They seem more entitled, empowered, and emboldened than any generation in our history.

And also somewhat myopic.

All this good news rests alongside a very different reality facing girls today. It doesn't cancel out gender disparity, especially when it comes to Guyland. Instead, the experiences of most girls and young women seem to run along a continuum, with Kindlon's Alpha Girls at one extreme. The other extreme tells a different story completely.

Consider, for example, the scene of ritual degradation called a "Circle the Fat" exercise, described by Margaret Soos, a pseudonymous ex-pledge at a California college. It is recounted in *Pledged*, journalist Alexandra Robbins's exposé of the secret life of sororities. It begins when the entire pledge class is led downstairs into the living room of the sorority house. Dressed only in their underwear, they are met by their sisters, who wear white robes. Large bed sheets cover the windows. The sisters hand them strips of white sheets and instruct them to blindfold themselves and lie facedown on the cold hardwood floor. Here's what happens next:

And that's when the men entered the room, whistling and howling . . . The men circled us . . . I was becoming disoriented and felt nauseated. Something smelled toxic. Then something cold came into contact with my thigh. I gasped. 'It's okay, baby,' said one of the men. 'I'm just helping to make you look good.' The cold moved to my inner thigh.

Some women quiver, cry out, or wince. "The fraternity guys are here to help us all become better sisters," the chapter president says. "You need to hold still and be quiet."

When the men are finished, they depart, their work of humiliation done. The pledges are led upstairs to an "education room." Their blindfolds are removed, and they stand nearly naked in front of a mirror. "There was a moment of confusion as each of us noticed that circles and 'X's' had been drawn on our bodies in permanent marker," recounts one pledge. "These [are] areas that needed some work," the pledgemaster said to them. When one girl started to sob, one of the sisters scoffed. "Don't be a ninny," she said. This is "just going to make you a better person."

Robbins writes that she originally had assumed that such rituals were the stuff of urban legend. But over and over again she heard these stories, of "Circle the Fat" and the "Bikini Weigh," in which the pledges are weighed in front of the sisterhood (or a fraternity) and the audience yells out the number displayed on the scale.

How do we reconcile the star athlete gearing up for her first semester at Princeton with the sorority sister who is so utterly preoccupied with social status that she's willing to submit to hazing rituals like those described above? Why would any young woman collaborate in her own humiliation like that?

There are plenty of girls who avoid the more dire pitfalls of female adolescence in America today—from eating disorders to self-mutilation, reckless promiscuity to binge drinking. Yet many do not. And while there are several reasons that might explain the kind of self-hating behaviors described above, none is more relevant to our conversation than the pressures exerted by the culture of Guyland.

That's right: Girls have to contend with Guyland just as much as guys do. Just as Guyland is the social world in which boys become men, so too is Guyland the context in which girls become women. How they navigate those troubled waters will do a lot more than raise or lower her self-esteem. It can determine what sort of life she will have.

Much of a girl's social status is determined by her relationship with guys, even today. To achieve high standing with guys, and thus with other girls, a girl must conform to Guyland's notions of what a girl should be. The world of girls that Robbins describes is part of Guyland. Make no mistake: Girls live in Guyland, not the other way around. Whereas guys are permanent citizens, girls are legal aliens at best. As second-class inhabitants, they are relegated to being party buddies, sex objects, or a means of access to other girls. While guys spend their time posturing for the validation of other guys, the girls who live in Guyland spend their time working tirelessly for the validation and approval of *those same guys*. Guys have the parties, supply the alcohol, and set the terms for social life. If a girl wants to play, she has to play by their rules.

Even though they may have been raised by forward-thinking mothers, many of these young women don't seem to be able to envision an alternative to Guyland, and without a different reality in mind, they can't critically analyze what is happening. Nor can they disengage without paying a high price—they have to kiss their social lives good-bye. Though there are certainly exceptions, it's hard to expect young women who are trying to find relationships, learn about their sexuality, and have fun on campus to buck the system to this extent.

Instead, each girl must negotiate Guyland for herself. She must decide when to go along with it and when to resist. Will she acquiesce and be accepted as a "babe," or will she defy it and be branded a "bitch"? Will she bond with her girlfriends and thrive in an atmosphere of female solidarity, or will she abandon her friends every time a new guy expresses an interest in her? Will she defend and protect her sisters, or will she betray them? Will she even think of them as her sisters?

Girls are necessary to Guyland. They enable guys, legitimate guys' behavior, normalize it, and make it seem natural and inevitable. To fully understand Guyland, we need to understand how women participate

in it, how they keep it going, and how they also, and might more effectively, resist it.

Sisterhood Is Powerless: The Sorority as Microcosm

From their earliest initiations into the world of Queen Bees, BFFs, and
cliques, girls learn two important messages: 1) after family, the bonds of
friendship with other women are the most durable and important bonds
of your life, and 2) your friends can turn on you in a heartbeat, they
are not to be trusted because they just might sell you out. Of course,
girls do form amazing—and amazingly resilient—friendships. And they
also betray each other. Young women embrace that contradiction, learn
to trust and not to trust, to reveal weakness and then be ostracized
for it, to share their secrets and find that suddenly everyone knows.
Young women want *Sex and the City*, but they get it coupled with *Mean
Girls*.

There is no doubt that women help to create the male-female
dynamics that animate Guyland. There is no doubt that women spend
an enormous amount of time policing the behaviors of their friends
and classmates. It may even be true that the closer the friendship, the
more closely women scrutinize each other's behavior. And, sure, part
of this scrutiny has to do with the dynamics of girls' lives themselves.
But the question remains: Who benefits when girls are unsupportive
and untrustworthy of each other, creating hierarchies to promote themselves at the expense of the others? Who benefits from this lack of
sisterhood?

In sorority rituals like the "Circle the Fat" or "Bikini Weigh," young
women are learning a valuable life lesson, and it's not about where their
cellulite is. They are also learning that men are the judges of attractiveness and that their so-called "sisters" are willing to betray them for
the approval and "fun" of their fraternity pals. They are learning, as
Rosalind Wiseman put it in *Queen Bees & Wannabes*, that "girls' social
hierarchy increasingly traps girls in a cycle of craving boys' validation,
pleasing boys to obtain that validation, and betraying the friends who
truly support them."

Girls have to play by the guys' rules. First, they have to be pretty, cute, and thin. Margaret Soos, whose description of the "Circle the Fat" ritual I discussed earlier, describes rush events in her sorority during which the heavier or less perfect sisters were forced to hang out in the house's kitchen, lest they be seen by pert and pretty potential pledges. In the spring of 2007, one sorority at DePauw University in Indiana purged all members who didn't fit the image that the national sorority now wanted to present. The "rejects" included girls who were overweight and minority students. Such concern was prompted by some suspicions that the prestige of the sorority on campus, especially in the eyes of the prestigious fraternities, had been slipping. A membership review by Delta Zeta's national administration invited a dozen members to remain living in the house—and twice that many were invited to leave. During a rush party, the national headquarters invited some "slender" members from Indiana University in nearby Bloomington to participate in place of the rejected women. Such a shameful display by a national sorority frantic about its image suggests something crucial: The core claims of eternal bonds of sisterhood are sometimes utterly hollow.

Second, girls definitely have to drink. The Commission on Substance Abuse at Colleges and Universities found that 76 percent of those women who did not binge drink in high school became binge drinkers if they joined a sorority—compared with less than 25 percent of those women who did not join one. Fraternity or sorority membership remains the best single predictor of binge drinking on campus.

And, finally, girls had better supply fresh meat. It's expected that sorority sisters will check out the first-year women, approach those who are hot or cool—that is, sexy or otherwise socially interesting— and invite them to the fraternity parties, reassuring these possibly wary young women that the guys are cool and friendly and will treat them with respect. The guys, as we've seen, often have other plans.

Many sororities and fraternities link up and share parties and social activities. The sororities become "Little Sisters" to the "Big Brother" fraternity guys. The Little Sisters will see themselves as "insiders" in the fraternity nexus, and, as such, entitled to the protection of the fraternity brothers from the potential sexual predation that might be accorded to women who are "outsiders." It's the outsiders, sociologist Mindy Stombler found in her study of Little Sister programs, who are pressured to have sex—often by the Little Sisters themselves!

But sometimes it does cross a line. Sometimes sisters even turn sisters out. In 1997, Robbins reports, a sorority girl announced that her pledge class had to sleep with an entire fraternity at another college. "You have to sleep with the brothers here in order for you to cross over," the pledges were told. "That's your duty." At first, one girl thought it was a joke. But when she was told again that all of the pledges had to have sex with the fraternity brothers—as well as that fraternity's pledges—she refused and depledged.

Girls learn, through experiences like these, where their sisters' allegiances really lie—with the guys. At one university, a sorority convinced a sister who was raped at a fraternity party not to report the rape because if she did, the fraternity brothers would "hate" them and wouldn't invite them to parties anymore. The pressure to be in good standing with the guys turned out to be far greater than the pressure to protect and defend their "sister." Guyland depends on female collaborators—if at least some women think that what they do is okay, then the women who don't can be dismissed as being uptight or bitchy.

These are extreme examples. But if this is happening in sororities, where young women join expressly because of the claims of sisterhood and vows of eternal friendship, you can imagine that it's happening throughout the other arenas where young women come of age in Guyland. And it is. Consider how some wannabe girls will mercilessly tease a fat girl, or a flat-chested girl, or any girl who doesn't look perfectly perky—and then immediately look to see if any boys saw her do it, just to make sure it registered. (This is the same dynamic as a male bully who waits for an audience of potential bystanders before launching his attack.) Or how guys make friends with girls—because they want to have sex with that girl's friend.

In Guyland, too often sisterhood can be powerless. Yet female solidarity is both a problem and a solution. There have always been women who collude with men in their own denigration, and there have always been women who defy sexism by bonding with other women. And there have always been women who use their friendships with other women as a sort of ballast against the tide of domination by guys' rules. Some girls choose their female friends over the guys—and thus over Guyland, even if it means being called "bitch" or "lesbo" or "freak" by the guys (and their female collaborators). Perhaps they just don't care; their self-esteem is strong enough to withstand that kind of peer pressure. Perhaps they have some core of self-respect that not only prevents them from becoming collaborators, but actually inspires them to join the Resistance.

Bitch or Babe?

Most of the time, a girl in Guyland seems to have a choice. She can either be a "bitch" or a "babe." A "bitch" does not model herself on a guy's expectations of her, but rather on her own expectations of herself. For her, the rewards of independence and self-respect far outweigh anything acceptance in Guyland has to offer. By identifying these independent-minded girls as bitches, guys can preemptively dismiss the rejection of Guyland that these girls represent. Since they refuse to play along, they're often shunned, excluded, or ridiculed. And their refusal may be sexualized, so they're likely to be gay-baited as well. After all, if you're not down with Guyland, then you must be a lesbian, right?

A "babe," on the other hand, conforms to a guy's visions of what a girl should be. The criteria goes something like this: She should be physically fit but not muscular, sexy but not slutty, pretty but naturally, not dumb but not too smart, a drinker and party girl but not a drunk (and definitely not sloppy), adoring but not needy. An unachievable fantasy.

Many girls carve out a place for themselves in Guyland by befriending the guys, either as "just friends" (or as "friends with benefits"). Indeed, cross-gender friendships are among the most important new features of adolescent and post-adolescent life. "My parents are, like, so *When Harry Met Sally*," says Kim, a junior at Brown.

> Like, they completely buy into that thing that Harry says, you know, that women and men can't be friends because sex always

gets in the way. Like they just don't believe that I have guy friends. Like my dad says, "He's a boy and he's your friend, so he's your boyfriend" and I have to say [she speaks very slowly and deliberately here] "No, Dad, he's a boy and he's my friend, but he is definitely not my boyfriend. He's my 'guy friend.'" I mean, well, okay, we hooked up once, but then we just became good friends and it's totally cool. We're friends.

Intimate friendships that do not include sex turn out to be advantageous. By becoming sisterly, a girl gains acceptance, gets invited to the right parties, and her status as a friend can offer her a certain amount of protection from sexual predation. Sexual friendships offer some of the same advantages, though (as we've seen) things can get complicated if both parties aren't in some kind of agreement about the limits involved.

Navigating cross-sex friendships in Guyland requires confronting the centrality of homosociality—"Bros Before Hos." In a sense, the friendship needs to be "de-gendered"—indeed, "masculinized" as it will center, at least publicly, on her participation in things he likes to do. They'll watch sports together, but probably not attend the campus production of *The Vagina Monologues*. She needn't mimic his behavior—she doesn't have to get blind drunk, hook up randomly, or watch WWE—but she needs to be comfortable with it. In a sense, she is "guyified." Around her, guys can relax. She's safe and somewhat sanitized—and that insures her safety as well.

Another way for a girl to avoid being either a babe or a bitch is to become a "bro." These girls prove their mettle in Guyland through shirking such "feminine" traits as intimacy, loyalty, and openness and appropriating guys' behavior: sports, drinking, and sexual promiscuity. This approach can often backfire. Says Kathy, a 26-year-old Cornell graduate:

I thought the only way I was going to fit in with the guys on campus was to sort of be one of them. You know, if you can't beat 'em, join 'em? Well, I joined 'em. I drank myself stupid, had plenty of hookups, and kept score just like the guys. It was ridiculous. They not only didn't like me—they had complete contempt for me. Acting as stupid and gross and fucked up as they were? As they *knew* they were? That did not increase my status! I didn't become one of the guys—I became one of the dogs, one of the pigs. Great.

"You seem a bit bitter about it now," I remarked.

Well, yes and no. The guys I knew made it pretty clear that they'd party with me because I was so much fun to hang out with, you know, just like them. I swear to God I even practiced how to spit. But they really didn't respect me acting like them. And it gradually dawned on me that they didn't respect themselves either—their contempt for me was sort of self-hatred. So that doesn't leave me feeling bitter, you know? That leaves me feeling pity for these guys. I mean, I'm way past that—steady boyfriend, good job, only moderate drinking. And my guy "friends"—I need to put that word in quotes—are like still wanting to be there, even if they are supposedly all grown up.

Kathy ultimately understood that female empowerment is really not about drinking a guy under the table, cussing like a sailor, or being a sexual predator. Certainly the goals of the feminist movement were not to enable women to be the best "bros" in town.

Playing by guys' rules puts women in a difficult spot. Since the traditional traits of femininity—kindness, patience, and nurturance—are antithetical to the definition of "success" in the public sphere—competency, assertiveness, ambition—women are constantly navigating between the two poles. When they are seen as competent and assertive, they're not seen as feminine; when they are seen as feminine, kind, and caring, they are not seen as competent.

There's an old expression in business circles that holds "men are unsexed by failure, but women are unsexed by success." For men, success confirms masculinity; for women, success *disconfirms* femininity—

it's seen as more of a tradeoff. To be taken seriously as a competent individual means minimizing, or even avoiding altogether, the trappings of femininity.

Several years ago, my students and I did a research project on the first women cadets at the nation's military academies. We interviewed about half of all the cadets in the first classes that had entered West Point in the mid–1970s, and then talked to about twenty from classes in the mid–'80s and mid–'90s. We also interviewed women from the very first classes at Virginia Military Institute and The Citadel. The women in those first classes at West Point described a similar dilemma. Said one:

> It was awful. I felt I had a choice between being a bitch or a babe. If I was serious, stern, and a good commander, no one would ever see me as a woman. But if I let down my guard for even a second, and did something as natural as smile, I'd be branded a babe. Every guy would come on to me, but no one would take me seriously as a soldier. What I could never be was just me—a good soldier and a woman.

Other women in those first West Point classes described how they avoided any public contact—let alone commiseration or solidarity—with the other female cadets. One told me:

> I learned pretty quickly to walk alone on parade grounds and to my classes from barracks. Every time I would walk with another woman, all the guys would like move over to let us pass, in a very grandiose gesture, you know, or they'd say something like "should I be afraid?" or "you gals plotting the revolution?" or something like that. I mean these were guys who were supposed to be the fiercest fighting machine on God's green earth and they were like cowering when two of us walked by.

She pauses, then laughs slightly in retrospect. "And it's not like we were even talking about them!"

Achieving "Effortless Perfection"

The good news on campus today is that more and more young women are beginning to recognize that the "bitch vs. babe" dichotomy is a false choice. Like their mothers, who "wanted it all"—a balanced career and family life—younger women want it all too. They want to be successful students, ambitiously pursuing their careers, and sexy women who will attract the right kind of guy. They want to be smart and pretty, feminine and successful. Yet this leaves many of them feeling like they have to live up to two impossible standards—they're expected to act "like a lady" while also acting "like a man." They have to be thin, pretty, and well dressed, even after they stay up all night studying for a final or writing a term paper. They also have to be tough and competitive, but they can't appear too eager in their assertiveness or it might be mistaken for aggression.

In a now-famous study of the life of women on its campus—from students to faculty to administrators to service staff—researchers at Duke heard a phrase that seemed to capture the core of this new femininity on campus: "effortless perfection." You can do it all, but you mustn't try too hard. In fact, you can't appear to be making any effort at all. In the study, Duke women said they felt they have to be "smart, accomplished, fit, beautiful, and popular, and that all this would happen without visible effort."

This goal is more wearing than it might seem. Said Jessica, a 21-year-old senior at Stanford:

I mean, just look at me today: I'm in jeans and flip flops and a sweatshirt, and this look is so casual, but do you know how long it takes to get ready in the morning and look like this? It's a studied look, and we work hard to appear that we don't care how we look. We work hard sometimes to conceal how hard we study. We work hard to eat, work out, stay fit, and never break a sweat. It's fucking exhausting!

Effortless perfection is an oxymoron. Impossible to achieve, it's a standard that demands that women work constantly, monitor their behavior at all times, and remain vigilant about either appearing lazy, stupid, or ugly—or even appearing that they spend any time at all working on it. Jessica's right: It is exhausting to make it look so easy.

In fact, "effortless perfection" may be the closest thing there is today to a "Girl Code." Girls are caught between the twin demands of entitlement and inequality: They believe that they can do anything they want, be anything they want to be, and yet when they go for it, they're judged by standards not of their own making. Young women face what we might call the Goldilocks dilemma—whatever they do, it's either too hot or too cold, too big or too small. And it has to be "just right"—although no one has told them what "just right" actually is. And they have to achieve it with no visible effort expended.

Hidden beneath the mandate of effortlessness is another, older mandate: lack of agency. It's okay to have it all, but it's not okay to want it all. It's not okay to work too hard to get it. It has to happen passively, somewhere beyond consciousness. The appearance of effortlessness is the way young women reconcile such conflicting demands. "I just happen to be beautiful and brilliant, I can't help it. Don't hold it against me." Effortless also counters the feminine taboo against competition. It's okay to win, but not okay to try to win.

What Do Women Want?: The Messages Guys Get

Tom came up to me as I was gathering up my notes at the end of a lecture and hour-long Q&A at his college. He stood to the side, waiting politely until the other students had gone and then he told me his dilemma, sheepishly, almost apologetically, and yet with more than a trace of bitterness and pain.

> I don't understand the girls—er, I mean, women—here. I mean, they say they want men to be more emotionally responsive and sensitive, that they want us to be good listeners and really caring. So I've become all that. I'm a really good friend, a good listener, sensitive, and all the rest. And they all want to go out with these macho assholes! I don't get it! What do women want?

Tom felt certain his question was unusual; indeed, he went on to tell me that he was sure it was different at other schools, and that his was a unique problem. In fact, it's the question I am asked most often by guys.

Molly, a senior at a large New England public university, asks the question I'm most asked by young women.

Jeff—that's my boyfriend—I mean, he is like really a great guy. He's my friend, you know, he really listens to me, is all sensitive and kind, and talks about his feelings. All that stuff. But when he's with his guy friends, something comes over him. He laughs at all sorts of sexist jokes, makes homophobic comments, and is just generally gross and offensive. What is up with guys when they are in groups?

What's up with guys is the Guy Code, the vows of silent complicity that men seem to take for fear that if they don't go along, they will be targeted themselves. Many guys *are* transformed when they are in groups of other guys. They do often become someone else, someone sometimes barely recognizable even to themselves. It's only when they're away from the group—alone with their girlfriends, or even with their female friends—that they can let their guard down. Close relationships with women, whether sexual or not, can offer guys a kind of respite from the relentless demands of Guyland.

Just because guys rule doesn't also mean that they feel powerful and in control. The hordes of smart, assertive, and confident young women may feel a bit overwhelming to many guys. "They don't know how to handle the independent girls, the smart ones, the ones who don't want to be tied down by guys because they want their careers first," one mother of a 22-year-old tells me. "It's like they get together with other guys and just circle the wagons."

This mother, herself a feminist veteran of all those struggles, raised her son to be empathic and understanding, sensitive and kind. "He wants a girlfriend," she tells me, "but now he ends up being the confidant, not the boyfriend. And he doesn't know how to deal with these young women who are still drawn by the strong silent type."

She pauses. "I was one of those," she confesses. "I know what a mistake that was."

Young women get such contradictory messages it's no wonder that trying to live up to them is as impossible as it is for guys to live up to the Guy Code. And it's no wonder that they then send out contradictory and confusing messages to guys.

Tom's concern was given voice years ago in an Anna Quindlen column in the *New York Times*. She called it the Boyfriend vs. Husband problem. Women, she argued, knew they were supposed to want Husbands—"upright, dependable, prone neither to wild partying nor to gross flirtation. He will show up for dinner on time and be the kind of father a kid can depend on for lots of meaty talks about life and honor." But at the same time, women simply couldn't stop themselves from being attracted to boyfriends—"entertaining, unprincipled, with a roving eye and a wickedly expressive brow above it."

To make her point, she offered a stark contrast, which I immediately incorporated into my class the next day. I invited the women in the class to imagine two different men. One is short, thin, with wispy thinning strawberry blond hair, and an honest open face. He loves you completely, will always be faithful: He'll be a great father, and a loyal friend. Now imagine the other. He is tall, dark, and roguishly handsome. He has a dark side, cold and cruel; he is a scoundrel, untrustworthy, and has never been faithful to a woman, and there is no reason to think he will start now. Which one would you choose?

My students looked confused and most seemed unhappy at the choice. Why did they have to choose at all? And were those the only choices? Half the women said they would choose the good and decent man, the honorable husband and father. The other half chose the swarthy and seductive boyfriend.

One woman in the class, Jeanine, simply wasn't buying it. "How about if I have sex with #2 and marry #1?" she asked. The class howled with laughter.

"Okay," I said, now referring to Quindlen's example. "Let's give them names. How about we call #1 'Ashley Wilkes' and #2 'Rhett Butler.' *Now*, whom would you choose?"

The class went silent. They had bumped up against the choice that Scarlett O'Hara made in what has been generally considered the most romantic movie of all time, *Gone with the Wind*. Of course, Scarlett chose Rhett—a man who, if you follow the narrative of the movie closely, actually rapes her. He picks her up and carries her up the stairs as she kicks and screams, fighting him off, clearly and unequivocally saying no. This being 1939, the film cuts to the next morning, when Scarlett awakens with an enormous cat-ate-the-canary grin and stretches to greet the sunlight streaming through her windows. Rhett read it right; she said no but meant yes. (Today he might be headed to jail.)

A few women hemmed and hawed, praising some of Rhett's better qualities. One or two tried to put Ashley down. But most felt stuck.

Not Jeanine, again. "Okay," she said. "I get it. But look, the problem is that Rhett Butler has never been loved *by me*. When *I* love him, he'll change." Again, the class erupted in laughter.

Jeanine had expressed, more concisely and eloquently than any self-help treatise, the core of women's romantic fantasy: A woman's love is transformative. It makes the Rhett Butlers of the world into Ashley Wilkeses—without sacrificing all the parts of Rhett Butler they found so compelling in the first place.

"But," as Quindlen wrote,

Lots of women fall for someone who is the life of the party, a dancing fool who has a weak spot for women, and then become enraged when they find themselves married to someone who is the life of the party, a dancing fool who has a weak spot for women. They expect matrimony to turn Jack Nicholson into Alan Alda. Yet they know that if they woke up one morning with Alan Alda, they'd soon yearn with all their hearts for just a little sturm and drang, a little rock and roll.

Women sustain Guyland because Guyland seems to be populated by Rhett Butlers, and they are much cooler than the Ashley Wilkeses of the college campus—the guys who study hard, are considerate of their feelings, and listen to them. Those guys are a bit nerdy, good friendship material, but they don't take your breath away. Better to latch on to the ones who treat you badly, with the hope that your love—and only your love—will transform him into a doting and attentive man, while he retains all the sexy guy-ness that drew you to him in the first place.

Many young women don't actually want what Ashley Wilkes has to offer—intimacy, commitment, a *serious* relationship. Who knows why? It might be that they're every bit as afraid of commitment as the guys are, and by choosing the guys who won't commit they can avoid looking at their own fears. Or perhaps they're so focused on their careers they don't have time for such foolishness—or the significant emotional investment they have to expend to sustain a relationship. Or maybe it's because they simply want to have fun in college, to play a bit more. They're just beginning their sexual adventures, and they're still looking forward to the promise of romance. They don't want to play house, instead they want to be swept away, to conquer and be conquered, to feel passion.

Of course, part of wanting what you can't have is inherent to desire in general—we tend to ascribe value in direct proportion to how hard a thing is to get. The coolest guys, the ones who are sought after by the most women (thus the least likely to choose any single woman since that would reduce their chances of scoring with numbers) are still the ones most women want. Getting the most popular guy is a coup. The Rhett Butlers of Guyland can be status symbols among women—they validate you, prove your worth. It's the feminine version of a "Trophy Wife."

Marriage: The City Limits of Guyland

Young women assume they will have both careers and families, and that they will be able to balance the two. Most plan to marry and have children, and they hope to have the flexibility and work/life options that will make it possible to continue their careers. And this is where things get complicated. Because in order to complete the project of becoming adults, they'd like to be able to count on the partnership of men. But given the cultural dynamics of Guyland, men their age are lagging far behind.

It's true that young men believe they will marry a woman who is committed to her career, and that fewer and fewer men report anticipating any emotional difficulties if she is more ambitious or earns more money (whether or not they experience actual difficulties might be a different story). It's also true that they expect to be involved fathers—far more involved, they say, than their own fathers were. Yet while women are preparing for adult life, guys are in a holding pattern. They're hooking up rather than forming the kind of intimate romantic relationships that will ready them for a serious commitment; taking their time choosing careers that will enable them to support a family; and postponing marriage, it seems, for as long as they possibly can. While girls are busy becoming women, boys seem content to idle in Guyland indefinitely.

Though marriage itself might be more of an issue for women who are beyond the age parameters of Guyland, the issue of commitment is nonetheless important for those who live in Guyland as well. The dynamics of Guyland are a powerful omen for what is to come. While most young men will eventually outgrow many of the more unattractive aspects of Guy culture—group porn watching, binge drinking, video game playing, predatory sexuality, puerile male bonding, and the like—the hookup culture can extend for years. Though the range of available female partners might diminish after college, the vagueness and lack of commitment that characterize guys' relationships with women often continue well into their thirties and even their forties. "Are we a couple?" seems to be a question women are condemned to repeat for a long time.

There is one simple reason why men haven't stepped up to the pace women have set for themselves: They don't have to. Why should they? The whole setup is skewed in their favor. As long as they continue to buy into the idea that marriage is the death of fun—an idea that is reinforced by the media, their peers, and even adult men at every turn—they will continue to prefer casual sex to long-term commitment. And as long as there is a steady stream of young women who will "hook up" in the hopes it might lead to something more, the burden for defining the relationship and securing commitment falls entirely on the women.

Most young women simply make their peace with Guyland. Not détente, in which each side gives ground—rather the women agree to put up with it in return for fun times now and the hope of more responsible and serious relationships later.

"I figured it was a done deal," says Amy, a 23-year-old recent graduate of Ohio State:

> I mean, the fix was in. The guys ran the whole show—they had the parties and organized social life. If you didn't go along with it, you had no social life. It was their way or the highway. So I went through all the motions, had a fine time of it, never got hurt or anything, and graduated. I made some good friends, and met my boyfriend, and now that we're living together, he's not like that at all anymore.

Lucy, her old roommate, back for a campus reunion, agrees:

> I mean what choice did I have? There simply was no other way. You know, that which doesn't kill you makes you stronger. And I definitely survived it—and now can get what I want. When the guys grow up a little . . .

The two women laugh loudly.

Many women put up with Guyland—for now—because they believe it is the only country in which they *can* live. They hope (and expect) that guys will eventually grow out of it, at which point their patience and forbearance will have paid off. Guys will have gotten all that stuff out of their systems and they'll settle down to the happy domestic life of a father and spouse.

And in many cases, it's not just wishful thinking. As we'll see in the next chapter, most guys do move on, grow up, settle down. But they often do so with regret and remorse, and not just a small amount of bitterness, at what women have "forced" them to give up. Countless movies and TV sitcoms remind men that marriage and parenthood are women's victories over the guys of Guyland, and that once they are permanently attached to nagging wives, they'll never again have sex or any other kind of fun again.

What Women Hear

Women believe that if they love him well enough, hard enough, and are as accommodating as possible, he'll change. They can "win" the war between the sexes. No wonder they collude! And no wonder those women end up, a decade later, the most avid consumers of those self-help books designed to help "smart women" stop making such "foolish choices."

Girls who learn to accommodate themselves to Guyland run the risk of becoming grown women who accommodate themselves to men's intransigence. Smart women learn from those self-help books to just leave him alone. Look at the contradiction: The cardinal rule of those books is that he is not going to change—no matter what you do. In other words, all that work was for naught. Your new task is not to try to change him, but to accommodate yourself to his intransigence. You have to change because he won't. Women have to accommodate themselves to guys' rules and learn to play by them. To my mind, those may be the most foolish choices of all.

Self-help shelves are crammed with books for women—by women. Women are seen as the experts in relationships—but also so woefully lacking in expertise that they need constant help in making relationships work. That's largely because these books all seem to counsel accommodation to Guyland—an accommodation that completely lets men off the hook.

While there are dozens of such books available at any one time, they all seem to offer similar advice. Take, for example, some recent prescriptions geared to young women in Guyland that turn out, in the end, to simply recycle old ideas in new packages. Wendy Shalit proposes that young women "return to modesty"—that they resist by just saying no. In her book *A Return to Modesty*, Shalit urges women to resist using men's standards as a barometer of freedom—indeed, she argues, it makes them more vulnerable to sexual predation and assault. Even worse, equating liberation with acting as piggishly as men do is a cruel seduction.

And while resisting Guyland as a barometer of female autonomy sounds like a pretty good idea, Shalit takes an odd turn, blaming feminism for holding out its false promise in the first place. Instead of independence, she suggests a recovery of the lost virtue of modesty, which, she argues, "gave women freedom to walk the street without having to fear being harassed, stalked, or raped, freedom for a girl to study in school without being sodomized, freedom to be alone with a man and still deserve respectful treatment."

But such a retreat to these lost pre-feminist virtues is just bad history. Life was hardly better for women before feminism. The reason that women weren't harassed in school was because they were prohibited from going. The reason that women didn't "fear" being battered or raped was because these things weren't crimes—they were simply the way things were. Men had their rights; women had no recourse. Where's the virtue in that?

At least Shalit comes by her modesty honorably; her return to virtue is at least, well, virtuous. Shalit intends hers to be a treatise in the moral philosophy of sex, and she models the modesty she asks from others. By contrast, the authors of the wildly bestselling *The Rules* see that return to pre-feminist modesty as a tactical weapon in the war between the sexes—a war, they believe, like Shalit, that women will lose if they act like men. Instead, they counsel accommodation, subterfuge, sabotage, and stealth. (What they don't see, of course, is that the rules they lay out play right into the rules already written by men.)

The Rules is a step-by-step guide promising to help young women land a husband through a step-by-step retreat through the 1950s and back to the '40s—the *1840s*, that is—when Catherine Ward Beecher, Sarah Hale, and others articulated the need for separate spheres and for women to be "the angel of the house," in Virginia Woolf's memorable phrase.

According to *The Rules*, women can't find husbands because they have been too busy being men's equals to connive to trap men in the time-tested ways that our grandmothers did—by holding out through manipulative coquetry. Women, they counsel, have to bury their competence, their ambition, their drive. And why? Because men will feel threatened. They are such pathetic creatures, completely preoccupied by surface appearances. "Don't leave the house without wearing makeup. Put lipstick on even when you go jogging!" they caution. Men are devoted to the chase and conquest, but not the simpler pleasures of domestic life. So the way to "catch" him is to let him chase you. Like Shalit's book, the message is clear—women's unhappiness is their own fault. Accommodating herself to men is the best chance a gal can have.

That, of course, is how Guyland works. It lets guys off the hook. Women have a choice: either embrace guys' styles as their own (in which case they are either parodic or lonely), or accommodate themselves to them (in which case their unhappiness is all their fault).

Beyond Subterfuge and Accommodation

There has to be another choice for women—a choice that involves men. And there is. A sizeable number of young adult women are searching for ways both to stop playing by men's rules and to find their own voices, their own sense of agency that can guide them into adulthood. To my mind, that choice is equality, a way to inspire women to find their own ethical core from which they can act in the world with authenticity and agency. Call it what you want: Most women who opt for this choice call it "feminism."

Among young women, discussions of "the F word" nearly always begin with the disclaimer "I'm not a feminist, but . . ." Young women assume that the feminist war has been waged—and won. They think the struggles for the right to work, to control their own bodies, to be safe in their own homes, or on dates, or at parties, are rights they can now take for granted, much as their mothers took for granted the right to vote or drive a car.

When my friends and colleagues hear a young woman say that she is "not a feminist, but . . ." they express disappointment, sensing from her a disengagement from the political struggles that still require so much attention and commitment. But I think we also need to listen to the last word, the "but"—and what comes next. Because when women say, "I'm not a feminist, but" what they are also saying is "but I agree with just about every single thing that feminists have demanded." Women fear that calling themselves feminists will result in their isolation: After decades of discrediting by pundits as ugly, man-hating, feminazis, they're wary. Yet they subscribe to just about everything for which feminists have stood for over a century. That is, they want all the rights, but resist the collective action that is required to achieve them.

In a recent op-ed in *The Daily Princetonian*, junior Chloe Angyal proposed a sort of individual "stealth feminism" for women who were afraid to be publicly labeled but still agreed with feminism's ideals of gender equality. She invited women to simply quit obsessing over their bodies, buying consumer products in the name of "empowerment," and make smarter sexual decisions. And she insisted that women stop calling each other sluts and whores, citing Tina Fey's line in the film *Mean Girls* that when women call each other those names they "send a strong message that it's acceptable for men to demean us."

Feminism dares to posit that the choice between bitches and babes is a false choice, and dares to imagine that women can be whole people, embracing and expressing ambition and kindness, competence and compassion.

And feminism also dares to expect more from men. Feminism expects a man to be ethical, emotionally present, and accountable to his values in his actions with women—as well as with other men. Feminism loves men enough to expect them to act more honorably and actually believes them capable of doing so. Feminism is a vision that expects men to go from being "just *guys*," accepting whatever they might happen to do, to being *just* guys—capable of autonomy and authenticity, inspired by justice. That is, feminism believes that guys can become men.

12 | "JUST GUYS"

*"Where lies the final harbor, whence
we unmoor no more?"*

—HERMAN MELVILLE
Moby-Dick

Adam Zwecker is no hero. He simply woke up one morning after a long night of standing barefoot on shards of broken glass, being pelted by raw eggs, and doing hundreds of push-ups in order to pledge a fraternity at Cornell, and decided he'd had enough. "That was one of the nights when you go home and you wonder 'What the hell am I doing?'" Zwecker told his campus newspaper. "The frat brothers tried to justify it by saying it would build unity for us, but it was kind of just a stupid, gross experience."

So he did something. He wrote a paper for a class titled "Hazed and Confused." His professor liked it and encouraged him to post it on the campus website, which inspired an intrepid administrator to set up an entire website devoted to exposing hazing on the Cornell campus (*www.hazing.cornell.edu*). Also included on the website are instructions on reporting hazing violations and allying across houses and teams to oppose hazing on campus.

Nor is a burly guy named John a hero. A lineman on the football team at a major Division I university, he was sitting with 100 of his teammates who were enduring a required workshop with Todd Denny, a men's violence prevention educator. The assembled group was visibly uninterested, loudly and distractingly joking around, relieved to have a few minutes off the practice field, and annoyed at having been singled out for such a workshop. Suddenly John stood up and shouted: "Everyone shut up and listen. This is important! I know—my girlfriend was raped!"

Another guy named Stafford was a participant in one of Denny's workshops at a university in Illinois. He told the assembled group about an experience he had had in high school.

I was at a kegger party where alcohol was flowing freely. I noticed a girl who was quite drunk being pulled by a guy toward an isolated room in the back of the house. He had targeted and separated her from the group and was clearly taking advantage of her condition. To their surprise I quickly stepped between them and confronted him with, "What do you think you're doing?" He menacingly retorted with, "Fuck off."

The young woman slurred, "Tell him to leave me alone." Standing face to face [to the antagonist] I said, "Back off, man," and held my ground, blocking his way. He feigned hitting me—but I didn't flinch. Seeing that I meant business, he looked perplexed and uneasy. After a few tense moments he released the girl's arm, muttered further obscenities, and walked away. I returned to the party with the girl, found one of her friends, explained the situation and she gave her a ride home.

Adam, John, and Stafford are just guys. They inhaled the same air and drank the same water as the other guys. They grew up on the same media images, hung out in the same locker rooms, and went to the same parties. And even though they had experienced some of the uglier sides of Guyland, they didn't get pulled in.

The truth is that most guys think that most of what happens in Guyland is stupid and gross. Sometimes it's far darker and more dangerous than that. Most guys think that binge drinking is brain-deadening, that hazing is sadistic torture, that sexual predation and assault is not only illegal but immoral. Most guys don't participate in these activities most of the time. But virtually all of them know guys who have. And most guys don't do anything about it. They are bystanders, and bystanders are complicit. Their silence implies support, or it's taken as support or acquiescence. Doing nothing allows something to happen.

I believe that they—and we all—can do better. Guys who are "just guys" can become *just* guys—guys who are capable of acting ethically, of doing the right thing, of standing up against the centripetal pull of Guyland. Guys can be everyday heroes. They can actually become men. For some it just happens; others need a lot of help.

Slouching Toward Manhood

Most guys actually do become men—eventually. They may try to convince themselves that they are proving their manhood by torturing each other through initiation, drinking themselves into unconsciousness, watching porn, blowing away virtual enemies, and hooking up with every willing—or sometimes unwilling—woman they meet. But that's not the way it happens. Most guys just drift into adulthood.

And they drift into adulthood individually. As we've seen, some of the more problematic activities of Guyland—hooking up and binge drinking, for example—decline precipitously after college. It turns out that these rites of passage require the substantial safety net of the college bubble to sustain such risky and potentially dangerous behavior.

For some guys, leaving Guyland is necessary to meet the demands of a job. The Guyland lifestyle is hard to sustain if you actually have to work regular hours, or longer. Many career trajectories require more time commitments at the beginning stages.

Says Dan, now 26:

> After I graduated, I thought I could party every night, like I used to in college. Hah! I would go out with my friends to some bars, hang out, play pool until 2, and then barely drag my ass to work in the morning. But I gradually began to see that I couldn't do both.

Dan pauses, and looks around the diner where we are talking, as if to see if anyone might recognize him.

Actually, I have to admit, I didn't exactly "begin to see" anything. My boss did. He told me he'd fire me if I didn't straighten up. I kinda weaned myself off my old friends and old habits. We get together still, on weekends, maybe, but never during the week. Now I even bring my work home with me. And, oh, P.S., I got a raise.

For others, the boredom of a dead-end job might spark a reconsideration of roads not taken. Professional training or jobs once ruled out as insufficiently creative or engaging might begin to look a bit more appealing. Says Frank, 25, now a third-year law student in Los Angeles:

You know, when I graduated, I wanted to move to Hollywood and write for TV. Well, I moved to Hollywood all right, and so did, it seems, every other college graduate in America. It was a circus. I was a waiter, I had no time to write, and I needed the money so I was also driving a delivery van in the mornings. I didn't exactly—uh, how shall I put this?—see my future in the food and beverage service industry. So I asked myself what would enable me to stay in the game? So I went to law school, and figure I'll be an entertainment lawyer. I still have every hope I will someday hold an Emmy. But maybe as producer.

For still other guys, the drift toward adulthood comes when they begin a relationship that feels like it could actually be the real thing. Like Simon, 26, who said:

I didn't plan to move in with Jessica; in fact, I think I kinda avoided the whole discussion. I was living with three guys from school, you know, and working, and hanging out with them, and then when Jess and I got more serious, I think I sort of expected that she'd just like hang out with all of us at my place.

She tried that—for about a week. No way she was going to be the den mother of this little Cub Scout pack. We were fucking pigs—beer cans and pizza boxes everywhere. And you know, the typical towels on the bathroom floor, never putting the seat down. She basically put her foot down—move in together or basically, like, lose her. So here I am—a somewhat happy almost-married man—at age 26!

Or maybe they get helped along with a little nudge. Jeff, for example, had just moved out of his family's house—at age 24, after living at home for the first three years after college:

I figured it was just time to sort of move on, you know. Did you ever see that commercial for—what was it, Burger King or Taco Bell or something—where the theme is "good to go"? This guy is like hanging out at his parents' house, sponging off them, and they pack up his stuff and send it off, and keep using that phrase as a sort of hint? Well, I finally sort of got the hint. I'm still not sure what I'm going to be doing for the rest of my life, but I gotta do something, right? So now I'm ready to find out.

But for all their different reasons, one factor remains constant: There is no playbook for becoming an adult, no road map. Young men often feel like they are making it up as they go along—in part because they are. "This is the one time in their lives when they're not responsible for anyone else or to anyone else," writes psychologist Jeffrey Arnett, perhaps young adulthood's most optimistic cheerleader. "So they have this wonderful freedom to really focus on their own lives and work on becoming the kind of person they want to be."

True, but freedom cuts both ways. To think you can do anything you want, be anyone you want to be, and be accountable to no one can be terrifying and daunting. Plus, irresponsibility doesn't age particularly well. What looked like freedom at age 24—hanging out, partying every night, getting a temp job with the hope that you will eventually make it as a rock star—doesn't look so enviable at age 40. For many guys, not making a decision about what they want to do with their lives *is* making a decision—a decision to do nothing.

What's more, freedom without context leaves you isolated from any sense of community and even more susceptible to peer pressure. Much of Guyland's excesses come not from the desire to stand out, but the obsession to fit in, to belong somewhere. Peer pressure hardly evaporates on one's eighteenth birthday. Indeed, in some cases it kicks into a higher and potentially more dangerous gear. As a society—as families, educators, and friends—we let guys down by failing to provide that guidance, or by assuming that they need no help from us.

Nurturing Resilience

What sort of help do these young men need? In order to answer that question, we first need to examine the constellation of factors that enable some young men to resist the pull of Guyland. Second, we must devise strategies for helping guys to feel empowered enough to resist being bystanders—to intervene, to stand up for what they know is right and fair, to act like honorable men, and defend the guys seen as so weak and vulnerable that they are tormented daily, or the woman targeted as a piece of meat.

Guys feel torn, sometimes, between proving their masculinity and expressing their humanity. How can we help them make the right choices for themselves—and do so publicly as a challenge to other guys? And how can we, as a society, make it clear that choosing between one's masculinity and one's humanity is a false choice—that one's humanity ought to be the highest expression of masculinity.

While some might suggest that the entire ideology of masculinity must be discarded, many elements of masculinity are enormously valuable; indeed, qualities such as honor, respect, integrity, doing the right thing despite the costs—these are the qualities of a real man. (And, I might add, a real woman. There is nothing inherently masculine about honor and integrity.)

Rather than pick apart the ideology, though, our task is more immediate. We need to encourage emotional *resilience* in guys—in our sons, our friends, our brothers—teach them to develop and hold fast to an ethical core that cannot be shaken from its foundation. How we go about nurturing this psychological resilience will vary with age. Enabling a 16-year-old to navigate hostile high-school hallways without becoming a target or an apathetic bystander may require more active engagement than supporting a 20-year-old who is trying to avoid the trappings of collegiate Guyland or a 25-year-old who is drifting, apparently aimlessly, waiting for his life to actually begin.

Profiles in Courage

I remember in primary school being deeply inspired by the stories in John F. Kennedy's book *Profiles in Courage*. His portraits of men who stood up for what was right—despite the fact that they paid a heavy price for their ethical positions—has inspired countless young people to do the right thing.

One group that has a lot to teach us is the kids who have been targeted, bullied, beat up, and gay baited, and survived. No, more than that—thrived. What enables an Adam Zwecker or a Dylan Theno to ride it out and emerge relatively unscathed? What empowers a Jamie Nabozny to steadfastly confront his abusers and insist on justice?

In my research I've talked with dozens of these kids. They were just regular guys, but they got beat up on the bus home from school, had garbage thrown at them from frat houses, were thrown up on by drunken partygoers, and were cruelly dismissed as losers by guys who they had thought were their friends. And just as their stories of torment and abuse sounded similar no matter where they came from and what kind of school they went to, their stories of resilience also had similar themes. To a man, they all spoke of at least one adult who made a difference, "someone who believed in me and stood by me."

Charismatic Adults

For some guys the influential adult might be one "charismatic adult"—a grownup who "gets" the boy, who sees him for who he truly is, who validates him, reassures him that he is all right, "a person with whom [he] can identify and from whom they gather strength."

In the book *Raising Resilient Children*, Robert Brooks, a psychologist at Harvard Medical School, and Sam Goldstein suggest that the charismatic adult is often another adult—a teacher, a coach, or clergy, or other family member such as an uncle, aunt, grandparent, and even older siblings. For guys, having a charismatic adult—perhaps one they brought with them from childhood, or one they meet later as a young adult, in college or the workplace—is crucial.

Says Douglas, 22:

> It was the strangest thing. I had this science teacher in high school, you know a guy who was just the most inspiring teacher you ever have, the one where you say to yourself, not "I want to grow up and be like him" but more like "I want to grow up to *be* him." He made me consider being a research chemist and not necessarily go into pre-med, the way I'd always thought I would. During freshman year, I kinda got out of control, you know, drinking and partying and stuff, and then I was sort of screwing up on my studying . . . well, I started hearing his voice talking to me. I even had a dream about him where he was like shouting to me from across this big ravine—like the one here on campus! I thought about him a lot, and how he had a tough life and struggled to make it. And when I came home over Christmas break that first year, I went back to my school, and like talked to him for like five hours. I feel like he pulled me back from a cliff I was about to fall over.

Of the charismatic adults in my own life—among the coaches and teachers and parents and friends—were two who stood out. From my earliest childhood, my maternal grandmother always listened to my ideas and took them seriously. She was the first person who really listened—someone who didn't *have* to. A professor in my English composition class in my first year of college, who probably wouldn't remember me if he were to meet me today, also had a lasting impact on me. Though my papers were filled with half-baked ideas, he must have seen something in those papers that was worth engaging. He sought me out and shared his own struggles to become a writer. I wanted to be like him—and I knew that required that I commit myself, for the first time, to serious work.

Far too often the burden for engaging with and guiding young men falls entirely on the parents. Adults outside the family assume guys won't want to talk to them, won't be interested, or won't have anything to contribute. Yet cross-generational friendships—not uncommon in many cultures—can be a crucial factor in helping guys envision possibilities for their own adult lives and should always be encouraged when appropriate.

Too Quick to Empty the Nest

Most charismatic adults do turn out to be parents. Research suggests we dramatically overestimate the importance of parents in our children's early lives, downplaying both the impact of heredity and the impact of peer groups and media. Just as important though, I believe we underestimate the role of parents in guys' lives from adolescence onward, as ballast against the impact of media and peers. And we do so at our peril.

Parents who stay close to their post-adolescent sons are the first line of defense against the worst elements of Guyland. They remind almost-men where they came from and that they are still accountable to a family code of honor. And yet, once post-adolescent children leave home, parents who were once "helicopter parents," hovering protectively over their children's every move, seem to transform instantly into absentee parents. "Well, they're on their own now," these parents might say. "There's nothing we can do to set them on the right path."

When their children are younger, parents seem so concerned with bolstering the children's self-esteem that they often shield them from the routine struggles out of which children are able to generate their own sense of self-respect. Self-respect is quite a different thing from self-esteem. Esteem requires only that you hold yourself in high regard, but it is unconnected to anything you have actually done. Self-respect is the fruit of action, of triumph over some hardship, of picking yourself up and getting back in the saddle. High self-respect means that you will, in the words of the parable, "fall down seven times, get up eight." High self-esteem means you're terrified of falling down once.

I have encountered so many young people whose parents have run interference for them, picked up after them, and unjustifiably told them that they were special—and who are now surprised that their actions have consequences to which they will be held accountable, that being special doesn't necessarily translate into preferential treatment in the outside world. From missing class or turning a paper in late to participating in hazing or drunk driving accidents, they assume that their parents, or other grownups, will bail them out and soothe any bruised egos. Or they think that they are untouchable because they've never been in trouble before. If we treat young adults like children, we do them no great service: We infantilize them and then we are shocked when they behave like babies.

Both fathers and mothers are important parts of the process of becoming an adult. (Let me be clear: Single parents—both women and men—can play as critical a role as the traditional two-parent family, and gay and lesbian parents can, and do, raise happy, resilient children. When it comes to family life, form is not nearly as important as content. Feeling loved and supported, nurtured and safe, is far more critical than the "package" it comes in.)

Mothers need to remain present in the lives of their sons—throughout their teens and twenties. By the time guys leave home, their mothers have often been on the sidelines for more than a decade, marginalized as irrelevant to the project of becoming a man. No, not merely irrelevant, but actually characterized as an obstacle, as the chief impediment to his manhood—holding him back, keeping him a "mama's boy," feminizing him, undermining his need to separate.

There could not be a worse characterization of a mother (or a worse model for how men should relate to women generally). These ideas have no basis in empirical fact; they're the holdover from antiquated Freudian notions about the boy's masculinity "project." There is virtually no empirical evidence that boys who stay close to their mothers become any less capable of manhood than those who reject her in a wrenching separation. In fact, there is some good evidence that separation from the person who has succored and nurtured him through his most dependent and vulnerable years has some negative consequences for his future relationships with women. Pulled from her side long before he is ready, he learns to distrust women, to steel himself against ever again revealing that vulnerability and neediness. He becomes a man all right—a cold, hard, and unfeeling one.

In fact, there is a lot of evidence that opposite-sex parents play a critical role in the healthy development of their children. For example, let's take the other opposite sex pairing—fathers and their daughters. Joe Kelly, cofounder of a group called Dads & Daughters, spends his life trying to encourage dads to stay connected. When dads are involved in their daughters' lives, their daughters develop greater self-respect, and thus are significantly less likely to be in abusive relationships, and less likely to be victims of date or acquaintance rape.

Mothers have an equally critical role to play with their sons. Mothers may enable their sons to stay connected to that part of themselves that is vulnerable or dependent, enable them to be open about their feelings, and remind them that women are not hos to get over on, but people they are capable of loving. Mothers are more likely to resist Guyland's mores, and to encourage their sons to resist them, as well.

It's ironic, though, that while we have vilified mothers as feminizing their boys, we've given a free pass to fathers when it comes to their grown sons. Even those pundits who proclaim fatherlessness as the cause of all social problems usually end up blaming mothers for keeping the dads away. Yet many dads willingly check out of their sons' lives far too soon, and stay away just as their sons really begin to need them. And there are the others who stick around and actually promote Guyland's values.

When a guy leaves home, his father often breathes an enormous sigh of relief. The kids are finally gone from the house! (Remember Josh in chapter 1?) How many fathers answer the phone when their son calls from college and say only, "Hold on, I'll get your mother"? How many declare their job "done"?

A friend, Bob, recently described his own experience with his son:

When Andy left home for college I thought, this is the moment I've been waiting for. I put in the long years, man, raising him, being there every fucking minute. Okay, I said, I'm 50. This is *my* time! I'm gonna learn how to sail. I'm gonna play more golf, do more fishing, have more sex with my wife—do you know how hard it is to have sex when he's in the next room and you're so damned tired? This is Bob's time. At least that's what I thought.

"What happened?" I ask.

He moved back in, that's what happened! I can't believe it. I mean, I would have rented out his damned room if I had my way. No, seriously, he's been living at home for the past year, and we're back being his parents, buying him food, and doing his laundry while he tries to figure out if more than a hundred grand spent on his education has actually prepared him for anything useful in the world!

"You sound a bit angry about it," I observe.
"You bet I'm angry about it. Dammit! This was my time. I'm really pissed that I have to give it up—again!"
Fathers often feel that they have sacrificed mightily for their families, that they left behind the fun stuff—hanging out with their buddies, being playful, irresponsible, and free—to get into harness as sober, respectable family providers. And they're right: they did sacrifice. For many men, the demands of being a provider and family man are filled with pressure and insecurity, having to bend to the will of moronic supervisors, placate mercurial clients, and kowtow to demanding bosses. And all for a family that barely appreciates them!
In essence, many men feel they gave up being guys in order to be men. And sometimes, they identify with their sons' active participation in Guyland, as their sons live out the lives that they, the dads, wish they could have lived until they turned 30.

When I tell moms about the gender asymmetry of the oral sex "epidemic," for example, or what the hooking-up culture actually is like, they seem shocked at how predatory it is, how the sex seems so disconnected from anything resembling even liking the other person. The fathers, though, get jealous. "You mean to tell me that these guys are getting, pardon my French, sucked off by, like, different girls all the time and that the girls are willing to do that?" says Dan, a 48-year-old father of a 19-year-old boy. "And then the guy can get laid and she doesn't even expect him to call her—let alone, like, be her steady boyfriend? Oh, what I wouldn't give to be 20 years younger."

In *Stiffed*, her exploration of the plight of American men, journalist Susan Faludi investigated the suburban southern California high-school group called Spur Posse. Spur Posse, you may recall, was a group of middle- and high-school boys who took the name from the jersey numbers of the San Antonio Spurs. The numbers (which the boys knew and, as we've seen in chapter 3, the girls didn't) became a currency among the boys to mark the number of different girls they had had sex with. Thus, when a guy shouted out "David Robinson!" his friends knew he'd had sex with 50 girls. The competition became so keen and the boys so predatory that there had been several date rapes and sex with girls as young as 10 years old.

When Faludi interviewed the fathers and mothers of the boys in the Posse, she found a striking difference. The mothers were outraged, distraught that their sons had treated girls so badly, and felt immediate connections with the mothers of the girls. Their fathers, though, seemed almost proud.

When a father connects with his son's sense of entitlement he becomes less of an ally to his son becoming a man. The father may have a momentary regression to Guyland himself, but he sacrifices his ability to help his son enter manhood. He—and not his wife—becomes the parent who holds him back.

When fathers resist the impulse to identify with Guyland, they can model empathic manhood and enrich their sons' lives with a concrete example of what honor and intregity look like. Fathers can show their sons that there are real alternatives to Guyland in which responsibility and accountability and self-respect are qualities that should be strived for, worlds in which saying no to Guyland does not make one any less than a man.

You Gotta Have Friends

Another way a guy can resist the perils of Guyland is to have an alternative pole around which some part of his life revolves. His parents can encourage some activity to which he can commit himself and in which he feels competent. The struggles to prove masculinity in Guyland come from fears of inadequacy, incompetence, weakness. If a guy feels good about this private passion, he can have the experience of competence and strength. It might also serve to give him social access to a world otherwise unavailable to him—a hiking club, a karate class, a religious group, or volunteer work at the local hospital can introduce him to people and ideas he might not encounter in his local high school. If guys have friends outside the orbit of their own high school, it is easier to believe that their own high-school cliques do not define the entire universe. Any of these activities will help to loosen the grip of Guyland and put it in perspective.

Guys also describe the importance of friendship in their lives. One male friend—particularly one who is not a target of bullying, but one who seems to be successful at masculinity—can stand in for an entire peer culture and validate a guy's sense of himself as a man. "If you go to school and people make fun of you every day, and you don't have a friend, it drives you to insanity," commented one high-school male student. A male friend can keep a guy sane.

Friendship is the currency of Guyland—the band of brothers. But often it's a counterfeit currency, based on suppression of emotion, false bravado, and toughness, a mutual recitation of allegiance to the Guy Code. Developing a genuine friendship—a real one—is difficult, perhaps the biggest risk a guy can take. It means being strong enough to show vulnerability, independent enough to brave social ostracism, courageous enough to trust another. A male friend reminds you that you are a man; he validates your gender identity. Even if everyone else says you're a wimp, a male friend provides a counterpunch, a reference point that says "no, you're not, because I'm your friend."

Ironically, another group of guys might have some valuable insights on how to nurture resilience: the guys who are relentlessly targeted, bullied, and gay-baited. That is, the very guys that other guys are trying so hard *not* to be! But the targets—whether they are gay or not—understand better than most how Guyland works, and have developed some strategies to survive it at its worst. While publicly befriending the target of the bullies' wrath may be too terrifying to be practical—after all, if you associate with them in public, you may be set up as a legitimate target yourself—many high schools today have Gay-Straight Alliances where students can communicate across these differences. Research on GSAs indicates that they significantly reduce homophobia in schools when—and only when—high status straight guys are part of the group. Which makes sense—it *is* called "Guyland" after all.

A female friend can also validate your heterosexuality. A female friend need not be a girlfriend, although she may be. His potential romantic interest in her—or her interest in him—validates a part of him that is constantly challenged in Guyland: his sexuality. That she shows interest negates all the things that might be said about him—all the epithets that equate homosexuality with femininity. Even if they are "just friends" she is able to remind him that other girls might like him, that he isn't a loser. It may be that the boys who are able to best resist the torments of incessant gay-baiting and the relentless questioning of manhood are those who have some girls among their friends.

More than that, girls who are friends are girls who are *people*. It is much harder to accept the dehumanization of women and girls that is the basic banter of Guyland, from the sexist put-downs to the sexual innuendoes to the predation and assault, if you can imagine these sorts of things being done or said to someone you know and care about. When a guy has a close female friend, he also is able to see concretely that the things other guys might say about girls simply aren't true. Or he can see the effect of such statements on her. Or it might personalize the sexual etiquette of the hookup, as he imagines his friend being the object of some predatory behavior. She might be the one at a party whom his friends are trying to get drunk. She might be the one some other guy is bragging about having hooked up with even though she didn't really want to.

The good news is that young people today are developing a capacity for friendships with members of the opposite sex that their parents often find hard to understand. Often these friendships depend on girls acting more like guys in public (drinking, hooking up, and the like) and guys acting more like girlfriends in private. This is why young women often ask their male friends why they behave like such boors in public when they are such nice guys in private.

Parents and real friends are the counterweights to Guyland, the stabilizing forces that anchor a guy's identity and enable him to withstand the storm of anxieties that will be exploited and the tests that he will be forced to endure.

Breaking the Silence

Transforming Guyland is going to take a lot more than changing individual guys' behaviors. This belief that psychological change among individual guys will dramatically change the culture indulges in what I call the "therapeutic fallacy"—that if, somehow, we could get every single guy into therapy, we could eliminate guy culture and rewrite the Guy Code. Why would we believe such a thing?

The only way to transform Guyland is to break the culture of silence that sustains the Guy Code. Guys do what they do in part because they believe they can get away with it, that other guys won't say anything, and that the community basically will support them. And they're right. Remember, the majority of guys are bystanders. And so it is the bystanders, the ones who know, and yet do nothing, whom we have to engage. Yet bystanders help create the culture of protection in which the most egregious and extreme behaviors occur. It is also true that many guys anguish over their silence, recognizing it for the cowardly complicity that it really is.

As a culture, we need to drive a wedge in between the perpetrators and the bystanders, severing the few from the many, and isolating their behavior. This wedge requires that some young men need to begin to challenge their peers, and this is risky. Think of all those whistleblowers—the ones who broke the culture of silence that surrounds military torture, corporate malfeasance, or other nefarious behaviors. At great personal risk, they threw back the veil that shields perpetrators from scrutiny. Their actions, in some cases, brought about drastic change. But being a whistleblower in Guyland is neither safe nor popular. We need to learn to support the guys who take this stance.

Let me give one example of how this works. I recently ran a workshop at an elite private college in the Northeast. This school is nestled into the side of a mountain with the classroom buildings in the middle of the campus, the dorms at the base of the hill, and the fraternities at the top. (Formerly an all-male school, there are no sororities on campus.) The administration was concerned about a sexist practice on campus in which women were being verbally and physically harassed as they walked down the path leading from the fraternities to the dorms—especially on Sunday mornings, after they had, presumably, spent the night with a guy in one of the frats. Men who returned to the frats from the dorms were said to be taking the "walk of fame" for having spent the night with one of the women. On the other hand, women returning to their dorms on the "walk of shame" were being hooted and jeered at, and called sluts and whores by frat guys who would assemble on balconies overlooking the path.

Working with some of these guys, I asked about the practice. One fraternity required all pledges to assemble on the balcony at 7 A.M. each Sunday. I met the pledges individually, and talked about it with them. Several expressed their disgust with the practice, but felt helpless to stop it, knowing that if they voiced their dissent individually, they'd simply get tossed out of the fraternity and life would continue as before.

I asked if any of them had ever seen a girl they actually knew on the walk. One or two had, and they tended to just stand silently when she walked by. I asked one guy what he thought she thought as she saw him on that balcony—even though he wasn't saying anything. "I guess she'd say 'some friend he is!' and be really pissed off."

I suggested to a few that the next Sunday they each might look around the balcony and see who else looked uncomfortable with such boorish behavior. Then, later that day, he could seek out his fellow pledge and express his discomfort—but privately. If the other pledge was receptive, I then suggested they make a solemn fraternal pact to *both* express their discomfort the next time it was demanded. If one guy does it, he can be too easily ostracized, but if two do it, I reasoned, they can create a safe space into which others might enter and express their feelings.

Two weeks after my visit I received a phone call from one of the pledges. He said he was surprised to still be a member of the fraternity, because he did what I had suggested. He and another pledge agreed to say something. And when they did, many of the pledges immediately agreed with them. The fraternity itself held a meeting about it, and several upper-class members also voiced their painful memories of their pledge experiences. The pledges were never again asked to assemble to harass the women, and the ritual ended.

Breaking one's own silence empowers others to break theirs, and the edifice often comes tumbling down. Only when guys can confront each other, and support each other in standing up for what is right, will the culture of entitlement begin to dissolve. Entitlement will end only when schools and families resume their role as moral arbiters, making it clear that they are watching, and that such behavior will not be tolerated. And it will end only when guys themselves break the silence, and have the moral compass to know right from wrong and the courage to stand up for what they believe in. Only in this way can we provide what psychologist Leonard Doob once called "inoculation against cruelty" that our guys so desperately need.

And desperately want. We often assume that guys do not want our help; I believe they are desperate for it. Most guys are desperate for permission to do the right thing, rather than swallow their complicity with the wrong thing. We must create an environment that sustains them at their best.

A Collective Effort

And creating that environment must be a collective effort. As young men begin to break the culture of silence, we, as a society, must also tear apart the culture of protection that envelops the most egregious of guys' behaviors. Communities must engage critically—compassionately but firmly—with these guys, not embrace them warmly. We must hold school administrators accountable when harassment and assaults and bullying take place on school grounds.

Sometimes an entire group of guys starts getting the message. Journalist Benoit Denizet-Lewis, in an article in the *New York Times Magazine* in 2005, described a return visit he made to his fraternity at Northwestern in which he had been a member a decade earlier. The university, in response to constant reports of alcohol-induced injuries and illness, had expelled five fraternities for hazing. Of the seventeen that remain, thirteen are alcohol free, and any new fraternity that wants to incorporate must also be dry. What's more, more than thirty schools have banned alcohol in all fraternity houses—including Iowa, Oklahoma, and Oregon.

While this presents some challenges to fraternities as the center of campus social life, and some feelings of competitive disadvantage for the dry houses as opposed to the wet ones, the general reaction has been positive. Except from alumni. They are furious about these changes; one angry alum reacted to Northwestern's decision by saying he "can't imagine that a fraternity can be fun without alcohol"—a most impoverished idea of both fun and fraternity life.

I'm not sure that banning alcohol entirely is the answer; after all, as Henry Wechsler asks, "[w]hat does dry really mean if they just go across the street?" And banning fraternities would surely generate so much opposition that a university president could stake his or her entire career on it.

There are other more obvious and less draconian options. For starters, consider what Chancellor John Wiley has implemented at the University of Wisconsin. For nearly a century, when parents dropped their children off at school, their parental duties were over and the university took over *in loco parentis*. But over the past thirty years, the trend has been for universities to retreat from students' extracurricular lives, unwilling to be babysitters or parental surrogates. With no one minding the store, alcohol abuse has soared. Lots of washing one's hands of the responsibility has led to lots of hand wringing over drinking and associated problems. *In loco parentis* has given way to *la vida loca.*

"Unambiguously, alcohol abuse is the No. 1 health and safety problem on every college campus," Wiley told the *New York Times.* "Just about every unpleasant incident, every crime, involves alcohol abuse by the victim or the perpetrator. The question is, what do you do that's effective to prevent it?"

What Wiley did was ramp up the university's role in monitoring the problem. A lot. With great fanfare, the university announced a new policy under which students who are found by the campus police to be intoxicated are taken to a detox center and contacted by a dean a few days later. As are their parents. The Wisconsin policy is notable because it brings parents back into their children's lives. The university reaches out, tells the parents about their concerns, and expects the parents to work together with the administration.

Under this policy, the administration requires that students write an essay about their experiences and examine their ethics and personal priorities. And apparently it's working. The number of repeat offenders has dropped significantly, and none of the sanctioned students have dropped out. Several other schools, such as Minnesota, Penn State, and St. Lawrence University, are either studying or implementing a similar policy.

Another strategy involves raising consciousness around this issue with law enforcement—both campus security and the community police force. Police officers often have experienced hazings of their own, either in the police academy or on the force, or during their own academic lives, and they tend to be more likely to explain such events away as minor infractions. "Maybe it's necessary for law enforcement officials to stop treating physical hazings as boys-will-be-boys misdemeanors and prosecute them as the assaults they are," writes syndicated columnist William Raspberry.

This seems to be increasingly the case. Police and district attorneys are now willing to file charges for hazing injuries and deaths. Schools may be held liable when harassment or assault takes place on their grounds. Individual administrators can be held accountable for the things that happen on their watch. In August 2007, two administrators at Rider University in New Jersey, Dr. Anthony Campbell, Associate Vice President for Student Affairs and Dean of Students, and Ada Badgley, the university's director of Greek life, were indicted in the hazing and drinking death of a freshman the previous March. This marked the first time that administrators who were not present at the scene were indicted. According to the grand jury, these administrators "knowingly or recklessly organized, promoted, facilitated or engaged in conduct which resulted in serious bodily injury" to two students who were pledging Phi Kappa Tau fraternity. One of these students, Gary DeVercelly, died after a night of excessive drinking at the fraternity house. The night before, he told friends that he would be forced to drink an entire bottle of vodka at the pledge event during "Code of Silence Week." By the time he arrived at the hospital, he was in a coma and had a blood alcohol level of 0.426—more than five times the legal limit.

After the indictment, Rider's president, Mordechai Rozanski, posted a message on the university website that said, "dangerous underage drinking occurred at an unregistered party in the fraternity house, resulting in the death of a student. Consequently, we have dissolved the Phi Kappa Tau chapter on our campus."

Apparently untouched by the death of one of their own, students rushed in—to defend the administrators. They set up a website to support the administrators and their fellow students who were charged. "If a student chooses to do it, that's not the dean of students' fault," said one, while another said that students have to "police themselves," and that DeVercelly "was responsible for his actions." Such evasions are indicative of the way the culture of protection works in Guyland. It is the bubble we must burst.

Teachable Moments

Colleges and universities claim to be about learning, so why not use the information systems of campus life to further those ends? In the late 1980s, Wesley Perkins, a sociologist at Hobart and William Smith Colleges in upstate New York, teamed up with Alan Berkowitz, a therapist on campus, to develop a "knowledge-based" anti-alcohol program.

They used the data from a survey asking students about their own drinking habits and their perceptions of the drinking habits of others. And what they found was interesting: Students regularly overestimated the amount their peers were drinking, but, what was more surprising, that overestimation actually predicted the amount that they themselves would drink. Students drink to the level they *perceive* is the social norm on their campus. "This misperception results in most moderate or light-drinkers consuming more than they would otherwise, encourages non-users to begin drinking, and is strongly correlated with heavy drinking," writes Berkowitz. It's almost like "keeping up with the Joneses"—but it's based on a misperception of what the Joneses are actually doing. In research with Henry Wechsler, Perkins found that the perception of campus drinking explained variations in drinking behavior better than any other explanation.

Berkowitz and Perkins's research informed the development of an alcohol awareness campaign on their then-beer-soaked campus. And sure enough, once students began to realize that they were drinking to keep up with their peers, rates began to drop. Within two years, Perkins found reductions of 20 percent or more in high-risk drinking rates. Hobart and William Smith is today far from an abstemiously dry campus—no one would advocate such a thing in the first place. But it is one where rates of alcohol abuse have dropped to within manageable levels.

Naturally, a program this successful has been widely adopted at many campuses around the country. At the University of Washington, Alan Marlatt and his colleagues have devised an individual feed-back mechanism, which gives students both their own scores and the campus-wide averages, so they can clearly see the differences. It provides an easy-to-read bar chart and a text that explains the numbers. For example, one student received a statement that he reported that he drank four times a week and drank six drinks on each occasion—which he estimated to be below the average of five times a week and seven drinks per occasion. The memo explained that the average student drinks only 1.5 times a week and about 3.5 drinks per occasion. This guy drank more than 91 percent of students—all the while thinking he was below average.

Social Norms programs might easily be adapted to hazing or sexual assault since many groups undoubtedly believe that their activities are no worse than, and perhaps even more lenient than, those of others. It's possible that such knowledge-based programs might begin to calm the overheated hazing that continues to claim so many lives.

Anti-hazing activist Hank Nuwer offers a variation on this in a new web-based course on hazing. Developed with an online educational consulting firm, the course, "Hazing: Rites and Wrongs of Passage," offers a 50-minute program that campus groups (like athletic teams or fraternities) can use to structure their initiations away from dangerous hazing rituals. Nuwer is an optimist; he believes that most national fraternities and campus administrators genuinely want to reduce the practice.

But that will be hard to do when so much seems to be on the line. Since so much of hazing and initiation depends on humiliation, or the threat of humiliation, maybe there are some ways to turn the tables, to reveal just how stupid and gross these rituals really are. A few anti-hazers have set up the hilariously funny spoof website, fratbeat.com, where crazed brothers debate the best crackers to use for the "Ookie Cookie" ritual, or describe other delightfully disgusting hazing rituals, all in the guise of supporting it. Like Jonathan Swift, it's so over-the-top that it might invite the fiercest defenders of the faith a glimpse of how the rest of the world actually sees them. Of course, it might just give them new ideas.

In the end we need to develop a new model of masculinity. Young men must understand on a deep level that being a real man isn't going along with what you know in your heart to be cruel, inhumane, stupid, humiliating, and dangerous. Being a real man means doing the right thing, standing up to immorality and injustice when you see it, and expressing compassion, not contempt, for those who are less fortunate. In other words, it's about being courageous. So much of Guyland encourages cowardice—being a passive bystander, going along with what seems to be the crowd's consensus.

Guyland is both a social space and a stage of life. It's unlikely to disappear—if anything the stage of life is likely to become more firmly entrenched. There are positive reasons for delaying marriage, exploring different career paths, playing the field, traveling, hanging out, exploring oneself and who one wants to be, and become, in this lifetime. But it must be time well spent.

And in order to do that, our task, as a society, is to decouple the stage of life from that social space—to enable young men to live through this stage more consciously, more honorably, and with greater resilience. To inject into that anomic and anarchic space called Guyland a code of ethics, of emotional responsiveness, and wholesome occasional irresponsibility.

Some of Guyland's most celebrated inhabitants seem to be getting that message—and passing it on. In response to the death of Scott Krueger (a pledge at MIT) during a drinking and hazing ritual, the national office of Phi Gamma Delta has produced a well-conceived video about high-risk drinking that is required for all their chapters. The local chapter of another fraternity accepts openly gay men and then works to make other brothers' homophobia the problem to be addressed. Sigma Phi Epsilon has embraced a new "balanced man program," which the fraternity developed in the 1990s to combat a culture of "boozing, drugging and hazing." They've simply and unilaterally done away with the pledge system; new members have virtually all the rights and privileges of brothers. The brothers are *presumed* to be men when they begin; they don't have to prove their manhood to their peers. Scott Thompson, the fraternity's national spokesman, told a journalist:

> New members don't pledge for a certain period of time, get hazed, get initiated, and then show up for parties until they graduate. In the Balanced Man Program, men join, and they are developed from the time they join until the time they graduate. Part of that development focuses on building a sound mind and sound body, a simple philosophy that we took from the ancient Greeks.

Here, in the words of a former frat guy, lies the hope of guys everywhere: that the culture of entitlement can become a culture of integrity—in which guys know that each person's integrity is equal to his own. That guys can be valued for their integrity and encouraged to be good, whole human beings. That the culture of silence can become a culture of honor, in which each guy feels honor bound to speak up, to act ethically, and to defend his core beliefs with respect toward the simple dignity of his friends. That the culture of protection become a culture of genuine brotherhood, in which each guy feels surrounded by support and care, knows that he is not alone, and that having left Guyland far behind, he has nothing left to prove.

ENDNOTES

CHAPTER ONE: Welcome to Guyland

4   **young people aged 21 to 25.** Lizzy Ratner, "Welcome to Murray Hell!" in the *New York Observer*, July 11, 2005, p. 17. I'm grateful to Lisa Machoian for her guidance to the Boston scene.

4   **anomic nomads looking for someplace to go.** I'm grateful to Steve Zyck, Dartmouth '04, for his help on Dartmouth grads.

15   **settle down, and get a life.** This section is based on my article, "Guy Lit—Whatever" in *Chronicle of Higher Education*, Review, May 26, 2006; *http://chronicle.com/weekly/v52/i38/38b01201.htm*

CHAPTER TWO: "What's the Rush?": Guyland as a New Stage of Development

25   **65 percent of men had reached them.** Sharon Jayson, "It's Time to Grow Up—Later" in *USA Today*, September 30, 2004, p. 1D.

25   ***New York Times* columnist David Brooks** David Brooks, "The Odyssey Years" in the *New York Times*, October 9, 2007.

28   **physically, socially, or economically.** E. C. Cline, "Social Implications of Modern Adolescent Problems" in *The School Review*, September 1941, pp. 511–14.

29   **adulthood that loomed ominously ahead.** Erik Erikson, *Childhood and Society* (New York: W. W. Norton, 1950) and *Identity: Youth and Crisis* (New York: W. W. Norton, 1968). Edgar Friedenberg and Paul Goodman each argued against Erikson's thesis, suggesting that the pace of life had shifted so much there was no time for a moratorium and discovery. See Edgar Friedenberg, *The Vanishing Adolescent* (New York: Dell, 1963) and Paul Goodman, *Growing Up Absurd* (New York: Vintage, 1962).

30   **masculinity in the eyes of other boys.** James Coleman, *The Adolescent Society* (New York: The Free Press, 1961). See also James Coleman, *Adolescents and Schools* (New York: Basic Books, 1965).

30   **smoking, and drinking when we're young.**) See Caroline Stanley, "Why
     Teens Do Dumb Things" in *www.healthykids.com*, accessed October 23,
     2004, describing the research of Dr. James Bjork.

31   **27.4 for men and 25.8 for women.** U.S. Bureau of the Census,
     Table MS–2: "Estimated Median Age at First Marriage by Sex, 1890 to
     Present" released September 15, 2004. In the first part of the century, the
     median age of first marriage fluctuated as the economy expanded and
     contracted; now, however, the median age creeps up steadily, seemingly
     disconnected from and uninfluenced by external factors. Numbers for 2004
     are slightly higher again: See Sam Roberts, "So Many Men, So Few Women"
     in *New York Times*, February 12, 2006, p. 3.

33   **remain loyal to a company."** Martha Irvine, "Young Workers Want It
     All, Now" in *Seattle-Post Intelligencer*, June 27, 2005; available at
     http://seattlepi.nwsource.com/business/230177_entitlement27.html
     (accessed 6/28/05); Stephanie Armour, "Generation Y Arrives at Work with a
     New Attitude" in *USA Today*, November 7, 2005, p. 6A.

33   **later, it was 67.9 percent, barely two-thirds.** Bob Herbert, "The Young
     and the Jobless" in *New York Times*, May 12, 2005.

34   **Labor Market Studies at Northeastern University.** Cited in Herbert,
     "The Young and the Jobless," Ibid.

34   **that gap had increased to 53 percent.** Mary Corcoran and Jordan
     Matsudaira, "Is it Getting Harder to Get Ahead? Economic Attainment
     in Early Adulthood for Two Cohorts" in *On the Frontier of Adulthood: Theory,
     Research and Public Policy*, Richard Settersten, Jr., Frank F. Furstenberg, Jr.,
     and Ruben G. Rumbaut, eds. (Chicago: University of Chicago Press, 2005),
     p. 357.

34   **remain dependent on their parents.** See: *http://www.commonwealthfund.*
     org/publications/publications_show.htm?doc_id=583404

34   **Americans' life experiences since 1972.** Tom Smith, "Generation Gaps in
     Attitudes and Values from the 1970s to the 1990s" in *On the Frontier of
     Adulthood: Theory, Research, and Public Policy*, Richard Settersten, Jr.,
     Frank F. Furstenberg, Jr., and Ruben G. Rumbaut, eds. (Chicago: University
     of Chicago Press, 2005), p. 182.

34   **no future job in the service sector."** Douglas Coupland, *Generation X*
     (New York: St. Martin's Press, 1994).

35   **poverty rates are twice the national average.** Elana Berkowitz, "Eyes on
     the Fries: Young People Are Coming of Age in the Era of the McJob,"
     published by *CampusProgress.org* on March 31, 2005.

35   **We were all still drunks back then.** Cited in Alexandra Robbins and Abby
     Wilner, *Quarterlife Crisis* (New York: Jeremy Tarcher, 2001), p. 113.

36 **young people in our history.** Elizabeth Fussell and Frank F. Furstenberg, Jr., "The Transition to Adulthood during the Twentieth Century: Race, Nativity, and Gender" in *On the Frontier of Adulthood*, p. 38.

36 **were living at home with them.** William Reese, *The Origins of the American High School* (New Haven: Yale University Press, 1995).

36 **more than doubled between 1992 and 2001.** Lou Dobbs, "The Generation Gap" in *US News & World Report*, May 23, 2005, p. 58.

37 **American families it's still a "full nest."** And we're not the only country where this is happening. In Britain, for example, they're talking about nesters, boomerang children, co-resident adults, or, my favorite, "kippers"— Kids In Pockets, Eroding Retirement Savings, which pretty much sums up what their parents think of the 50 percent of college graduates who have returned home. In Japan, 70 percent of women between age 30 and 35 live with their parents, and in Australia, only 14 percent of people in their early twenties are independent.

38 **neither kids nor adults, but betwixt and between.** Sharon Jayson, "It's Time to Grow Up—Later" in *USA Today*, September 30, 2004, p. 1D; Lev Grossman, "Grow Up? Not So Fast" in *Time*, January 24, 2005, pp. 42–54.

38 **name for that for years: moocher."** Letters, *Time*, February 14, 2005, p. 6.

39 **have been resolved by time and experience.** Jeffrey Arnett, *Emerging Adulthood: The Winding Road from the Late Teens through the Twenties* (New York: Oxford University Press, 2004), p. 181.

40 **what they really want to do," said one.** In Jeffrey Arnett, *Emerging Adulthood*, p. 41.

40 **for any age group except men over 70.** James E. Cote and Anton L. Allahar, *Generation on Hold: Coming of Age in the Late Twentieth Century* (New York: New York University Press, 1996), p. 59.

40 **that human beings are naturally good.** Tom Smith, director of the General Social Survey, cited in *Time*, January 24, 2005, p. 53.

41 **develop[ing] greater consideration for others."** Jeffrey Arnett, "Are College Students Adults?" (See also Arnett, *Emerging Adulthood*, p. 210.)

41 **their own road map," commented another.** Alexandra Robbins and Amy Wilner, *Quarterlife Crisis*, pp. 121, 6.

41 **a word about gender in their work.** Neither of the two major works cited here—Arnett's *Emerging Adulthood* and The MacArthur Foundation-sponsored *On the Frontier of Adulthood*—has a single reference to "masculinity," "manhood," or even "men" in the Index.

41-42 **women in separate spheres of endeavor."** James E. Cote and Anton L. Allahar, *Generation on Hold*, p. 84.

42 **and men were men," are long gone.** "Those Were the Days" by Lee Adams and Charles Strouse, sung in the opening credits of *All in the Family*.

43 **Every man's armor . . . "** Norah Vincent, *Self-Made Man*. New York: Viking, 2006, p. 130.

CHAPTER THREE: "Bros Before Hos": The Guy Code

44 **hear someone say, "Be a man!"** This workshop idea was developed by Paul Kivel of the Oakland Men's Project. I am grateful to Paul for demonstrating it to my classes.

45 **Willam Pollack calls.** See William Pollack, *Real Boys: Rescuing Our Sons from the Myths of Boyhood* (New York: Henry Holt, 1998).

45 **four basic rules of masculinity:** See Robert Brannon and Deborah David, "Introduction" to *The Forty-Nine Per Cent Majority* (Reading, MA: Addison-Wesley, 1976).

49 **just means taking away your manhood.** Richard Kim, "A Bad Rap?" in *The Nation*, March 5, 2001, p. 5.

50 **goin' to get something on you."** John Steinbeck, *Of Mice and Men* (New York: Scribner's, 1937), p. 57.

51 **completely in control, and therefore safe.** Eric Nagourney, "Young Men with No Attachments" in *New York Times*, January 4, 2005.

51 **and 93 percent of road ragers are male.** Mary Blume, "The Feminist Future of the Automobile" in *International Herald Tribune*, October 8, 2004, p. 11.

53 **Pollack calls it** See Pollack, *Real Boys*.

54 **to be diagnosed with Attention Deficit Disorder.** See, for example, Brad Knickerbocker, "Young and Male in America: It's Hard Being a Boy" in *Christian Science Monitor*, April 29, 1999.

54 **as unworthy, incomplete, and inferior.** Erving Goffman, *Stigma* (Englewood Cliffs, NJ: Prentice-Hall, 1963), p. 128.

56 **writes psychologist James Garbarino.** James Gilligan, *Violence* (New York: Putnam, 1996), pp. 67, 110. Darcia Harris Bowman, "Male Adolescent Identity and the Roots of Aggression: A Conversation with James Garbarino" in *Adolescents at School*, edited by Michael Sadowski (Cambridge: Harvard Education Press, 2004), p. 79.

56 **unsure of itself that it had to be proved."** Margaret Mead, *And Keep Your Powder Dry* (New York: William Morrow, 1965), pp. 151, 157.

57 **presumed they would fight more often!** See Geoffrey Gorer, *The American People: A Study in National Character* (New York: Norton, 1964), p. 38; J. Adams Puffer, *The Boy and His Gang* (Boston: Houghton Mifflin, 1912), p. 91.

57 **after the humiliating defeat in the Civil War.** Boys would take little

chips of wood from the woodpile, place them on their shoulders, and dare others to knock them off, thus providing the initiating offense that would justify fighting.

57   **and beat 'em into the goddamn concrete."** Kit Roane, "New York Gangs Mimic California Original" in *New York Times*, September 14, 1997, p. A37.

60   **sometimes—it favors someone different.** Anna Quindlen, "The Great White Myth" in *New York Times*, January 15, 1992.

62   **you'll be the next one inside the ring."** Michael Kaufman, personal communication, July 11, 2005.

64   Bernard Lefkowitz, *Our Guys*. (Berkeley: University of California Press, 1997).

CHAPTER FOUR: High School: Boot Camp for Guyland

71   *The "War Against Boys"?* Some of this section is based on " 'What About the Boys?' What the Current Debates Tell Us—And Don't Tell Us—About Boys in School" in *Michigan Feminist Studies*, 14, 1999, pp. 1–28.

71   **diagnosed with Attention Deficit and Hyperactivity Disorder (ADHD).** See for example Brad Knickerbocker, "Young and Male in America: It's Hard Being a Boy" in *Christian Science Monitor*, April 29, 1999.

71   **lower class rank and fewer honors than girls.** Knickerbocker, "Young and Male." URL for this article is *http://www.csmonitor.com/durable/1999/04/29/fpls3-csm.shtml*

71   **he says, that "boyhood is defective."** Article in *New York Times* and Elium book are cited in Susan Faludi, *Stiffed* (New York: William Morrow, 1998), p. 46; Gurian is cited in G. Pascal Zachary, "Boys Used to Be Boys, But Do Some Now See Boyhood as a Malady" in *Wall Street Journal*, May 2, 1997.

71   **mainly wish to control and to suppress boys."** Cited in Debbie Epstein, Janette Elwood, Valerie Hey, and Janet Maw, "Schoolboy Frictions: Feminism and 'Failing' Boys" in *Failing Boys* (Buckingham: Open University Press, 1998), p. 7.

72   **healthy, and, by implication, best left alone."** Christina Hoff Sommers, *The War Against Boys* (New York: Simon and Schuster, 2000), p. 75.

74   **liberal arts curriculum is seen as feminizing.** Tamar Lewin, "American Colleges Begin to Ask, Where Have all the Men Gone?" in *New York Times*, December 6, 1998, p. A26. See also Michele Cohen, "A Habit of Healthy Idleness: Boys' Underachievement in Historical Perspective" in *Failing Boys*, edited by Debbie Epstein, Janette Elwood, Valerie Hey, and Janet Maw (Buckingham; Open University Press, 1998), p. 28.

75 **how you feel and that's what I don't like.** Wayne Martino, "Gendered Learning Practices: Exploring the Costs of Hegemonic Masculinity for Girls and Boys in Schools" in *Gender Equity: A Framework for Australian Schools* (Canberra: 1997), p. 133.

75 **without it being rejected as a wrong answer.** Wayne Martino, "Gendered Learning Practices," p. 134. See also Wayne Martino and Bob Meyenn, *What About the Boys?: Issues of Masculinity in Schools* (Buckingham: Open University Press, 2001).

75 **that boys are having trouble in school?** Susan McGee Bailey and Patricia B. Campbell, "The Gender Wars in Education" in *WCW Research Report*, 1999/2000.

75 **are what get in boys' way in school?** It's also hard to square this woman-blaming with the collapse of school funding across the country. Many of the after-school programs that have been eliminated because of tax cuts have had serious impact on boys—team sports, bands, art and music classes—not to mention the disappearance of remedial programs and new teaching initiatives as schools struggle to comply with federal achievement mandates established by the No Child Left Behind Act, which has resulted in channeling the remaining resources toward core curriculum and away from noncurricular activities.

76 **teachers intervene only about 3 percent of the time.** "Out but not down" in *Anchorage Daily News*, June 24, 1999; Kelley Carter, "Gay Slurs Abound" in *Des Moines Register*, March 7, 1997, p. 1. See also Susan Fineran, "Sexual Minority Students and Peer Sexual Harassment in High School" in *Journal of School Social Work*, 11, 2001.

76 **ethnographic account "Dude, You're a Fag."** C. J. Pascoe, *Dude, You're a Fag* (Berkeley: University of California Press, 2007).

77 **be punched in the face than called gay.** Cited in Rebecca Jones, "I Don't Feel Safe Here Anymore," in *American School Board Journal*, 186 (11) November, 1999.

77 **And those are fighting words.** Robert Young and Helen Sweeting, "Adolescent Bullying, Relationships, Psychological Well-Being and Gender Atypical Behavior: A Gender Diagnosticity Approach" in *Sex Roles*, 50(7–8) April, 2004, pp. 565–574. See Human Rights Watch, *Hatred in the Hallways* (Washington, D.C.: Human Rights Watch, 2001). See also Stephen Frish, Ann Phoenix, and Rob Pattman, *Young Masculinities* (London: Palgrave, 2002).

77 **pretending to have intercourse with him.** *Montgomery v. Indep Sch Dist No 709*, 109 F. Supp. 2d 1081, 1089–93, D. Minn. 2000. See also Mark Stodghill, "Duluth School District Sued by Former Student" in *Duluth News Tribune*, March 13, 1999, available at: *http://www.youth.org/loco/PERSON/ Project/Alerts/States/Minnesota/lawsuit2.html* (accessed July 23, 2005).

78   **with impunity." The court awarded him $250,000.** Robert Cronkleton, "Taunted Teen Wins Federal Suit" in *Kansas City Star*, August 12, 2005. Quote from administrators is in Response of Defendants, p. 7; interview with Dylan Theno, November 10, 2005. See both the Complaint and Response at the website of Arthur Benson, Theno's attorney: *www.arthurbenson.com* (accessed August 19, 2005).

79   **internal bleeding that resulted from Huntley's beating.** *Nabozny v. Podlesny*, U.S. Court of Appeals, Seventh Circuit 92 F.3d 446, July 31, 1996.

81   **author of a study in *Seventeen* magazine.** J. H. Hoover, R. Oliver, and R. J. Hazler, "Bullying: Perceptions of Adolescent Victims in the Midwestern USA" in *School Psychology International*, 13, 1992, 5–16. Melissa Holt and Dorothy Espelage. "A Cluster Analytic Investigation of Victimization among High School Students: Are Profiles Differentially Associated with Psychological Symptoms and School Belonging" in *Journal of Applied School Psychology*, 19(2), pp. 81–98; Nan Stein, "Sexual Harassment Meets Zero Tolerance: Life in K–12 Schools" in *Zero Tolerance*, William Ayers, Bernardine Dohrn, and Rick Ayers, eds. (New York: The New Press, 2001), p. 145.

81   **harassment as a serious problem in their schools.** "From Teasing to Torment: School Climate in America; A Survey of Students and Teachers" conducted for GLSEN by Harris Interactive, 2005.

81   **just as distressing as the face-to-face kind.** Michael Lemonick, "The Bully Blight" in *Time*, April 18, 2005, p. 145.

81   **and *Queen Bees & Wannabes* first revealed.** Letter to *New York Times*, August 30, 2004. See also Rachel Simmons, *Odd Girl Out* (New York: Harcourt, 2002), and Rosalind Wiseman, *Queen Bees & Wannabes* (New York: Crown, 2002).

82   **fearing they will be the targets of bullies.** Cited in Sandra Boodman, "Teaching Bullies a Lesson" in *Washington Post*, June 5, 2001, p. HE12.

82   **a marker for more serious violent behaviors."** Tonja Nansel, Mary D. Overpeck, Denise Haynie, W. June Ruan, and Peter Scheidt, "Relationships between Bullying and Violence among US Youth" in *Archives of Pediatrics & Adolescent Medicine*, 157(4), April 2003.

82   **25 percent have criminal records before they turn 30.** On social status, see Juvonen, Graham, and Schuster, 2003; Coleman quotes in Lemonick, 2005, p. 145; on rates of criminality, see Kelly, 1999, p. C4.

83   **evident than among high-school athletes.** See Hank Nuwer, *High School Hazing: When Rites Become Wrongs* (New York: Franklin Walls, 2000); see also, Kevin Bushweller, "Brutal Rituals, Dangerous Rites" in *American School Board Journal*, August 2000; available at *www.asbj.com/2000/08/0800coverstory.html* (accessed October 25, 2004).

83 **the public to dismiss them as inconsequential.** Nadine Hoover and Norman Pollard, "Initiation Rites in American High Schools: A National Survey" (Alfred, NY: Alfred University, 2000) available at: *www.alfred.edu/news/html/hazing_study.html*

84 **canceled the last game of the season.** See *Seamons v. Snow*, 206 F.3d 1201 (10th Cir. 2000); see also, *School Law Bulletin*, Fall, 2000, p. 28.

86 **at best perverse and at worst criminally insane.** Kevin Bushweller, "Brutal Rituals, Dangerous Rites" in *American School Board Journal*, August 2000; available at *www.asbj.com/2000/08/0800coverstory.html* (accessed October 25, 2004).

87 **massacre ends when they turn the guns on themselves.** This is different from the "older" form of lethal school violence, in which a young boy of color brings a concealed handgun to his urban school and singles out a particular person to shoot—for having committed some offense. Those types of shootings have actually declined in recent years, in part due to heightened security (metal detectors and armed security personnel in the halls). But such a decline may also be an artifact of measurement: The number of lethal shootings that occur within a block of a school, by a student at the school, has risen significantly. As long as it doesn't happen on school property, it is not counted as school violence.

87 **and that revenge was one of their motives.** See Michael Kimmel and Matthew Mahler, "Adolescent Masculinity, Homophobia and Violence: Random School Shootings, 1982–2001" in *American Behavioral Scientist* 46(10), June 2003, pp. 1439–58.

88 **constantly made fun of," commented one boy.** E. Gaughan, J. Cerio, and R. Myers, *Lethal Violence in Schools: A National Survey Final Report.* (Alfred, NY: Alfred University, 2001).

88 **I am malicious because I am miserable."** Richard Lacayo, "Toward the Root of the Evil" in *Time*, April 6, 1998, pp. 38–39; H. Chua-Eoan, "Mississippi: In a Dramatic Turn, an Alleged One-Man Rampage May Have Become a Seven-Pointed Conspiracy" in *Time*, October 20, 1997, p. 54.

88 **his sanity that, "People respect me now."** J. Blank, "The Kid No One Noticed" in *US News & World Report*, December, 1998, p. 27.

89 **rumor that Harris and Klebold were lovers.** N. Gibbs and T. Roche, "The Columbine Tapes: In Five Secret Videos They Recorded Before the Massacre, the Killers Reveal Their Hatred—and Their Lust for Fame" in *Time*, December 20, 1999, p. 40.

89 **put up with nearly every day for four years.** Ralph Larkin, *Comprehending Columbine* (Philadelphia: Temple University Press, 2007), p. 91

90 **says Leon, from Long Beach, California.** Cited in Human Rights Watch, *Hatred in the Hallways* (New York: Human Rights Watch, 2001).

91 **more aggressive than a comparison control group.** See, for example, S. G. Kellam et al. "The Course and Malleability of Aggressive Behavior from Early First Grade into Middle School" in *Journal of Child Psychology, Psychiatry and Allied Disciplines* 35(2), 1994, pp. 259–81.

92 **from what we were about to do to each other.'"** Michael Thompson cited in "Boys to Men: Questions of Violence," *The Harvard Education Letter,* July/August 1999; transcript available at *www.edletter.org/past/issues/1999-ja/ forum.shtml* (accessed August 2, 2005).

92 **knew the attacker was planning something.** Nicole Crawford, "New Ways to Stop Bullying" in *APA Monitor*, 33(9), October 2002, p. 65. (American Psychological Association)

93 **weeks later, the boy killed himself.** Jeff Walsh, "Profiles in Courage" available at: *http://www/cyberspace.com/outproud/oasis/9602/oasis-profiles.html* (accessed July 20, 2005).

CHAPTER FIVE: The Rites of Almost-Men: Binge Drinking, Fraternity Hazing, and the Elephant Walk

96 **friends can rest easy; a job well done.** This description of "power hour" is adapted from the research of my student Ryan Hubbell. I am grateful for his assistance.

96-97 **have to bend over to make this work.)** In a variation, the pledge reaches his hand through his own legs to grab the penis of the guy standing behind him.

97 **and it is over; Jason has made it.** Lionel Tiger also mentions this ritual in "Males Courting Males" in *The Hazing Reader,* edited by Hank Nuwer (Bloomington: Indiana University Press, 2001), p. 15.

98 **other times they are relatively benign.** See David Gilmore, *Manhood in the Making* (New Haven: Yale University Press, 1990).

99 **the source of love, food, and nurturing.** Since this story is about the boy's masculinizing project, I will use only the masculine pronoun, specifically.

99 **custom, convention, and ceremony."** Victor Turner, *The Ritual Process* (New York: Aldine, 1969).

101 **this time a birth from men."** Robert Bly, *Iron John* (Reading, MA: Addison-Wesley, 1991).

102 **They may even believe in it.** It is true that in some African cultures, notably Nilotic tribes like the Samburu, Maasai, Rendille, the boys go off by themselves, live alone in the bush, and the village elders stay out of their way—that is, until the final ceremonies. I am grateful to my friend and colleague David Gilmore for pointing this out.

103 **average is pretty significant itself!)** Cited in Alexander Cockburn, "Emblems of the Bush Age: Adrift in a Sea of Booze" at: *http://counterpunch.org/cockburn12012007.html*

103 **one symptom of either abuse or dependence.** Henry Wechsler and Bernice Wuethrich *Dying to Drink: Confronting Binge Drinking on College Campuses* (Emmaus, PA: Rodale 2002), pp. 4, 21.

103 **generally disapproved of their doing so."** Helen Lefkowitz Horowitz, *Campus Life: Undergraduate Cultures from the End of the Eighteenth Century to the Present* (Chicago: University of Chicago Press, 1987), p. 211.

104 **Hispanic, and Asian students do not binge drink.** Wechsler, pp. 35, 36.

105 **more than one in five females (21 percent).** Helen Lefkowitz Horowitz, *Campus Life: Undergraduate Cultures from the End of the Eighteenth Century to the Present* (Chicago: University of Chicago Press, 1987), p. 249.

105 **development of new nerve cells and destroys older ones.** See, for example, J. Obernier, A.A.M. White, H. S. Swartzwelder, and F. T. Crews, "Cognitive Deficits and CNS Damage after a 4-day Binge Ethanol Exposure in Rats" in *Pharmacology and Biochemical Behavior*, 72, 2002, pp. 521–32; J. A Obernier, T. W. Bouldin, and F. T. Crews, "Binge Ethanol Exposure in Adult Rats Causes Necrotic Cell Death" in *Alcohol Clinical Experimental Research* 26(4), 2002, pp. 547–57; and K. Nixon and F. T. Crews, "Binge Ethanol Exposure Decreases Neurogenesis in Adult Rat Hippocampus" in *Journal of Neurochemistry*, 82, 2002, pp. 1087–93.

105 **recognize the ultimate consequences of one's actions."** Paul Steinberg, "The Hangover that Lasts" in *New York Times*, December 29, 2007, p. A31.

106 **in the terrorist attacks on the World Trade Center.** Henry Wechsler and Bernice Wuethrich, *Dying to Drink: Confronting Binge Drinking on College Campuses* (Emmaus, PA: Rodale Press, 2002), p. 4; For Iraq War casualties, see *http://icasualties.org/oif/*

106 **vomiting was tolerated and even celebrated."** Amherst College report, cited in Helen Lefkowitz Horowitz, *Campus Life*, p. 277.

107 **party the first week of the new college year."** Cited in Benoit Denizet-Lewis, "Ban of Brothers" in *New York Times Magazine*, January 9, 2005, pp. 36, 35.

107 **juice, coffee, and schoolbooks combined.** Henry Wechsler and Bernice Wuethrich, *Dying to Drink: Confronting Binge Drinking on College Campuses* (Emmaus, PA: Rodale Press, 2002), p. 4, 108; see also David Hanson, *Preventing Alcohol Abuse: Alcohol, Culture and Control* (Westport, CT: Praeger, 1995).

107 **friendship networks rather than intergenerationally.** M. Fondacaro and K. Heller, "Social Support Factors and Drinking among College Student Males" in *Journal of Youth and Adolescence* 12, 1983, pp. 285–99.

107 **network of friends, the more you will likely drink.** Wechsler, p. 58. See, also for example, Brian Borsari and Kate B. Carey, "Peer Influences on College Drinking: A Review of the Research" in *Journal of Substance Abuse*, 13, 2001, pp. 391–424; Kenneth Leonard, Jill Kearns and Pamela Mudar, "Peer Networks among Heavy, Regular, and Infrequent Drinkers Prior to Marriage" in *Journal of Studies on Alcohol*, 61, 2000, pp. 669–73.

108 **different gauge for one's own behavior.** Intervention strategies using this "social norms" approach, in which surveys inform students of what actually is happening instead of what they imagine is happening, are enormously effective. I discuss them in chapter 12.

111 **the resulting wound was "only a cigarette burn."**) "Branding Rite Laid to Yale Fraternity" in *New York Times*, November 8, 1967, p. 80.

111 **The most recent study of collegiate hazing** Elizabeth J. Allan and Mary Madden, "Hazing in View: College Students at Risk (Initial Findings from the National Study of Student Hazing)," March 11, 2008, available at: http://www.hazingstudy.org/publications/hazing_in_view_web.pdf

113 **line between men's space and women's space.** See David Gilmore, *Manhood in the Making*, p. 166; Thomas Gregor, "No Girls Allowed," in *Science*, 82, 1982; and Daphne Spain, "The Spatial Foundations of Men's Friendships and Men's Power" in *Men's Friendships*, edited by Peter Nardi (Thousand Oaks: Sage Publications, 1992), p. 76.

113 **thought we were real immature."** Cited in Robert Rhoads, "Whales Tales, Dog Piles and Beer Goggles: An Ethnographic Case Study of Fraternity Life" in *Anthropology and Education Quarterly*, 26(3), 1995, p. 318.

114 **at some predominantly white universities.** See, for example, Walter M. Kimbrough, *Black Greek 101: The Culture, Customs and Challenges of Black Fraternities and Sororities* (Madison, NJ: Fairleigh Dickinson University Press, 2003).

115 **some of which required hospitalization. . . ."** Lisa Leff, "24 Students at U-Md. Charged with Hazing" in *Washington Post*, May 5, 1993, C1, C10.

115 **and permanence in an uncertain and impermanent world."** Quoted in Lisa Faye Kaplan, "Beyond Piercing: Branding Heats Up as the Ultimate Way to Send a Message with your Body" in *Detroit News*, July 28, 1997, available at: *http://detnews.com/1997/accent/9707/28/07280008.htm*; Ricky L. Jones, *Black Haze: Violence, Sacrifice and Manhood in Greek Letter Fraternities* (Albany: SUNY Press, 2004), p. 119; Posey, Sandra Mizumoto, "The Body Art of Brotherhood," in *African American Fraternities and Sororities: The Legacy and the Vision*, edited by Tamara Brown, Gregory Parks, and Clarenda Phillips, (Lexington: University of Kentucky Press, 2005), p. 289.

115 **one former pledge told journalist Hank Nuwer.** Hank Nuwer, *Wrongs of Passage: Fraternities, Sororities, Hazing, and Binge Drinking* (Bloomington: Indiana University Press, 1999), p. 49.

116 **his father's experience in a fraternity at Indiana in the 1930s.** Cited in Hank Nuwer, *Wrongs of Passage*, p. 125.

117 **build a gigantic fraternity system!"** William F. Buckley, Jr., "The Clubhouse" *About Men: Reflections on the Male Experience*, edited by Edward Klein and Don Erickson (New York: Poseidon, 1987), p. 256, 257.

118 **student fatality every year involving hazing.** Hank Nuwer, *Wrongs of Passage*.

118 **His blood alcohol level was 0.328.** Aimee Heckel, "Alcohol Caused CU Pledge's Death" in *The Daily Camera*, October 5, 2004; Elizabeth Mattern Clark, " 'Hazing' Claimed Life of Pledge" in *The Daily Camera*, October 9, 2004.

118 **newspaper negatively impacts so many CU students."** Christine Reid, "Letters to Students Draw Fire" in *The Daily Camera*, October 20, 2004.

120 **admit liability when faced with a potential claim."** Hank Nuwer, *Wrongs of Passage*, p. 16.

120 **school for namby-pambies and Lizzie boys.** Ibid., p. 109.

122 **brotherhood, it's about power and control."** Elaine Korry, "A Fraternity Hazing Gone Wrong" on NPR.com available at: *www.npr.org/templates/story/story.php?storyId=5012154*

CHAPTER SIX: Sports Crazy

125 Thanks to Jean-Anne Sutherland and Daren Painter for their description of *Goodfellas*.

127 **they watch and play, and what they talk about.** My thinking about sports has been so deeply influenced by the work of Mike Messner and Don Sabo that the questions I asked and the ways I listened to the answers was invariably filtered through their pioneering work. Their thoughts and friendship inspired this chapter.

134 **includes access to those private spaces.** Varda Burstyn, *The Rites of Men: Manhood, Politics and the Culture of Sport* (Toronto: University of Toronto Press, 1999).

135 **modern ritual more sublime than the fantasy draft."** Erik Barmack and Max Handelman, *Why Fantasy Football Matters (And Our Lives Do Not)* (New York: Simon Spotlight, 2006). Anton Kazobowski, "Selling the Dream" in *egaming* review, September, 2005, available at: *http://www.funtechnologies. com/images_fun/press/eGaming%20Review%20article_Sept%2005.pdf;*

Abigail Lorge, "In Fantasy Leagues, the Field is Level" in *New York Times*, July 28, 2007, p. D6.

136 **And we're thinking, we can't have that."** Max Handelman, cited in Abigail Lorge, "In Fantasy Leagues, the Field is Level" in *New York Times*, July 28, 2007, p. D6.

136 **increased by more than 400 percent to 8.3 teams per campus.** Cited in Michael A. Messner, *Out of Play*, p. 2.

137 **men's teams citing discrimination as women's teams.** Michael A. Messner, *Out of Play: Critical Essays on Gender and Sport* (Albany: SUNY Press, 2007), p. 2.

137 **the field and take a hit from Ronnie Lott."** Ibid. p. 37.

137 **in which if women get more, men have to get less.** In reality, full athletic equality could be achieved without cutting any men's sports. All you'd have to do is implement one small reform. Currently, most Division I collegiate football teams carry—and outfit—about 125 players, 85 of whom are on scholarship. NFL teams, by contrast, carry 53 players, of whom 48 may suit up for a game. All you need to do is scale back collegiate football to the level that professional teams find perfectly adequate. Reassign those 37 scholarships and you can field every sport that doomsayers fret about losing.

138 **women's sports, virtually exclusively tennis and golf.** Michael A. Messner, *Out of Play*, pp. 156–7.

138 ***The Stronger Women Get, the More Men Love Football.*** Mariah Burton Nelson, *The Stronger Women Get, the More Men Love Football* (New York: Quill, 1995).

139 **nearly 400 all-sports stations in the U.S.** Russell Adams, "Sports Talk Radio: On the Air and on a Roll" in *Sports Business Journal*, February 16, 2004; see also David Nylund, "When in Rome: Heterosexism, Homophobia and Sports Talk Radio" in *Journal of Sport and Social Issues*, 28(2), May, 2004, pp. 136–68.

139 **eight out of ten listeners are male.** John Fetto, "Here's the Pitch: Growth of Sports Broadcasting on Radio" in *American Demographics*, April 1, 2002.

140 **85 and 90 percent of the audience is male.** Russell Adams, "Sports Talk Radio: On the Air and on a Roll" in *Sports Business Journal*, February 16, 2004; available at: *http://www.sportsbusinessjournal.com/index.cfm?fuseaction=page.feature&featureId=1159*

140 **So my dad and I bond also.** See David Nylund, *Beer, Babes, and Balls: Masculinity and Sports Talk Radio* (Albany: SUNY Press, 2007).

140 **you win the admiration and respect of your community.** See, for example, Christopher Burke, "Fans Find a Voice on the Airwaves" in *Yale Daily Herald*, January 17, 1997; available at:

http://www.yaleherald.com/archive/xxiii/1.17.97/sports/editorial.html

141 **the New York Knicks or the Los Angeles Dodgers."** G. Farred, "Cool as the Other Side of The Pillow: How ESPN's *SportsCenter* has Changed Television Sports Talk" in *Journal of Sport and Social Issues*, 24(2), 2000, pp. 96–117.

CHAPTER SEVEN: Boys and Their Toys: Guyland's Media

144 **The brothers of Alpha Beta Gamma at Colorado State University** The fraternity is fictionalized; the observations are accurate.

145 **two hours a day just playing video games.** Donald Roberts, Ulla Foehr, Victoria Rideout, and Mollyann Brodie, *Kids and Media @ the New Millennium: A Comprehensive Analysis of Children's Media Use* (Menlo Park: The Henry J. Kaiser Foundation, 1999).

146 **bet $200 million online every single day.** Kevin Conley, "The Players" in *The New Yorker*, July 11 and 18, 2005, p. 56.

151 **subtle and, very possibly, [intellectually] improving."** Steven Johnson, *Everything Bad Is Good for You* (New York: Riverhead Books, 2005); John Beck and Mitchell Wade, *Got Game* (Cambridge: Harvard Business School Press, 2004); "Chasing the Dream," in *The Economist*, August 4, 2005; Kenneth Terrell, "Bone Up at Video Game U" in *US News & World Report*, December 26, 2005, p. 68. See also Malcolm Gladwell, "Brain Candy" in *The New Yorker*, May 16, 2005.

152 **frequency of play has serious adverse effects."** Cheryl Olson, "Media Violence Research and Youth Violence Data: Why Do They Conflict?" in *American Psychiatry*, 28, June, 2004, pp. 144–50; Mark Giffiths, "Video Games and Health" in *British Medical Journal*, 331, July 16, 2005, p. 123. See also Mark Griffiths, "The Therapeutic Value of Video Games in Childhood and Adolescence" in *Clinical Child Psychology and Psychiatry*, 118, 2003.

153 **agitated and aggressive after playing video games.** See, for example, Craig Anderson and B. J. Bushman, "Effects of Violent Video Games on Aggressive Behavior, Aggressive Cognition, Aggressive Affects, Physiological Arousal, and Prosocial Behavior: A Meta-Analytic Review of the Scientific Literature" in *Psychological Science*, 12, 2001, pp. 353–58; Craig Anderson and K. E. Dill, "Video Games and Aggressive Thoughts, Feelings and Behavior in the Laboratory and Life" in *Journal of Personality and Social Psychology*, 78, 2000, pp. 772–90.

154 **games "the most fun family entertainment."** Video game data are drawn from Michel Marriott, "The Color of Mayhem" in *New York Times*, August 12, 2004, G3; *www.idsa.com;www.digiplay.org.uk*

154 **genre are male, the percentages vary enormously.** See, for
example, M. D. Griffiths, Mark N. O. Davies, and Darren Chappell,
"Online Computer Gaming: A Comparison of Adolescent and Adult Gamers"
in *Journal of Adolescence*, 10, 2003; James D. Ivory, "Still a Man's
Game: Gender Representations in Online Reviews of Video Games" in *Mass
Communication and Society* 9(1), 2006.

154 **cyber-swords in online game competition.** "Cloudburst of Ghoul Slayers"
in *The Economist*, November 26, 2005, p. 54.

154 **(75 percent male, 50 percent over 19 years old).** Mark Griffiths, Mark
N. O. Davies, and Darren Chappell, "Breaking the Stereotype: The Case of
Online Gaming" manuscript, Nottingham Trent University, 2005.

155 **"It was a little too realistic for them."** William Lugo, interview,
February 2, 2005.

155 **one's real life can only pale by comparison.** *Continental*, January, 2008, pp. 61–2.

155 **more than a few somewhat uncomfortable."** Interview with Nina
Huntemann, November 1, 2005. *Game Over* is available from the Media
Education Foundation, www.mediaed.org

155 **pandering to "the lowest common denominator."** Seth Schiesel, "The
Year in Gaming: Readers Report" in *New York Times*, December 31, 2005, B21.

156 **But games let you *do* something."** Dan Houser, quoted in Seth Schiesel,
"Gangs of New York" in *New York Times*, October 16, 2005, section B, p. 1.

157 **are cartoon versions of hypermasculine stereotypes.** See Derek Burrill,
"Watch Your Ass: The Structure of Masculinity in Video Games" in *TEXT
Technology*, 13(1), 2004, pp. 89–112.

157 **they make Barbie look well proportioned.** The one game where gay
relationships exist is *The Sims*, since the game makes it possible for same-sex
characters to live together, share a bed, kiss, have a baby, etc. (Nina
Huntemann, personal communication, December 19, 2005.) And, of course,
The Sims is the one game that "real guys" can't stand!

158 **happens to know how to handle a grenade launcher.** See, for example,
Helen Kennedy, "Lara Croft: Feminist Icon or Cyberbimbo?" in *Game
Studies*, 2(2), December 2002.

159 **it was 43.2 percent who were under 18.** "Youth Betting on Cards
Rising, National Annenberg Risk Survey Shows," press release, March 14,
2005, Annenberg Public Policy Center, University of Pennsylvania.

159 **started playing poker on my computer instead."** Jonathan Cheng, "Ante
Up at Dear Old Princeton: Online Poker as a College Major" in *New York
Times*, March 14, 2005, pp. A1, B4.

161 **Jimmy Neutron all the time," says one guy.** Cited in Ron Rentel, *Karma
Queens, Geek Gods and Innerpreneurs* (New York: MacGraw Hill, 2007), p. 173.

163 **It's an "authentic" expression.** Nelson George, *Hip Hop America* (New York: Penguin, 1998), p. xi.

163 **take from the hypermasculine 'black buck.'"** Mark Anthony Neal, "Hip Hop's Gender Problem" in *Africana* May 26, 2004; available at: *http://archive. blackvoices.com/articles/daily/mu20040526hipgender.asp* (accessed December 20, 2005).

164 **frustration than we do this dream world."** Cited in Bakari Kitwana, *Why White Kids Love Hip Hop: Wankstas, Wiggers, Wannabes and the New Reality of Race in America* (New York: Basic Books, 2005), p. 41.

164 **70 percent and 80 percent of hip-hop consumers are white.** Julie Watson, "Rapper's Delight: A Billion Dollar Industry" in *Forbes.com* February 18, 2004; available at: *www.forbes.com/2004/02/18/cx_ jw_0218hiphop.html* (accessed December 24, 2005); see also figures cited in Bill Yousman, "Blackophilia and Blackophobia: White Youth, the Consumption of Rap Music, and White Supremacy" in *Communication Theory*, 13(4), November 2003, p. 367.

164 **"just a cultural safari for white people."** Powell is cited in Bakari Kitwana, *Why White Kids Love Hip Hop: Wankstas, Wiggers, Wannabes and the New Reality of Race in America* (New York: Basic Books, 2005), p. 53. Unfortunately, I'm not persuaded by Bakari Kitwana's argument that white suburban consumption of hip-hop heralds the arrival of new racial politics in America, a new inclusiveness and opposition to racism on the part of white music consumers. Consumption of the "other's" culture may easily coexist with discrimination against the other in real life; indeed, the consumption of the other's culture may make such discrimination less transparent, and thus more palatable to the white majority.

164 **without being followed," noted one observer.** Melvin Donaldson, cited in Bakari Kitwana, *Why White Kids Love Hip Hop* (New York: Basic Books, 2005), p. 148.

165 **authenticity by speaking in another group's tongue.** Anthony Bozza, *Whatever You Say I Am: The Life and Times of Eminem* (New York: Crown, 2004), p. 31. My own interpretation of Eminem's meaning and importance has been greatly influenced by conversations with Steven Zyck, and his "Undressing Eminem: Intersection and Abjection in the Formation of a Cultural Icon," B.A. Honors Thesis, Dartmouth College, June 2004. He, also, will likely be disappointed by my less-than-ironic appreciation of Eminem.

166 **express their anger, impotence, confusion, and longing.** Nina Silber, *The Romance of Reunion: Northerners and the South, 1865–1900* (Chapel Hill: University of North Carolina Press, 1993), p. 130; see also Eric Lott, *Love and Theft: Blackface Minstrelsy and the American Working Class* (New

York: Oxford University Press, 1993), and Michael Paul Rogin, *Blackface, White Noise: Jewish Immigrants in the Hollywood Melting Pot* (Berkeley: University of California Press, 1998).

167 **communications professor Bill Yousman.** Bill Yousman, "Blackophilia or Blackophobia: White Youth, The Consumption of Rap Music and White Supremacy" in *Communications Theory*, November 2003.

CHAPTER EIGHT: Babes in Boyland: Pornography

170 **14 million web pages in 1998 to 260 million in 2003.** Jessica Williams, "Facts that Should Change the World: America Spends $10bn Each Year on Porn" in *New Statesman*, June 7, 2004.

170 **Internet, 100 are adult-sex oriented.** Stacy L. Smith and Ed Donnerstein, "The Problem of Exposure: Violence, Sex, Drugs and Alcohol" in *Kid Stuff: Marketing Sex and Violence to America's Children*, edited by Diane Ravitch and Joseph Viteritti (Baltimore: The Johns Hopkins University Press, 2003), p. 83.

170 **surreptitiousness is no longer part of the equation."** Pamela Paul, *Pornified: How Pornography is Transforming Our Lives, Our Relationships, and Our Families* (New York: Times Books, 2005), p. 4.

171 **unmarried (71 percent) and young (median age is 26).** Laramie Taylor, "All for Him: Articles About Sex in American Lad Magazines" in *Sex Roles* 52(3/4), 2005, p. 155.

171 **been "diminished by the women's movement."** Time Adams, "New Kid on the Newstand" in *Observer*, January 23, 2005.

172 **harder, and have more sexual endurance.** Circulation figures cited in David Brooks, "The Return of the Pig" in *The Atlantic Monthly*, April, 2003.

174 **trusted, lusted after, and sexually confident themselves.** David Loftus, *Watching Sex: How Men Really Respond to Pornography* (New York: Thunder's Mouth Press, 2002), pp. 54, 114.

174 **though it tells the truth about men."** John Stoltenberg, *Refusing to Be a Man: Essays on Sex and Justice* (Portland, OR: Breitenbush Books, 1989), p. 121.

174 **when I swim or run, I feel good afterward."** Lillian Rubin, *Erotic Wars* (New York: Farrar Straus, 1991), p. 102.

175 **you never will. It's really frustrating."** Pamela Paul, *Pornified*, p. 40.

176 **with a video camera looking for young women.** I am grateful to Robert Jensen for alerting me to these sites. See his *Getting Off: Pornography and the End of Masculinity* (Boston: South End Press, 2007), p. 15.

177 **worked within the fabric of their own lives.** Michael Kimmel, ed., *Men Confront Pornography* (New York: Crown, 1990).

178 **visits to prostitutes," writes the poet David Mura.** David Mura, "A
Male Grief: Notes on Pornography and Addiction" in Michael Kimmel, ed.,
Men Confront Pornography (New York: Crown, 1990), p. 125.

178 **that second it's all right, that chasm's not there."** Michael Putnam,
"Private 'I's: Investigating Men's Experiences with Pornographies" Ph.D.
Dissertation, CUNY Graduate Center, 2001.

179 **The little black dots, they are easy.** ". . . Those Little Black Dots" by Tom
Cayler, from *The Rat Piece* by Tom Cayler, Kay Cummings, and Clarice
Marshall. Reprinted by permission in Michael Kimmel, ed., *Men Confront
Pornography* (New York: Crown, 1990), p. 52.

179 **almost-men experience it with anger and contempt.** Cited in Michael
Kaufman, *Cracking the Armour* (Toronto: Penguin, 1993), p. 144. Kaufman's
analysis of pornography is particularly insightful.

180 **violence, not the sex, that exerts a greater influence.** See Alan
McKee, "The Relationship between Attitudes towards Women, Consumption
of Pornography, and Other Demographic Variables in a Survey of 1,023
Consumers of Pornography" in *International Journal of Sexual Health,* 19(1), 2007;
Edward Donnerstein and Daniel Linz, "Mass Media, Sexual Violence and Male
Viewers: Current Theory and Research" in Michael Kimmel, ed., *Men Confront
Pornography* (New York: Crown, 1990); Neil Malamuth and Ed Donnerstein,
eds., *Pornography and Sexual Aggression* (Orlando: Academic Press, 1984).

181 **to abuse the women in their lives," writes Loftus.** David Loftus,
Watching Sex, p. 70.

181 **among black men were about half the rates of white men.** Edward
Laumann, John Gagnon, Robert Michael, and Stuart Michaels, *The Social
Organization of Sexuality* (Chicago: University of Chicago Press, 1994),
p. 82.

186 **If you can't get off to it, it is not "good" porn.** A 2001 MSNBC.com poll
found that three-fourths of online users of pornography masturbated to
images they found online; cited in Pamela Paul, *Pornified,* p. 26.

186 **they get even with the women they can't have."** Cited in Robert Jensen,
Getting Off, p. 69–70.

187 **turned into a competitive moment with other guys.** "Sexual Violence
in Three Pornographic Media: Towards a Sociological Explanation" (with
Martin Barron), in *Journal of Sex Research,* 37(2), May 2000, pp. 161–68.

189 **poor, nasty, brutish and short."** Thomas Hobbes, *Leviathan* [1651],
reprinted in Michael Kimmel, ed., *Classical Sociological Theory* (New York:
Oxford University Press, 2007), p. 7.

189 **real women," as feminist writer Naomi Wolf argues.** Naomi Wolf, "The
Porn Myth" in *New York,* October 20, 2003.

189 **their girlfriends unless they act like porn stars."** David Amsden, "Not Tonight, Honey. I'm Logging On" in *New York*, October 20, 2003.

CHAPTER NINE: Hooking Up: Sex in Guyland

193 **complex dance that he called "rating-dating-mating."** Willard Waller, "The Rating and Dating Complex," in *American Sociological Review*, 2, October, 1937: 727–34.

193 **depends on dating more than anything else."** Ibid., p. 730.

195 **there will likely be no future commitment."** Tracy A. Lambert, "Pluralistic Ignorance and Hooking Up" in *Journal of Sex Research*, 40(2), May, 2003, p. 129.

195 **(28 percent) have hooked up ten times or more.** Our numbers seem to square with other surveys, or, perhaps, run a bit to the conservative side, since we have a large sample of colleges in our pool, and virtually all other surveys were done only at the researcher's university.

196 **very vagueness and ambiguity that characterizes it.** See, for example, Andrea Lavinthal and Jessica Rozler, *The Hook up Handbook: A Single Girl's Guide to Living It Up* (New York: Simon Spotlight, 2005). p. 3.

196 **from, in my opinion, kissing to having sex" says another.** See Kathleen Bogle, *Hooking Up: Understanding Sex, Dating and Relationships in College and After* (New York: New York University Press, 2008), p. 26.

197 **good friend and they're telling you all the details.** Quotes from students at Radford University come from research by my colleague Danielle Currier, whose in-depth interviews parallel the survey research of the online study. I am grateful to Danielle for sharing some of her findings.

198 **for a woman there's still some loss of value."** Laura Sessions Stepp, "Study: Half of All Teens Have Had Oral Sex" in *Washington Post*, September 15, 2005; Sharon Jayson, "Teens Define Sex in New Ways" in *USA Today*, October 18, 2005.

198 **rituals for what has become known as "the girl hunt."** See, for example, David Grazian, "The Girl Hunt: Urban Nightlife and the Performance of Masculinity as Collective Activity" in *Symbolic Interaction* 30(2), 2007.

199 **participants are drinking or drunk," says one study.** Norval Glenn and Elizabeth Marquardt, *Hooking Up, Hanging Out, and Hoping for Mr. Right: College Women on Dating and Mating Today.* New York: Institute for American Values, 2001. p. 15.

200 **her book, *Unhooked*, "is a small price to pay for exoneration."** Laura Sessions Stepp, *Unhooked: How Young Women Pursue Sex, Delay Love and Lose at Both,* (New York: Riverhead, 2007). p. 115.

201 **so annoying when you start dating them."** Benoit Denizet-Lewis, "Friends, Friends with Benefits and the Benefits of the Local Mall" in *New York Times Magazine,* May 30, 2004, p. 32.

201 **pushed aside or drawn closer at our whim.** Laura Sessions Stepp, *Unhooked,* pp. 40, 174.

202 **then play video games or something. It rocks.** Ibid., p. 32.

202 **outside of relationships, guys don't need relationships."** Ibid., p. 34

203 **any night and you know that's fine with them.** Bogle, *Hooking Up,* manuscript, Ch. 6, p. 6, Ch. 4, p. 7.

204 **Asian students are *far* less likely to do so.** The median number of hookups for white males, juniors and seniors, was 6 (3 for white women). The median for black and Latino males was 4, and for Asians it was zero.

209 **had intercourse every time they hooked up," she writes.** Bogle, *Hooking Up,* Ch. 5, p. 20.

210 **end it," because "they're like bored with it."** Paula England, Emily Fitzgibbons Shafer, and Alison Fogarty, "Hooking Up and Forming Romantic Relationships on Today's College Campuses" in *The Gendered Society Reader* (Third Edition) edited by Amy Aronson and Michael Kimmel (New York: Oxford University Press, 2007), manuscript, p. 7.

211 **90 percent of both boys and girls are sexually active.** See Peter Bearman and Hannah Bruckner, "Promising the Future: Virginity Pledges and First Intercourse" in *American Journal of Sociology,* 106(4), January, 2001, pp. 859–912.

212 **just as likely to practice oral sex as nonpledgers.** Angela Lipsitz, Paul D. Bishop, and Christine Robinson, "Virginity Pledges: Who Takes Them and How Well Do They Work?" Presentation at the Annual Convention of the American Psychological Association, August 2003.

212 **kissing with tongues broke their abstinence pledge.** See Bearman and Bruckner, 2001, and Lipsitz, Bishop and Robinson, 2003.

212 **they "kept" their vows had experienced oral sex.** Lipsitz, et al., 2003.

213 **impair their ability to develop those relationships—ever.** Laura Sessions Stepp, *Unhooked,* pp. 13, 28, 58, 4.

213 **those grandmothers!—could never have imagined.** For examples of this, see Laura Sessions Stepp, *Unhooked;* and Norval Glenn and Elizabeth Marquardt, *Hooking Up, Hanging Out and Hoping for Mr. Right.*

214 **postponing marriage, so they have time to play the field."** Cited in Sharon Jayson, "What's Up with Hookups?" in *USA Today,* February 14, 2007.

215 **your body and make yourself emotionally invulnerable."** Laura Sessions Stepp, *Unhooked,* p. 243.

221 **Pollyanna view of sexuality on the rest of the nation.** See, for example, Cathy Young, *Ceasefire! Why Women and Men Must Join Forces to Achieve True Equality* (New York: The Free Press, 1999); and Katie Roiphe, *The Morning After: Sex, Fear, and Feminism* (Boston: Little Brown, 1993).

222 **resolve never to make that mistake again.** Camille Paglia, "Rape and Modern Sex War" in *Newsday*, January 27, 1991; reprinted in Camille Paglia, *Sex, Art, and American Culture* (New York: Vintage, 1992), p. 51.

222 **half were by a guy that the woman was dating.** Bonnie Fisher, Francis Cullen, and Michael Turner, "The Sexual Victimization of College Women" (Washington, D.C.: National Institute of Justice and Bureau of Justice Statistics, 2000). It is available at: *http://www.ncjrs.gov/pdffiles1/nij/182369.pdf*

222 **are reported only to friends, or to no one at all.** While women comprise the largest proportion of victims of sexual assault, male victims are not uncommon: about 23 percent of women and 4 percent of men state that they have been forced to have sex against their will. Male perpetrators are most common in assaults against women (21.6 percent were assaulted by men, and .3 percent by women), but in assaults against men, the gender balance is about equal (1.9 percent were assaulted by men, 1.3 percent by women).

223 **with alcohol or targeting an intoxicated woman."** Rana Sampson, "Acquaintance Rape of College Students" Problem-Oriented Guides for Police series, Number 17 (Washington, D.C.: U.S. Department of Justice, Office of Community Oriented Policing Services, 2002), p. 6. The best empirical research on party rape is by Elizabeth Armstrong and her colleagues; see, for example, Elizabeth Armstrong, Laura Hamilton, and Brian Sweeney, "Sexual Assault on Campus: A Multilevel, Integrative Approach to Party Rape" in *Social Problems*, 53(4), 2006, pp. 483–99.

224 **they could be certain of getting away with it.** Neil Malamuth and Karol Dean, "Attraction to Sexual Aggression" in *Acquaintance Rape: The Hidden Crime*, Andrea Parrot and Laurie Bechhofer, eds. (New York: Wiley, 1991), p. 234 et passim; see also Neil Malamuth, "Rape Proclivity Among Males" in *Journal of Social Issues* 37, 1981, pp. 138–57. This Attraction to Sexual Aggression Scale (ASA) has been used numerous times, and is well tested for reliability. Finally, see James Breire and Neil Malamuth, "Self-reported likelihood of sexually aggressive behavior: Attitudinal versus sexual explanations" in *Journal of Research in Personality*, 17, 1983, pp. 315–23.

224 **seem to corroborate the statistics provided by women.** Cited in Katha Pollitt, *Reasonable Creatures: Essays on Women and Feminism* (New York: Knopf, 1994).

224 **if they believed they could get away with it?** Interestingly, these chilling rates are similar across race and class. Only among Asian Americans, for whom "loss of face" played a significant role in preventing sexual aggression, was there a significant decrease in the likelihood to commit rape. Apparently, peer pressure works differently for Asian Americans and whites. Whites fear "loss of face" by *not* participating; Asian Americans fear a loss of face if they do. See Gordon Nagayama Hall, David DeGarmo, Sopanga Eap, Andrea Teten, and Stanley Sue, "Initiation, Desistance and Persistence of Men's Sexual Coercion" in *Journal of Consulting and Clinical Psychology* 74(4), 2006, pp. 732–42; Gordon Nagayama Hall, Andrea Teten, David DeGarmo, Stanley Sue, and Kari Stephens, "Ethnicity, Culture and Sexual Aggression: Risk and Protective Factors" in *Journal of Consulting and Clinical Psychology*, 73(5), 2005, pp. 830–40.

225 **their own beliefs are shared by many others."** Frederike Eyssel, Gerd Bohner, and Frank Siebler, "Perceived Rape Myth Acceptance of Others Predicts Rape Proclivity: Social Norm or Judgmental Anchoring?" in *Swiss Journal of Psychology* 65(2), 2006, p. 93.

229 **violence to even the playing field, to restore equality.** See Tim Beneke, *Men on Rape* (New York: St. Martin's Press, 1982); see also Tim Beneke, *Proving Manhood: Reflections on Men and Sexism* (Berkeley: University of California Press, 1997).

229 **upon every male within eyesight of them."** Letter to the editor, *New York Times*, June 12, 1992.

230 **I question the amount of consent a lot.** Cited in Armstrong, Hamilton, and Sweeney, "Sexual Assault on Campus," p. 491.

231 **exposés in *Sports Illustrated*, where he was a columnist.** Rick Reilly, "What Price Glory?" in *Sports Illustrated*, February 27, 1989; Rick Reilly, "It Only Gets Worse at Colorado" in *SI.com* February 16, 2004; available at *http://premium.si.com/pr/subs/siexclusive/rick-reilly/2004/02/16/reilly0223*

232 **this is what you get when you come to Colorado."** David Gray, police statement; CU 03–0426, p. 2; also David Gray, police statement, CU 03–0428, p. 4.

232 **You didn't give me no girls.' "** Deposition of Allen Mackey, 12/05/03, p. 245; deposition of Daric Wilhite, 3/12/04, p. 64.

232 **me a good time. Suck my dick."** Deposition of Lisa Simpson, 8/13/03, p. 236.

233 **which even the athletic director called a "sham."** Deposition of E. J. Kreis III, 10/21/03, p. 35.

233 **He was a good player, after all.** Deposition of Richard Byyny, 1/14/04, p. 181.

233 **very threatening or serious position," she said.** Robert Weller, "CU Recruiting Probe Leader Won't Step Down Despite Comments" in *Denver Post*, February 10, 2004; available at: *http://www.denverpost.com/cda/article/print/0,1674,36%7E30780%7E1945541,00.html*

234 **think that the world is handing out things to you . . .** Cited in Jeffrey Benedict, *Athletes and Acquaintance Rape* (Newbury Park, CA: Sage 1998), p. 11.

235 **sexual assault awareness workshops for players.** Gandolf cited in Jill Niemark, "Out of Bounds: The Truth about Athletes and Rape" in *Mademoiselle*, May 1991; Andrea Parrot, *Sexual Assault 101: Sexual Assault Prevention Education or College Athletes.* (Holmes Beach, FL: Learning Publications, 1994).

235 **who was gang raped during a recruiting visit.** "Ex-SMU Recruit Indicted on Sex Charges" in *Rochester Democrat and Chronicle*, February 16, 1991.

235 **types of suggestions because the competition is so fierce . . .** Terry Holland, interviewed on "All Things Considered" February 23, 2004.

236 **baseball player is going to be able to play next week.** Jeffrey Benedict, *Athletes and Acquaintance Rape*, p. 30.

236 **that's the impression you're giving them.** Joe Watson, "Risky Behavior Not Policed at ASU Football Recruiting" in *State Press* (Arizona State University), February 25, 2003.

237 **the most impressively comprehensive programs in the country.** Jackson Katz, personal communication, April 30, 2004.

238 **write psychologists Mary Koss and John Gaines.** Mary P. Koss and John A. Gaines, "The Prediction of Sexual Aggression by Alcohol Use, Athletic Participation, and Fraternity Affiliation" in *Journal of Interpersonal Violence*, 8(1), 1993, p. 95.

238 **aggression the means by which the bond is renewed."** Peggy Reeves Sanday, *Fraternity Gang Rape: Sex, Brotherhood, and Privilege on Campus* (New York: New York University Press, 1990), pp. 19–20.

238 **binds the brothers to the fraternity body."** Peggy Reeves Sanday, *op. cit.*, p. 37.

238 **that we were a group of up and coming young cats."** Nathan McCall, *Makes Me Wanna Holler: A Young Black Man in America* (New York: Vintage, 1995), p. 47.

238 **beings on the face of the earth—black females."** Ibid.

239 **from a group of stronger people," writes Robin Warshaw.** Robin Warshaw, *I Never Called it Rape*, p. 103.

239 **Only 16 percent were spontaneous.** Menachim Amir, 1971, p. 142; Susan Brownmiller, *Against Our Will: Men, Women and Rape* (New York: Simon and Schuster, 1975), p. 199.

239 **men can distance themselves from their violence."** Todd W. Crosset, "Male athletes' violence against women: A critical assessment of the athletic affiliation, violence against women debate" in *Quest,* 51(3), 1999, p. 250.

240 **clearly spelled out in a printed college directive."** Charlton Heston, "Winning the Cultural War," lecture at the Harvard Law School Forum, February 16, 1999, available at: *http://www.houstonprogressive.org/hestonlaw.html.*

240 **blurted out one young man to a reporter.** Jane Gross, "Combating Rape on Campus in a Class on Sexual Consent" in *New York Times,* September 25, 1993.

241 The "splash guard" was initially developed by Michael Scarce.

CHAPTER ELEVEN: Girls in Guyland: Eyes on the Guys

242 **author of *Alpha Girls: Understanding the New American Girl and How She Is Changing the World*** Dan Kindlon, *Alpha Girls: Understanding the New American Girl and How She Is Changing the World* (New York: Rodale Press, 2007).

244 **"just going to make you a better person."** Margaret Soos, "With Friends Like These" in *OC Weekly,* August 27, 1999, cited in Alexandra Robbins, *Pledged: The Secret Life of Sororities* (New York: Hyperion, 2004), pp. 259–60.

248 **often by the Little Sisters themselves!** Mindy Stomber, " 'Buddies' or 'Slutties': The Collective Sexual Reputation of Fraternity Little Sisters" in *Gender & Society* 8(3), 1994.

248 **pledges—she refused and depledged.** Alexandra Robbins, *Pledged,* p. 61.

248 **and wouldn't invite them to parties anymore.** Michele Collison, "Although Fraternities Bear Brunt of Criticism for Hazing, Activities of Sororities, Too, Stir Concerns on Campuses" in *The Chronicle of Higher Education,* October 10, 1990.

256 **roving eye and a wickedly expressive brow above it."** Anna Quindlen, "Life in the 30s" in *New York Times,* January 21, 1987.

262 **man and still deserve respectful treatment."** Wendy Shalit, *A Return to Modesty* (New York: Free Press, 1999), p. 113.

262 ***The Rules* is a step-by-step guide** Ellen Fein and Sherrie Schneider, *The Rules: Time-tested Secrets for Capturing the Heart of Mr. Right* (New York: Warner Books, 1995). This book has been so successful that the current bestseller list has several of its offspring offering the same advice.

263 **Put lipstick on even when you go jogging!"** Ibid., pp. 19, 17, 78, 110.

264 **In a recent op-ed in *The Daily Princetonian*** Chloe Angyal, "How to Be a Feminist Without Anyone Knowing" in *The Daily Princetonian,* February 28, 2008; available at: *www.dailyprincetonian.com/2008/02/28/20285*

265 **but it was kind of just a stupid, gross experience."** Noah Grynberg, "Effects of Hazing Last Long After Pledging Process" in *The Cornell Daily Sun*, January 26, 2007.

266 **explained the situation and she gave her a ride home.** Todd Denny, *Unexpected Allies: Men Who Stop Rape* (Victoria, BC: Trafford Publishing, 2007); personal email communication, 9/21/2007.

271 **who believed in me and stood by me."** See Robert Brooks, "Education and 'Charismatic' Adults: To Touch a Student's Heart and Mind" available at his website: *http://www.drrobertbrooks.com/writings/articles/0009.html*

273 **should always be encouraged when appropriate.** See William Marsiglio, *Men on a Mission* (Baltimore: Johns Hopkins University Press, 2008).

279 **Ironically, another group of guys** Melinda Miceli, *Standing Out, Standing Together: The Social and Political Impact of Gay-Straight Alliances* (New York: Routledge, 2005).

283 **most impoverished idea of both fun and fraternity life.** Benoit Denizet-Lewis, "Ban of Brothers" in *New York Times Magazine*, January 9, 2005, p. 36.

284 **mean if they just go across the street?"** Hank Nuwer, *Wrongs of Passage*, p. 28.

284 **what do you do that's effective to prevent it?"** Samuel G. Freedman, "Calling the Folks about Campus Drinking" in *New York Times*, September 12, 2007, p. B6.

284 **writes syndicated columnist William Raspberry.** William Raspberry, "Brothers? Time to Treat Frat Hazings as Assaults" in *Virginian-Pilot*, April 24, 1998, p. B11.

285 **excessive drinking at the fraternity house.** Winnie Hu and Jonathan Miller, "Five Charged in Death of a Fraternity Pledge" in *New York Times*, August 4, 2007, B4.

285 **DeVercelly "was responsible for his actions."** Winnie Hu and Jonathan Miller, "Five Charged in Death of a Fraternity Pledge" in *New York Times*, August 4, 2007, B4; Darryl Isherwood, "Support Builds at Rider" in *Times of Trenton*, August 6, 2007.

286 **drinking behavior better than any other explanation.** Alan Berkowitz, "Fostering Healthy Norms to Prevent Violence and Abuse: The Social Norms Approach" in *Preventing Sexual Violence and Exploitation: A Sourcebook* edited by Keith Kaufman (Woods and Barnes, 2007). H. Wesley Perkins and Henry Wechsler, "Variations I Perceived in College Drinking Norms and its Impact on Alcohol Abuse: A Nationwide Study" in *Journal of Drug Issues*, 26(4) 1996, pp. 961–74. Wechsler has since

launched a critique of the Social Norms approach, in part because, ironically, it has been so successfully used around the country.

286 **alcohol abuse have dropped to within manageable levels.** H. Wesley Perkins, ed., *The Social Norms Approach to Preventing School and College Age Substance Abuse: A Handbook for Educators, Counselors and Clinicians* (San Francisco: Jossey-Bass, 2003).

286 **all the while thinking he was below average.** L. A. Dimeff, J. S. Baer, D. R. Kivlahan, and G. A. Marlatt, *Brief Alcohol Screening and Intervention for College Students* (New York: Guilford, 1999).

288 **philosophy that we took from the ancient Greeks.** Benoit Denizet-Lewis, "Ban of Brothers" in *New York Times Magazine*, January 9, 2005, p. 74.

INDEX

predatory sex or rape and, 227–29, 231, 234
prolonged adolescence and privilege, 11–12
restoration of, media entertainment, 152, 165–67
sex, women, and, 172, 175–77, 181, 234, 242–43
"street dilemma" and, 175, 177
unrealistic job expectations, 32–33
Erikson, Erik, 29, 39
ESPN, 125, 137, 139, 145
Essex, Vermont, 86
Evergreen State College, 191
Everyone Loves Raymond (TV series), 26
Everything Bad Is Good for You (Johnson), 151
EXPN.com, 138

Faludi, Susan, 17, 277
fantasy. *See also* video games
"babe" as, 249
empowerment and, 150, 155–56
lack of preparation for adult relationships and, 192
media entertainment and, 147, 148, 167–68
pornography as, 173–74, 175
sports leagues, 134–36
women as threats to, 136, 155–56
women's, of changing men, 261–63
women's, romantic, 257–58
Farred, Grant, 141
Fein, Ellen, 262
feminism, 71–72, 255–56, 263–64
Antioch rules (Code of Conduct) and, 240
gender equality and male anxiety, 172
girls' rejection of, 242–43
men's loss of entitlement and, 173
men's magazines and, 171–72
sex and, 192, 211
sexual assault and, 221–24
Fey, Tina, 264

FHM, 5, 145, 171
Field of Dreams (film), 136
fighting. *See* violence
Fitzgerald, F. Scott, 105
Fondacaro, Mark, 107
Francis, Joe, 176
fraternities, 2
alcohol and, 2, 6, 9, 10, 97, 103–10, 121, 244, 247, 259, 266, 285–86
Alpha Beta Gamma, 144, 147–48
on black campuses, 114–15
Delta Kappa Epsilon, 111
dissolving, Rider College, 285
hazing (*see* hazing)
Phi Gamma Delta, 288
predatory sex or rape and, 233–38
reforming, 283–85, 287, 288
Sigma Phi Epsilon, 288
"walk of fame/walk of shame," 281–82
Freedman, James O., 119–20
Freud, Sigmund, 52, 99, 164, 274
Friends (TV show), 4
friendships
college, continuing, 1, 2–3
cross-sex, 32, 249, 279–80
"friends with benefits," 3, 190, 209, 220, 249, 250
male, positive, 278–80
sports and, 133–34
women's, 246–49
"friendsters," 4

gambling and online poker, 2, 3, 144, 145, 146, 148, 159–60
Game Over: Gender, Race and Violence in Video Games (documentary), 155, 157
Garbarino, James, 53, 56
gay-baiting/gay bashing, 6, 9, 77–80, 88
gender
homosexuality and nonconformity, 76–77
initiation rites and, 113
policing of, 47–51, 76–77

gender (*cont.*)
promiscuity and, 192
stereotyping, 72
video games and, 154–55
"gender intensification," 41–42
Generation X (Coupland), 34
Gen X'ers, 34
Gen Y'ers, 34
George Washington University, 203, 205
Gilligan, Carol, 73
Gilligan, James, 55–56
Gilmore, Anne, 231, 232
Girl Code, 254
Girls Gone Wild, 175–76, 182
Glenn, Norval, 212
Glen Ridge, New Jersey, 64–66
Goffman, Erving, 54–55
Goldolf, Edward, 234
Goldstein, Sam, 272
Gone With the Wind (Mitchell), 257
Goodfellas bar, 125
Grand Theft Auto (*GTA*), 144, 149, 158, 166–67
Grey, Zane, 128
Griffiths, Mark, 152, 154–55
Gurian, Michael, 71
Guthrie, Woody, 166
Guy Code, 7, 43, 44–69, 150, 256
abstinence and, 212
boy's psychological development and, 51–54
code of silence, 61–62
Columbine shooters and, 89–90
conformity and, 255
culture of entitlement and, 59
defined, 45
desire to feel validated as a man, 116
emotional consequences of, 54
gender and academic subjects, 73–75
getting laid and, 175, 219, 225
honor and, 57
origins, 46–47
pressure to conform, 54–55, 61–62, 75
"Real Guy's Top Ten List," 44–45

violence as restoration, 55–57, 58–59, 75–76
Guyland
age bracket, 5, 6
athletes and fraternity members at epicenter, 233
binge drinking in, 103–4 (*see also* alcohol)
"Bros Before Hos" (homosociality of) 13, 14–15, 67, 169, 186–88, 207, 230, 250
as consumers, 5, 145–50, 164
as crippling young men, 168
culture of complicity, 67
culture of entitlement and, 59–61, 162–63, 165–67, 227, 282, 288
culture of privilege and, 37
culture of protection and, 42, 63–64, 68–69, 118, 283–85
culture of silence and, 61–62, 64, 67, 108, 267, 280–82
defined, 4, 9
definition of freedom, 117
disconnect from society, 40
dress code, 7, 48, 144
entertainment, media, 144–68
experts on "twixters," 38–40
failure to conform, responses, 50–51
fun in, 9
getting inside, 21–23
indeterminacy as chief characteristic, 39–40
initiations in, 99–100
leaving for adulthood, 267–70
motto of, 67
Negative Playbook, 49
in other countries, 13
Peter-Pan mindset, 4, 168
pornography, 169–89
profile/dominant patterns, 8–13
prolonged adolescence and, 25, 27, 130, 136, 147, 192, 205–8, 259
put-downs, most frequent, 48
racial and ethnic differences, 183–85

racism and, 141–42
as selective, boys vs. men, 55
sex in, 192, 215 (*see also* "hooking up";
pornography)
sports and, 123–43
sports talk as *lingua franca* of, 142
as stage of life, 6–7, 24–28, 287–88
supervision absent, 101
three cultures of, 57–64
transforming, 280–89
war between the sexes and, 182, 279
why now, 16–18
women as threats, 103
women in, 244–64, 279
"guys," 7, 14, 42

Hall, G. Stanley, 28
Hamilton, Steve, 34
Handelman, Max, 135
Harris, Eric, 89–90
Harvard University, 104–5
"Hazed and Confused" (Zwecker), 265
hazing, 57, 110–14, 265–66, 267
  age limit, 121
  among noncampus groups, 121
  branding, 111, 114–15
  Cornell exposé, 265
  deaths from, 6, 17, 58, 117–18, 122,
    284–85, 288
  Delta Kappa Epsilon, 111
  "elephant walk," 97
  high school, and rites of passage,
    83–86
  homoerotic sadism, 61, 112–13
  how to make schools safe from, 90–93
  humiliation and, 113
  Mepham High School incident,
    65–66, 68
  minorities and, 114–15
  "Ookie Cookie," 113, 287
  prevalence of, on campus, 111
  purpose of, 86
  reforming fraternities and, 284–85,
    287

rituals, 96–97
sadomasochistic, 10
sense of worthlessness and, 114
sorority hazing, 111, 243–44, 246
"teabagging," 113
voluntary participation in, reasons,
  115–17
"Hazing: Rites and Wrongs of Passage"
  (Nuwer), 287
Henry V (Shakespeare), 239
Heston, Charlton, 240
Higgins, Patrick D., xiii–xiv
High Fidelity (Hornby), 15
high school
  academic subjects and boys, 73–75
  as boot camp for Guyland, 70–94
  boy crisis blamed on girls, 71
  "boy crisis" in, 71–76
  bullying, 6, 17, 57, 76–80
  drinking, 102
  drop-outs, boys as, 54, 71
  "elephant walk," 112
  gays and lesbians targeted, 76–80
  girls' verbal bullying and aggression,
    81–82
  graduates, percentage, 36
  hazing and rites of passage, 83–86
  homoerotic sadism in, 61
  how to make schools safe, 90–93
  legal protection in, 79, 93
  pervasive predation, 80–82
  school shootings, 87–90
  sports and anti-intellectualism, 29–30
  teachers as mentors, 272–73
Hobart College, 285–86
Hobbes, Thomas, 189
Holland, Terry, 235
homophobia, 9, 13, 48–51, 112, 141, 163,
  288
  "that's so gay," 9, 48, 76
homosexuality, 3
  gays and lesbians targeted, 76–80
  heterosexual patterns resembling gay
    male community, 196

Index | 323

women/girls
abuse of, 181
academic subjects and, 73–75
alcohol and, 103, 199–200, 215, 244, 247, 250–51, 266
antagonism/animosity toward, 12, 18, 136, 139–40
average age of becoming a parent, 31
average age of marriage, 31
"babe" or "bitch," 245, 249–52
"Bros Before Hos" and, 67, 230
changing men, desire for, 261–63
college enrollment, 72–73
contemptuous language and, 182, 185, 187, 279
date-rape, 10, 57, 224–27
dating, 2, 201–2
eating disorders, 244
empowerment, 251
femininity, traits of, 251–52
gender stereotyping, 72
girls, Guy Code of silence and, 62
girls vs. women, 13–15
"guyification," 14, 250–51
Guyland and, 14, 242–64
hazing by girls, 86
homosexual men and, 49
"hooking up" and, 195–216
induction into womanhood, 99–100
initiation rites and replacing mother, 98–100
low place of, to men, 47
male delayed adulthood and women's freedom, 31
male friendships, 32, 249, 279–80
markers of adulthood, age at each stage, 25
marriage goals, 258–60
misogyny of rap music, 163
perfection and, 253–54
pop psychology blaming of matriarchy for boys' problems, 71

pornography and, 152, 169–89
portrayal, in media entertainment, 152, 157–58, 167
as possessions, 47
put-downs and locker-room talk about, 19
rape and sexual assault, 217–41
as reminder of adulthood, 136
sex and, 169–70, 174–75, 195–216, 244, 247–48, 281
sexual experience, differing from male, 197–98
sexualized images of, 171
sexual patterns on campus, history of, and, 192–94
sorority hazing, 111, 243–44
sports, sex-segregation of, 138–41
sports and, 136–38
sports as girl-free zone, 134
as threats, 103, 134, 143, 167, 227–29
Title IX, 136, 137
validation by men/boys, 246–52
verbal bullying by girls, 81–82
video games and, 151, 154, 155
virginity pledge, 211–12
what it means to be a woman, 44
what women want in a man, 254–58
Woodham, Luke, 88
Wordsworth, William, 93
working-class guys, 12–13
Wright State University, 204–5
Wrongs of Passage (Nuwer), 117

Yale University, 218
Yeats, William Butler, 1, 53
Young, Cathy, 221, 222
Yousman, Bill, 166–67
"youthhood," 39
YouTube, 156

Zillman, Dolf, 180
Zwecker, Adam, 265, 271